AF844430

Murat Birdal is Assistant Professor in the Department of Economics at Istanbul University. He received his Ph.D. in Political Economy from the University of Southern California.

LIBRARY OF OTTOMAN STUDIES

Series ISBN: 978-1-84885-245-7

See www.ibtauris.com/LOS for a full list of titles

7. *The Ottoman Empire and the World around it*
Suraiya Faroqhi
978 1 85043 715 4

8. *Ottoman Reform and Muslim Regeneration*
Weismann Zachs
978 1 85043 757 4

9. *Governing Property, Making the Modern State: Law, Administration and Production in Ottoman Syria*
Martha Mundy and Richard Saumarez Smith
978 1 84511 291 2

10. *The Crescent and the Eagle: Ottoman Rule, Islam and the Albanians, 1874–1913*
George Gawrych
978 1 84511 287 5

11. *Guarding the Frontier: Ottoman Border Forts and Garrisons in Europe*
Mark L. Stein
978 1 84511 301 8

12. *Ottomans, Turks and the Balkans: Empire Lost, Relations Altered*
Ebru Boyar
978 1 84511 351 3

13. *Ottoman Propaganda and Turkish Identity: Literature in Turkey During World War I*
Erol Koroglu
978 1 84511 490 9

14. *Ottomans Looking West? The Origins of the Tulip Age and its Development in Modern Turkey*
Can Erimtan
9781845114916

15. *Women in the Ottoman Balkans: Gender, Culture and History*
Amila Buturovic and Irvin Cemil Schick (eds)
978 1 84511 505 0

16. *Innovation and Empire in Turkey: Sultan Selim III and the Modernisation of the Ottoman Navy*
Tuncay Zorlu
978 1 84511 694 1

17. *Artisans of Empire: Crafts and Craftspeople Under the Ottomans*
Suraiya Faroqhi
978 1 84511 588 3

18. *The Political Economy of Ottoman Public Debt: Insolvency and European Financial Control in the Late Nineteenth Century*
Murat Birdal
978 1 84885 298 3

19. *Ottoman Women: A Social History from the Nineteenth and Twentieth Centuries*
Duygu Koksal and Anastassia Falierou
978 1 84511 778 8

20. *The Young Ottomans: Turkish Critics of the Eastern Question in the Late Nineteenth Century*
Nazan Çiçek
978 1 84885 333 1

21. *The British in the Levant: Trade and Perceptions of the Ottoman Empire in the Eighteenth Century*
Christine Laidlaw
978 1 84885 335 5

22. *The Ottoman Origins of Modern Iraq: Political Reform, Modernization and Development in the Nineteenth Century Middle East*
Ebubekir Ceylan
978 1 84885 425 3

23. *Cities of the Mediterranean: From the Ottomans to the Present Day*
Meltem Toksözö and Biray Kolluoğlu (eds)
978 1 84885 127 6

THE POLITICAL ECONOMY OF OTTOMAN PUBLIC DEBT

Insolvency and European Financial Control in the Late Nineteenth Century

MURAT BİRDAL

TAURIS ACADEMIC STUDIES
an imprint of

I.B.Tauris Publishers
LONDON • NEW YORK

Published in 2010 by Tauris Academic Studies
An imprint of I.B.Tauris & Co Ltd
6 Salem Road, London W2 4BU
175 Fifth Avenue, New York NY 10010
www.ibtauris.com

Copyright © 2010 Murat Birdal

The right of Murat Birdal to be identified as the author of this work has been asserted by the author in accordance with the Copyright, Designs and Patent Act 1988.

All rights reserved. Except for brief quotations in a review, this book, or any part thereof, may not be reproduced, stored in or introduced into a retrieval system, or transmitted, in any form or by any means, electronic, mechanical, photocopying, recording or otherwise, without the prior written permission of the publisher.

Library of Ottoman Studies 18

ISBN 978 1 84885 298 3

A full CIP record for this book is available from the British Library
A full CIP record for this book is available from the Library of Congress

Library of Congress catalog card: available

To my family,
Banu, Zeynep, İlker, İnci and Sinan

CONTENTS

LIST OF TABLES

LIST OF FIGURES

GLOSSARY

Ayan	Local notable
Bahşiş	Bribe
British Consols	Long-term government bonds issued in Britain
Bourse	Stock exchange
Dönüm	An Ottoman unit of area (1 *dönüm* = 919 square meters)
Efendi	Ottoman title, gentleman
Egyptian *Reftieh*	Duty on tobacco exports to Egypt
Esham	Bonds issued by the Ottoman government
Fatwa	Religious edict
Feddan	A unit of area used in Egypt (1 *feddan*= 4,200 square meters)
Havale	Payment order
Hoca	Muslim preacher
İltizam	Tax farming
İmam	Leader of the congregational prayer in Islam
Kaime	Form of paper money issued in the Ottoman Empire
Khedive	Title borne by Egyptian rulers after 1867
Kolcu	Surveillance unit of the tobacco monopoly
Lots Turcs	Securities of the Ottoman Lottery Loan 1870–72
Malikane	Life-term tax farm
Muharrem	The first month in the Muslim calendar
Muhasebeci	Accountant
Muhassıl	Tax collector
Muhtar	Village headman
Mültezim	Tax farmer

Nargile	Water pipe
Nazır	Minister
Nezaret	Office
Okka	An Ottoman unit of weight (1 *okka* = 1,280 grams)
Öşür	Tithe
Paşa	An honorary title granted to senior ministers and generals
Porte	Refers to the Ottoman court where government policies were established
Ramazan	Muslim month of fasting
Sarraf	Money lender
Sergi	Promissory notes issued by the Ottoman government
Sheriat	Islamic law
Sipahi	Cavalrymen assigned as the administrator of the *tımar* land
Softa	Muslim theological students
Şeyhülislam	Chief of religious affairs in the Ottoman state
Tekke	Religious gathering place
Tımar	Benefice holding
Tömbeki	A tobacco used when smoking a water pipe
Vilayet	Ottoman province

PRINCIPAL ABBREVIATIONS

ASIR	Administration of Six Indirect Revenues
BIO	*Banque Impériale Ottomane*, Ottoman Bank
CFB	Council of Foreign Bondholders
FDI	Foreign Direct Investment
GFD	Global Financial Database
Fr	Francs
LE	*Livre Égyptienne*, Egyptian Pounds
LT	*Livre Turque*, Ottoman Lira (LT 1.1 = £1= Fr 22.727)
OPDA	Ottoman Public Debt Administration
Pa	Para (LT 1= Pa 4000)
Ps	Piastres (LT 1= Ps 100)

A NOTE ON THE PRONUNCIATION OF TURKISH WORDS

C,c = 'j' as in juice
Ç,ç = 'ch' as in church
Ğ,ğ = not pronounced, lengthens the preceding vowel
I,ı = without a dot, as 'er' in farmer
İ,i = with a dot, as 'ee' in see
Ö,ö = as in the umlaut 'ö' in German
Ş,ş = 'sh' as in sheep
Ü,ü = as in the umlaut 'ü' in German

PREFACE AND ACKNOWLEDGEMENTS

A Turkish proverb says 'debt is a man's whip (motivation). From the mid-19th century on, Turkish officials adopted this saying as their motto and made a career out of foreign borrowing. As with many young Turks in 1980s, I became familiar with the words 'foreign debt' and IMF from my early teens. I witnessed the socio-economic transformation under the military dictatorship, which played a crucial role in the implementation of the IMF policies. As Turkish society underwent a traumatic transformation, I endeavored to understand the relationship between the IMF austerity measures and the military coup, which laid the foundations for the 'structural adjustment'.

My early studies focused on identifying a pattern of insolvency and economic transformation imposed on the debtor countries. Turkish insolvency was an especially compelling case, since the measures imposed by the creditors were the driving force behind two major economic transformations experienced by the Turkish economy, a century apart. As I delved deeper into the case of Ottoman insolvency, I was struck by the similarities between the OPDA and the IMF. At least as important were their differences, which helped to distinguish the needs and mechanisms of 19th century imperialism from those of the capitalist world system of our times. This book is the product of this lengthy effort to understand the role of foreign indebtedness in the economic transformation of debtor countries with a focus on the distinguishing aspects of the Ottoman experience. It is an attempt to go beyond both the nationalist historical accounts that present the OPDA merely as an instrument of European imperialism and liberal accounts that portray it as a vanguard of economic reform and modernization. Both of these approaches have an exclusive focus on one side of the coin. In contrast, this work emphasizes the dialectics between imperialism and economic modernization. It illustrates the pivotal role of the OPDA in the penetration of European imperialism as well as in the modernization of the economy and the reorganization of state bureaucracy (particularly in fiscal matters), which in turn facilitated the influx of foreign investment into the empire.

This book is a revision of my doctoral dissertation submitted to the University of Southern California. Among many who made this work possible, my advisor Timur Kuran deserves a special place. His academic and editorial guidance was essential to the completion of this project. He tirelessly read numerous drafts and raised issues that had previously gone largely unnoticed in the literature. Other members of my committee were Howard Sherman and the late Hayward Alker, whose suggestions contributed to the originality of my work. I am also grateful to Barış Kablamacı, the late Burhaneddin Ulutan, Erdoğan Keskinkılıç, Erol Manisalı, Farideh Motamedi, Hakan Ongan, the late Haydar Kazgan, İzzettin Önder, Judith Stiehm, Mehmet Akbulut, Metin Coşgel, Murat Bayız, Nora Hamilton, Pablo Heidrich, Rahşan Akbulut, Şelale Tüzel, Şevket Pamuk, the late Türkel Minibaş and Zeynep Türkyılmaz who provided their valuable comments and help during the course of this research.

I am greatly indebted to David Annetts whose criticism and editorial contribution was indispensable to revising this work into a book. I should also express my gratitude to Allison McKechnie and Joanna Godfrey, my editor at I.B. Tauris, for their generous help and support. I owe thanks to the Istanbul University Library, Ottoman Bank Archives and Research Center and Lorans Tanatar Baruh for the images used in the book.

My sincere thanks go to all the institutions that provided me with generous sponsoring. The research for this book has been supported in part by a Turkish Higher Education Council fellowship, *İktisatlılar Vakfı* of Istanbul University School of Economics Alumni, University of Southern California Center for International Studies dissertation fellowship and Robert L. Friedheim fellowship.

Finally, I am grateful to my family, my daughter Zeynep, my wife Banu, my parents İnci and İlker and my brother Sinan for their enduring love, understanding and support throughout this research. I am blessed to have them.

1

INTRODUCTION

In the mid-1870s and 1880s many debtor countries faced severe external debt service problems and eventually had to agree on new contracts for the settlement of their debts. This process always involved power asymmetries in favor of the creditors. In some cases, the lenders were satisfied with institutional changes aimed at securing the repayment of their loans and the creation of opportunities to further their economic and political ambitions. In other cases, the lenders went even further and seized direct control of the fiscal revenues of the debtor countries. Among these debtors, the Ottoman Empire presents a unique case of an Empire gradually dissolving and peripheralizing within the capitalist world economy. This book analyzes the external debt crisis in the Ottoman Empire by focusing on the institutional changes following the establishment of the Ottoman Public Debt Administration (OPDA), and its role in the peripheralization of the Ottoman economy.

The peripheralization of the Ottoman Empire brought about a weaker state apparatus, but also a more efficient one in terms of facilitating the operations of the world economy. This meant a relative diminution in the state's ability to interfere with the flows of factors of production in the world economy, as well as specialization in certain products, transfer of new technologies to these sectors, improvement in the means of transportation, and the creation of a more efficient bureaucracy. Within this framework, this book demonstrates the dual role played by the OPDA. On the one hand, the function of the OPDA supports the 'colonization through lending' arguments due to its pivotal role in the peripheralization of the Ottoman Empire and in securing and furthering the interests of the countries directly or indirectly represented in the administration. On the other hand, the OPDA initiated several measures that improved the condition of the sectors under its control by introducing new technologies, and increasing their productivity. It also generated positive externalities for several other sectors of the economy. Moreover, the administrative system set up by the OPDA contributed to the development of state entrepreneurship in the Empire and laid the foundations of the early republican economy based on state enterprises.

Previous studies analyzing the integration of the Ottoman Empire with the global economy focus on the 1838 British Free Trade Agreement as a major determinant of expanding external trade. Typically, they overlook the period of stagnation in the growth of Ottoman external trade after the 1870s and the second period of expansion in the 1890s. By contrast, this book argues that the external trade potential of the Empire was determined by the limitations of a pre-capitalist economy based largely on subsistence production. In this context, it focuses on the institutional reforms initiated by the OPDA that restructured the export-oriented sectors of the Ottoman economy, played a crucial role in the construction of railways, contributed to the gradual dissolution of subsistence production, and boosted the external trade of the Empire. Moreover, it emphasizes that the expansion of foreign trade in the 1890s was accompanied by a drastic increase in foreign direct investment after the establishment of the OPDA, which created a safer environment for foreign investment.

Theoretical background

There are two main strands of thought dealing with international capital movements and the external debt of sovereign borrowers. The first follows the classical international trade theory whereby capital movements between two countries are analyzed with reference to differences in interest rates and their implications on exchange rates.[1] After the Second World War, the focus of the theory shifted to the development problems of the underdeveloped countries, emphasizing the necessity to mobilize external resources for higher levels of economic growth. This theory focuses on the gap between planned investments and the expected savings, aiming to determine the necessary optimal borrowing required to initiate the growth process and thereby secure the repayment of the loans.[2] The second approach regarding international capital movements is the World System/Dependency approach, which has its roots in the Imperialism theories of the early twentieth century.[3] In contrast to the former literature's focus on the dyadic relationship between the capital exporting and capital importing countries, these theories focus on the capital accumulation process in the world economy. Accordingly, they adopt a historical approach, treating the problem of external debt within the core-periphery framework, and discuss the phenomenon of indebtedness in the periphery within the context of a general theory of development and underdevelopment.

Although these two theories focus on different parts of the problem, they are not mutually exclusive. The first approach is ahistorical and fails to explain the dynamics behind recurring defaults. Moreover, it does not account for the role of politics in sovereign lending, and in the allocation of foreign funds in the debtor countries. The followers of this approach typically build models on how sovereign lending should occur rather than explaining the rationale behind how it actually took place. In exploring the background of Ottoman borrowing, this book makes use of certain arguments developed by this literature. The scope of this work, however, is far broader.

In an effort to analyze the OPDA's role in the 'peripheralization' of the Ottoman Empire, this book draws on the concepts developed by the 'world system/ dependency approach'. This approach typically challenges the assumption that an understanding of social change within a particular region in the world system can be reached by focusing on the dynamics and changes occurring within these boundaries alone.[4] Drawing on the well-known core-periphery framework, the dependency school argues that the worldwide capitalist accumulation process, instead of creating uniformity, deepens inequalities among nations and social formations by polarizing them as 'core' and 'periphery'. Capital accumulation in the core is 'auto-centric', governed by its own internal dynamics. Yet, in the periphery it is dependent upon the core-periphery relationship, meaning it is determined by external dynamics.[5]

The theory also warns us not to build a unidirectional cause and effect relationship from the core to the periphery. The capitalist world system is generated by the adaptation of every single internal formation to the unified whole, the world economy. The reproduction of every internal formation stimulates the reproduction of both other internal forms and the unified whole. Hence, capital accumulation in the core and underdevelopment in the periphery are interdependent processes. It is through this interaction that the hegemony of the core over the periphery is established and maintained. Therefore, in accordance with the formulation of the relationship between core and periphery, peripheralization is identical with 'entering the worldwide division of labor and thus ceasing to be a self contained unit of reproduction'.[6]

Historical studies on external debt reveal a sequence of decade-long surges in foreign lending that generated four outstanding periods of global debt service incapacity among sovereign borrowers in the late 1820s, the mid-1870s, the early 1930s and the early 1980s.[7] Empirical studies in world system theory illustrate that capital flows from the core to the periphery coincide with periods of economic recession at the core of the world system, leading to a decline in profit rates.[8] At this stage investment in the periphery becomes more attractive, and this potential induces capital outflow from the core to the periphery. This capital flow can be in the form of foreign government bonds or bank credits to the private sector in the periphery. However, the lack of necessary institutions limits the efficient allocation of financial resources, restraining economic growth in the periphery. These capital flows are interrupted by economic stagnation in the core economies, causing a serious decline in world trade, and leading to frequent defaults or rescheduling of external debt on behalf of the peripheral economies.[9] World system theorists argue that debt settlements serve to restore the hegemony of the core over the periphery and to restructure the world economy in accordance with the growing needs of the core economies.

This study does not delve into a lengthy discussion of long-term business cycles. Rather, it focuses on the role of the debt settlement in creating a safer and more profitable environment for future capital flows into the Ottoman Empire and the imposition of a model of integration with the world economy that facilitates the flow of raw materials from the periphery to the core and the flow of consumer goods in the opposite direction. As argued by a regime theorist, Krasner, sovereign lending often results in violations of the Westphalian model through coercion and imposition.[10] More often than not, defaults lead the lenders to seize control of the sources of revenue in debtor countries (collection and allocation of taxes). Therefore, even though lending to a sovereign is not the most secure of enterprises, it plays a crucial role in the peripheralization process as a vehicle through which the domestic autonomy of the weaker polities is compromised.[11]

A vital question that demands an answer is, given its foreseeable consequences, why would a ruler or a sovereign state resort to foreign debt that may eventually force it to concede its domestic autonomy? Krasner maintains that rulers of borrowing countries would have preferred terms that did not include such invitations, but their actions were still voluntary. Considering their desperate need for external resources, capital with a loss of domestic autonomy was better than the status quo of no capital at all.[12] In this sense external debt can be understood as a 'mutually contingent', 'Pareto-improving' contract, which often includes invitations that concede debtors' sovereignty.

A well-known criticism of the world system/ dependency approach is that it has a structural-functionalist bias, since it endeavors to explain history according to the functions of specific events and regions in relationship to the overall structure of the world system. According to this critique, the world system approach underestimates the internal dynamics of the specific economies while overrating the external dynamics (dynamics of the world economy). As such, it fails to explain the substantial differences in the debt patterns and economic performances of the debtor countries. Second, core-periphery analysis depends crucially on the consideration of an institutional structure that shapes the different economic performances of the core and periphery. As North emphasizes, to be more convincing these studies need to identify the institutional framework that produces the systematic uneven consequences implied by the theory.[13]

The theoretical approach of this book aims to combine the core-periphery analysis with an institutional analysis, focusing on the role of formal and informal institutions as a set of rules that shapes the actions of the economic and the political actors. With a multi-level analysis – from the world system to the individual actors – many changes that are considered as exogenous can be internalized through an institutionalist approach. Moreover, world system theory can be provided with a 'better understanding' of the institutional mechanisms that would surely help to explain different responses from the periphery to the same set of institutions imposed by the core economies. In this context, this book aims to analyze the consequences of the institutional reforms introduced by the OPDA, by explaining the actions and the reasoning of all the agents in each and every relevant sector controlled by the administration. For this purpose it asks the following questions: while the existing production and trade networks were being altered, how was the incentive structure restructured and which social group(s) benefited or lost out in the aftermath of this transition?

The Ottoman Public Debt Administration (OPDA)

Rising balance of payment deficits, and the increasing need for external sources to finance the military (during the Crimean War) forced the Ottoman Empire to take its first official foreign loan in 1854. Unproductive use of these external resources (for example, for importing military equipment and consumption by the state bureaucracy) resulted in a growing debt burden; consequently, the Ottoman state had severe debt service problems. In 1875, when the Empire became bankrupt, more than half of its revenues were committed to the debt service.

In 1881, Sultan Abdülhamid II issued the Decree of *Muharrem* establishing the Ottoman Public Debt Administration (OPDA). It should also be noted that by the decree, besides securing additional loans, the government hoped to avoid placing the Turkish finances directly in the hands of foreign powers, which was another option considered by the European states, proposed at the Berlin Congress in 1878.[14]

The Ottoman Council of Foreign Debt was ostensibly private in spite of close ties between its members and their home governments. The council consisted of two members from France, one each from Germany, Austria, Italy, and the Ottoman government itself, and one from Britain and Holland together. The foreign members of the council were selected by the banks, bondholders or, in the case of Italy, by the Rome Chamber of Commerce. The council established the Ottoman Public Debt Administration (OPDA).

The Decree of *Muharrem* entrusted to the OPDA the direct administration, receipt, and encashment, by means of agents acting under its authority, of the revenues and other sources ceded to the service of debt. It had the power to appoint and dismiss its employees, who were considered to be functionaries of the state. The government was also bound to give the OPDA, in the exercise of its administration, all the general assistance compatible with the existing institutions, and to provide military protection to ensure the security of its principal seats and local services. The administration was largely independent from the Ottoman government. The government was allowed to send a commissioner to the regular meetings of the administration and examine its books, but beyond this point it could not interfere with its operations. In case of a disagreement between the government and the council, an arbitration panel consisting of four members (two appointed by the council, two by the government and a fifth chosen by the arbitrators if necessary) would be formed to resolve the matter.

Under the terms of the decree, the revenues from the salt and tobacco monopolies, the stamps and spirits tax, the fish tax, the silk tithe of certain districts, the Bulgaria tribute, the revenue of Eastern Rumelia and the surplus of the Cyprus revenue were irrevocably ceded to the OPDA, until the debt was liquidated. As the Ottoman government continued to borrow from abroad, the control of the administration over the resources of the Ottoman economy extended far beyond the assignments of the decree. Until the outbreak of the First World War in 1914, the OPDA functioned as a 'state within the state' controlling around one-third of state revenues.

The OPDA was at the center of public attention from the early days of its operation. As a foreign-controlled administration it was perceived as a severe blow to Turkish pride, which made it the target of the nationalist critiques of the Young Turks.[15] Yet, the criticism seldom went beyond the discursive level and never evolved into a thorough analysis of the administration. During the Ottoman period, the only writer who provided a detailed and coherent analysis of the administration was a Russian socialist, known as Parvus Efendi, who endeavored to expose the role played by the OPDA and the Régie Company in the penetration of Western imperialism into the Empire.[16]

The early studies of the OPDA are mostly by foreign writers.[17] These works lack an analytical background and merely provide a narrative of the Ottoman external debt and the administration of the revenues under the OPDA. Their most important contribution is their reliance on primary sources such as the archives of the OPDA and the Council of Foreign Bondholders, as well as the personal accounts of prominent figures within the OPDA. The later studies of the OPDA by Turkish historians largely repeated the findings of the earlier second-hand sources.[18] Almost all of these works treated the OPDA as an agent of imperialism. However, they did not even attempt to provide an analytical mechanism to explain the OPDA's function in the penetration of European imperialism into the Empire.

This book, while laying out the institutional foundations of Western imperialism in the Ottoman Empire, also points out the pitfalls of the prevailing nationalist historical accounts, which portray the OPDA as one of the foremost causes of Ottoman underdevelopment and a major obstacle to Ottoman modernization in the nineteenth century.[19] These accounts overlook the fact that the establishment of the OPDA was a direct consequence of Ottoman underdevelopment rather than its direct cause. After all, the major cause of heavy foreign borrowing was the Ottoman state's inability to catch up with the technological and military developments in the West, which made it increasingly vulnerable to foreign military threats. Moreover, the significant improvements later achieved by OPDA in the revenues under its control also illustrate the administrative and organizational backwardness of the Ottoman state machinery as compared to its Western counterparts.

There is no doubt that the OPDA contributed to the underdevelopment of the economy, particularly through its pivotal role in the transfer of economic surplus from the Empire to the core economies. First of all, the main purpose of the OPDA was the collection of taxes to pay the shares of the foreign bondholders. In this case, more efficient tax collection meant a larger tax burden on the impoverished agricultural population and a greater capital outflow from the economy. Second, most members of the administration also held positions in foreign corporations operating in the Ottoman Empire. In case of a disagreement between the government and these corporations, the administration usually sided with the interests of the latter. And perhaps most important of all, by limiting the state's control over the appropriation and utilization of the economic surplus, it terminated the sporadic efforts of the palace to recreate Ottoman centralism. In these respects, the role of the OPDA lends support to the 'colonization through lending' arguments.

Furthermore, this work demonstrates another facet of the OPDA that has been overlooked in most historical accounts. As mentioned before, with the Decree of *Muharrem* the OPDA had received the right to administer, collect, and to hold in deposit the revenues resulting from the development of the sources of income ceded to the bondholders. In this framework, the OPDA initiated several measures including administrative reforms and technology transfers that not only facilitated growth in sectors under its responsibility, but also generated positive externalities for other sectors. The administrative reforms initiated by the OPDA also set an example for the Ottoman bureaucracy. Double-entry bookkeeping, first introduced by the BIO (La Banque Impériale Ottomane) and later by the OPDA to state accounting, was later adopted by the Ottoman state as the standard accounting principle.[20] As discussed in detail later, the institutional reforms initiated by the administration contributed to the development and modernization of state entrepreneurship in the Empire, and formed the backbone of the early republican economy.

The 'dual role' of the OPDA emphasized in this study is parallel to what Sunar calls the 'paradox of peripheralism'.[21] Discussing the role of the English in the Reform Period (1839–76), Sunar points out a very common disagreement that has divided students of nineteenth century Ottoman history:

> some have praised the English as true precursors of Turkish modernization, while others have condemned the English as Imperialists solely responsible for Ottoman underdevelopment.[22]

Similar disagreements may be observed when it comes to other institutional changes imposed by foreign powers, such as the establishment of the OPDA, which occurred during the peripheralization of the Ottoman Empire. Despite the disagreement over the role of the OPDA (or Britain in the former case), arguments on both sides are based on the assumption that these concepts – 'modernization' and 'peripheralization' or 'underdevelopment' – are mutually exclusive.

Incorporation into the world economy is generally defined as becoming an integral part of the division of labor and responding to the imperatives of the drive for accumulation of capital.[23] According to this argument, peripheralization requires restructuring of the state machinery to form a state that operates within an interstate system as opposed to a self-centered and self-responsive 'world Empire'. İnalcık defines this transition as a change in the 'concept of state'.[24] On one hand, this means the relative diminution of the state's ability to interfere with the flows of factors of production in the world economy; on the other, it means specialization in certain products, improving the means of transportation, creation of a more efficient bureaucracy, and the transfer of new technologies and information into these areas. Therefore, this book argues that the peripheralization process triggered by the OPDA brought about not only a weaker state apparatus but also a more efficient one in terms of facilitating the operations of the world economy.

In the literature, the OPDA is often portrayed simply as an official agent of foreign powers or Western capitalism.[25] This approach perceives Western capitalism as a monolithic entity and overlooks the fact that different capitalist groups, even with the same country of origin, might have conflicting interests on a variety of issues. The members of the

OPDA were directly appointed by the bondholder organizations of the countries concerned. Hence, they were responsible first to the bondholders. There is no doubt that these representatives were under the influence of their governments, sometimes even handpicked by them. But on many occasions they also came into conflict with the general policies of their governments by protecting the interests of their bondholders, which were closely tied to the performance of the Ottoman economy.[26]

Another argument observed in the nationalist critiques of the period is that foreigners forced loans on the government at usurious rates.[27] As discussed in detail later, the Ottoman government complained that they could not borrow when they were in need. They never complained, however, that they were forced to borrow when it was not necessary. The high rates on foreign loans stemmed mostly from mistrust in Ottoman finances and reform attempts. Also, with the formation of the OPDA, the risk premiums on foreign loans declined drastically due to the strong enforcement mechanisms for sovereign compliance during the OPDA era. Moreover, unable to command confidence in the financial markets by its own means, the government aimed to benefit from the credibility of the OPDA. Therefore, when necessary, the government voluntarily transferred more sources of revenue to the control of the OPDA in order to raise new loans at more favorable terms. Hence, in a manner that echoes the argument developed by North and Weingast in their seminal paper on the economic consequences of the Glorious Revolution, the constraints on the sovereign enabled the Ottoman government to regain access to foreign capital markets with lower risk premiums.[28]

Peripheralization of the Ottoman Empire in the nineteenth century and the role of the Ottoman Public Debt Administration

It is difficult to pinpoint the beginning of the transformation of the Ottoman Empire from a self responsive, auto-centric 'world Empire' into a peripheral economy governed by the dynamics of the world economy.[29] Nevertheless, there is a near-consensus in the literature that the incorporation of the Ottoman Empire into the world economy gained momentum in the nineteenth century.

Previous studies emphasized the crucial role played by the 1838 British Free Trade Agreement in the peripheralization of the Ottoman economy in the nineteenth century. The agreement was not the first capitulation granted to foreign powers, nor was it the last. However, by introducing restrictions on the establishment of state monopolies and abolishing export restrictions for the first time, it went far beyond the privileges granted to foreigners in the previous capitulations and took the form of a major restriction on the Porte's fiscal sovereignty. Moreover, by exempting foreigners from internal duties, it gave foreign merchants an advantage over their local counterparts. It also facilitated the penetration of European goods into the interior parts of the Empire.

There is a consensus in the literature that the 1838 Trade Agreement served as a major determinant of the expanding external trade of the Empire in the nineteenth century.[30] This consensus is supported by empirical evidence, which also illustrates the stagnation in the growth rate of Ottoman external trade after the 1870s and another period of expansion in the 1890s, as observed from Figure 1.1. This book aims to explore the role of the OPDA in the second period of expansion in Ottoman external trade after the 1890s. From this perspective, it argues that the external trade potential of the Empire was determined by the limitations of a pre-capitalist economy based largely on subsistence production, lacking the infrastructure for further expansion of external trade. In this context, it focuses on the institutional reforms initiated by the OPDA that restructured the export-oriented sectors of the Ottoman economy, played a crucial role in the construction of railways, and hence contributed to the gradual dissolution of the subsistence production, and boosted the external trade of the Empire in this period. Moreover, it emphasizes that the expansion of foreign trade in the 1890s was accompanied by a drastic increase in foreign direct investment after the establishment of the OPDA, which created a safer environment for foreign investment. This is also the distinguishing element of the peripheralization process experienced in the OPDA period.

Organization of the book

Chapter 2 commences with an analysis of the Ottoman financial crisis, and the dynamics behind the demand for external loans in the pre-OPDA period. Despite mounting financial problems, the Ottoman government managed to meet its budget deficits until the 1850s without resorting directly to foreign credit, by various means such as the debasement of the coinage, the issue of securities, and printing banknotes. However, the treasury crisis brought about by the cost of the Crimean War in 1854 forced the Ottoman Empire to reconsider the borrowing opportunities in foreign markets. Debasement of the coinage or the issue of paper currencies had already led to severe problems. Local bankers, who played an intermediary role between the government and foreign capital, asked for rates well above the prevailing average market rates in return for undertaking the risk of lending to the government. Under these circumstances, the Ottoman government contracted its first foreign loan, under the official guarantee of its allies Britain and France, and embarked on a path that would lead ultimately to its insolvency.

The second part of Chapter 2 provides an in-depth analysis of the debt contracts made in the pre-OPDA period and the institutional reforms carried out by the government to improve the Empire's credit. In order to issue bonds in external markets, the debtor country must show some effective guarantees of its capacity for future repayment. In the Ottoman case, the Porte still had not established a budget system; the existing accounts of the treasury were unreliable and hardly monitorable. Under these circumstances, it was very difficult for the government to issue loans secured on the general revenues of the treasury and additional revenues had to be pledged as collateral. The more liquid and monitorable the collateral, the more confidence it would command in the foreign markets. For every attempt to raise a new loan the Porte had to rely more on less attractive collaterals, which gradually brought an increase in the risk premiums charged on these loans. Following the 1860s, the Porte initiated several institutional reforms in order to gain credibility in the European markets. These reforms or reform attempts included several measures that aimed to improve the reliability and the monitorability of the financial accounts. In some cases, the government went as far as delegating the collection of certain central government revenues to a foreign-owned bank, the BIO, or setting up a largely independent commission to control and approve the budgets. Nevertheless, European investors continued to question the sincerity of the government and risk premiums remained very high on the series of bonds issued in this period. The skepticism of the investors was often justified as the reforms were not fully carried through after the loans had been secured.

Chapter 3 explores theoretical issues in sovereign lending and aims to explain the drastic fall in risk premiums on foreign loans, as well as the significant increase in foreign direct investment following the establishment of the OPDA. The chapter starts with a discussion of the problems of monitoring and enforcement of sovereign compliance in international lending and lays out the factors that affect the risk premium through a game theoretical model.

Figure 1.1 Ottoman foreign trade: 1830–1913

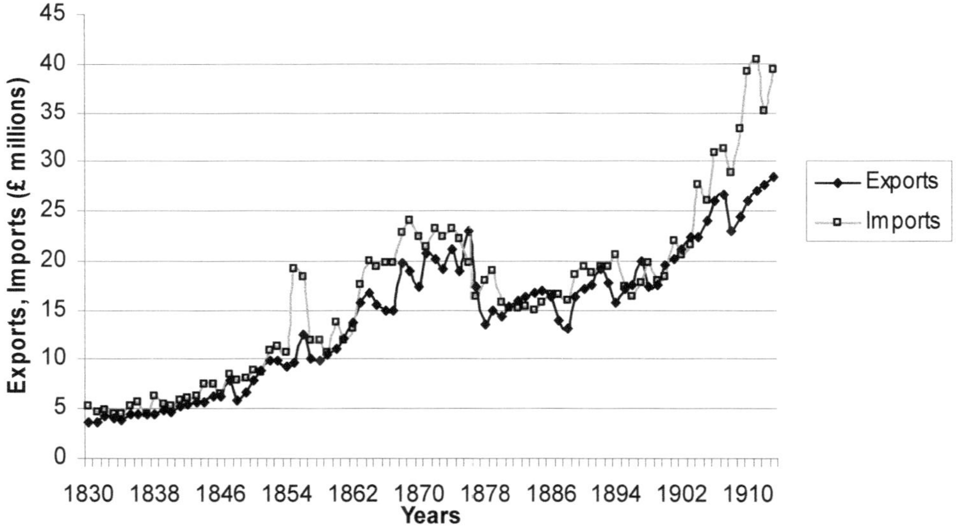

Source: Pamuk, 1994: 24.

Historical evidence shows that in the absence of international enforcement mechanisms, mistrust between the creditors and the debtor countries limits the cross-border credit flow and damages both sides in the credit markets. Hence, each side seeks to develop a mechanism to overcome this problem. On the supply side, the creditors seek to develop credible threats. The principal penalty available to creditors is to block the defaulters' access to outside sources. However, the enforcement of this penalty requires coordination among private creditors and their home governments. On the demand side, debtor countries seek to develop commitment mechanisms to further their access to foreign credits with lower interest rates.

The creation of the OPDA in 1881 was a result of the European pressure for debt settlement following the default in 1875. For creditors, the OPDA represented a cooperative effort to secure the repayment of foreign loans and to develop a monitoring and enforcement mechanism for future direct or indirect investments in the Empire. For the Ottoman Empire, on the other hand, the establishment of the OPDA constituted a severe blow to Ottoman pride and sovereignty. For the first time in its history, the Ottomans were forced to surrender a considerable portion of the state's most liquid revenues to the unconditional control of a 'foreign' commission, which constituted a 'state within the state'.

Nevertheless, it is also true that the establishment of the OPDA provided an instrument for committing credibly to the terms specified in the debt contracts and to the protection of foreign investment in the Empire. This commitment created a safer environment for foreign capital and gave the Ottoman government greater access to foreign capital markets at lower risk premiums. Moreover, the existence of the OPDA encouraged foreign direct investment in the Empire at an unprecedented rate. A considerable amount of the FDI during this period went to railway schemes, which not only facilitated domestic economic activities but also enabled the penetration of Western goods into the interior parts of the country. This chapter aims to further our understanding of the changing nature of the European economic penetration of the Ottoman Empire and the institutional infrastructure that allowed this penetration to proceed. In this context, it provides answers to the following questions: Why did the nature of capital flow change after the OPDA? Why did the foreign direct investment take place in this period, not before? How did a government which had defaulted before, and hence already had a bad reputation as a borrower, regain access to foreign capital markets at considerably lower risk premiums?

Chapter 4 provides an in-depth analysis of the management of revenues under the OPDA, tracks the sources of increase in these revenues, and describes the obstacles encountered by the administration. The OPDA, considered as 'the outpost of European imperialism', also provided a good example of the best features of European financial management. In many respects the administrative system introduced by the OPDA contrasted greatly with the financial administration of the Ottoman government. The OPDA introduced new technologies to the relevant sectors under its responsibility, improved the regulations, and made the necessary legislative changes concerning the development of its revenues. Significant improvements achieved in the OPDA revenues, and the introduction of new institutions in relevant sectors, also generated positive externalities for other sectors of the economy.

Chapter 4 also points out that the international treaties imposed on the Porte by the European powers restricted the administration's ability to improve its revenues. In several cases, including wine duties, stamp and patent laws, the OPDA officials complained about the unfair conditions imposed by these treaties and asked for their revision. Hence, despite being widely regarded as the 'outpost of European imperialism' in the Empire, the OPDA itself suffered from the impositions of the hegemonic powers. These examples also illustrate the nature of disagreements on foreign policy issues towards the Empire that arose among European capitalists with conflicting interests in the Ottoman economy. The bondholders or other investors whose interests were tied to those of the Ottoman economy called for more protective measures, while European merchants pushed for less protection and increasing privileges, regardless of the adverse consequences on the overall condition of the economy.

Chapter 5 provides a detailed study of the tobacco monopoly farmed out by the OPDA to the Régie Company, which was formed by a consortium of European banks. The Régie Company was not only the largest foreign investment in the country, but also the largest corporation. The capital of the company made up around 23 percent of total foreign direct investment in the Ottoman Empire in 1881–1914. It held the tobacco monopoly for 42 years, from 1883 until the contract was terminated in 1925, two years after the foundation of the Turkish Republic.

One immediate effect of the Régie on tobacco economy was a considerable fall in the number of tobacco cultivators. This was mostly due to the elimination of small producers as well as high fees, low purchase prices, and excessive regulations applied to remaining growers. Tobacco cultivators often complained that the monopoly suppressed purchase prices whilst inflating retail prices to the frustration of consumers. Smuggling flourished under these conditions, and became a major obstacle to the success of the company. Throughout its operation, the Régie remained a focus of public opposition. It was regarded as a symbol of Western imperialism and exploitation, mostly due to its controversial methods in dealing with the cultivators and its infamous surveillance unit, *kolcus*, which was held responsible for the death of thousands.

Despite the Régie's significant place in the Ottoman economy during the last four decades of the Empire, there is no in-depth study of the company in the literature. Chapter 5 aims to fill this gap by providing a portrayal of the Régie system, and identifying the actors who lost and gained from the institutional arrangements introduced by the company. The majority of the data used in the chapter come from first-hand sources, the annual reports of the Régie Company and the Corporation of Foreign Bondholders.

2

OTTOMAN BORROWING IN THE PRE-OPDA PERIOD: THE PATH TO THE DECREE OF *MUHARREM*

The crisis in Ottoman finance and reform attempts

In the Ottoman Empire, the land was principally owned by the Sultan and was rented to the peasants in return for taxes. Until the sixteenth century, taxation was primarily based on the *tımar* institution. *Sipahis* were state employees who were assigned by the Sultan as administrators of state land and were responsible for the collection of taxes. In return, *sipahis* were obliged to use these revenues locally to maintain a local army, and provide the central administration with a predetermined number of cavalry units in times of war.[1] Although very common, the *tımar* system was not practiced in all conquered territories. In many remote areas, such as Eastern Anatolia, Iraq, Egypt, Yemen, Romania, Moldavia and the Maghrib, the Ottoman government collected tributes through local officials and left the local administrations largely unaltered to avoid popular unrest. This practice also minimized the transaction costs in tax collection. Local governments were likely to be in a better position to minimize the costs of measuring and collecting variable taxes, due to their closer proximity to the tax base.[2]

Until the second half of the sixteenth century, the existing decentralized military structure based on the *tımar* system functioned well, and the Empire continued to expand. During this period, the financial position of the Ottoman Empire was underpinned by the revenues obtained through rapid territorial expansion. Therefore, the state did not feel the need to alter the tax system in order to increase the revenues collected at the center. However, in the late sixteenth century, advances in arms technology, mainly the introduction of firearms, created a need for a modern central army. This development undermined the basis of the *tımar* system in two ways. On one hand, it led to the replacement of light cavalry provided by *sipahis* with infantry. On the other hand, the establishment of a central Imperial army required the development of new financial sources. Hence, it increased the pressure on the state to collect the tax revenues at the central treasury. This led to the gradual dissolution of the *tımar* system and its replacement by the *iltizam* system.

İltizam was based on tax-farm auctioning and subcontracting, thus providing the cash flow required for financing the central Imperial army. In late medieval and early modern Europe, domestic borrowing by sovereigns was financed by the banking houses.[3] In the Ottoman Empire, domestic borrowings were mainly handled through these tax-farming arrangements by which individuals possessing liquid capital assets advanced cash to the government in return for the right to farm the taxes of a given region or fiscal unit for a fixed period of time. In this period, former government officials, merchants and certain other wealthy individuals became the new tax collectors. The emerging local elite, *ayans*, gradually turned economic control over their territories into political power and became involved in numerous provincial revolts against the central government.

In need of immediate resources for financing the modernization of the military, the government began to increase the length of the tax-farming contracts, demanding an increasingly higher proportion of the auction price in advance.[4] This trend led to the introduction of the *malikane* system in 1695, in which the revenue source was farmed out on a life-term basis in return for a large initial sum and annual payments.[5] Nevertheless, neither of these attempts to reform the tax collection system brought a long-term solution to the Ottoman budget deficits, which were often financed by debasements in the coinage. Towards the end of the eighteenth century, for the first time, the Ottoman administration considered borrowing from abroad. However, due to the economic difficulties in Europe arising after the French Revolution, and the reluctance on the Ottoman side, this possibility was not pursued any further, until after 1854.

In 1839, the Ottoman administration introduced extensive tax reform as part of the administrational reorganization under the *Tanzimat* reforms. An important measure related to tax reform was that all the taxes would in future be collected by the salaried government agents, *muhassıls*.

This system worked favorably in the case of many urban taxes. In rural areas, however, the government encountered great difficulties in the collection of tithes, *öşür*, which accounted for a considerable part of state revenues.[6] The major motive behind the implementation of the tax reform in these areas was to curb the power of the provincial elite, the *ayans*, and restore central authority. Yet the economic consequences of this political move turned out to be costly for the treasury. First of all, there were simply not enough new bureaucrats willing and able to act as salaried *muhassıls*, returning all their collections to the treasury. The existing tax farmers had already turned into businessmen and such an arrangement was not profitable for them; hence they opposed the reform. Under these conditions, the salaried agents sent out to the countryside faced many difficulties due to their lack of local knowledge and connections. Consequently, the new system failed to fulfill expectations and *öşür* revenues fell drastically in 1840, forcing the government to revert to the tax farming system.[7] It was only after the accession of Abdülhamid II in 1877 that the tax farms were abolished by a law passed by the parliament. The same law established the department of cultivation and sheep tax for the collection of *öşür* revenues. Even then, the opposition of the tax farmers delayed the establishment of the new system throughout the Empire until late in the reign of Abdülhamid II.[8]

Another major restriction on the development of state revenues was the commercial treaties (capitulations) imposed on the Ottoman Empire by the European powers.[9] The capitulations granted extraterritorial privileges to foreign subjects conducting business in the Empire under Islamic law. Initially, these privileges were granted voluntarily by the rulers with the main motive being the stimulation of interregional trade in the Empire, which would lead ultimately to an increase in their tariff revenues.[10] However, with the gradual decline of the Ottoman Empire in world politics, the capitulations took the form of impositions restricting the sovereignty of the rulers and instruments of discrimination against the local population. By the nineteenth century, the destructive consequences of these treaties on the state finances were so evident that it was even admitted by Adam Block, the representative of the British and Belgian Bondholders in the OPDA:

> The fetters of a contractual trade regime deprive the State of the legitimate means of raising money to defray those expenses without which political and administrative reform is an impossibility.[11]

According to Adam Block, the system of free trade as practiced in the Ottoman Empire restricted every attempt at industrial expansion, impeded the development of its considerable resources, and created *de facto* foreign monopolies, thus contributing to the impoverishment of native enterprise. Block's opinion on capitulations was shared by Charles Morawitz, a foreign observer and a specialist on the Ottoman economy, who argued that the restrictions imposed by the capitulations were among the major obstacles to reform in the Empire.[12]

The first major restriction imposed by the capitulations was that the Ottoman government was deprived of its sovereign rights to set customs duties in a way that maximized its revenues whilst protecting local industry. European governments exercised such rights; indeed, at a time when most of the European powers were endeavoring to protect their own industry and agriculture from foreign protection, the same powers were constantly pressurizing the Porte to lower customs barriers.[13]

In the Ottoman Empire, customs taxes were among the charges sanctioned by the Islamic law, *sheriat*, and were traditionally imposed at the *öşür* rate of 10 percent for foreign and 2.5 percent for internal trade.[14] The capitulations granted to European powers starting in the sixteenth century lowered the duty on foreign goods below 5 percent. After the capitulations of 1673, granted first to France, both exports and imports were fixed at a uniform rate of 3 percent *ad valorem*. Additionally, the buyers of foreign goods paid a supplementary duty of 2 percent, while exporters of foreign goods had to pay higher duties and were subjected to many prohibitions and monopoly restrictions, particularly in the case of essential goods such as wheat and rice. An extra 8 percent internal duty was also imposed on goods carried by land.[15]

Among the capitulations, the most controversial one – because of its perceived destructive effects on native production – was the 1838 Trade Agreement, also known as the Baltalimanı Treaty. In contrast to the previous capitulations, this treaty did not directly lower the customs duties. Tariffs were even raised to 5 percent on imports and 12 percent on exports. However, it removed all monopolies and restrictions on foreign trade, hence foreign subjects were allowed to export or import all sorts of goods without restrictions.[16] The agreement would apply to all parts of the Empire including Egypt, where Mehmed Ali had established an elaborate system of state monopolies and a protective foreign trade policy.[17] Moreover, the crucial element of the agreement regarding duties was the privileges granted to foreign subjects in terms of internal duties. According to the terms of the treaty the transit duties imposed on goods were dropped to 3 percent for foreigners, even as local merchants continued to pay 8 percent. Hence, the resultant tax regime put local merchants at a profound disadvantage when competing with their foreign counterparts.[18]

In 1861, at the insistence of the Porte, new treaties were signed with foreign powers, raising import duties to 8 percent and providing for the gradual reduction of export duties to 1 percent. Further attempts at modification of the treaties were rejected by the powers until 1907, when the import duties were raised to 11 percent with the support of the OPDA, which took control of these revenues under the assignments of the Decree of *Muharrem*. Both the OPDA and the Ottoman government constantly appealed to the foreign powers for a further 4 percent increase in import duties, which could only be realized in 1914.[19] After the Ottoman government's entry into the war, the capitulations were abolished and a more protective trade policy was adopted. In this context, in 1916, the uniform *ad valorem* tax was replaced by differentiated specific duties designed to yield more revenue and protect the developing local industries.[20]

While trade protection has its obvious disadvantages, such as preserving inefficient industries in their existing form, the free trade regime as practiced in the Ottoman economy prevented the state from taking any protective measures to stimulate the development of infant industries. As confirmed by Adam Block's comments, it was not only local producers who sought protection. A very large portion of the foreign direct investment in the Empire went to monopolies or sectors that were not exposed to foreign competition, such as the tobacco industry, railways, tramways, ports, gas, electricity and waterworks. In this context, it is hardly surprising that the foreign-owned tobacco monopoly was also the largest foreign enterprise in the economy. In addition, due to these unilateral compromises, the Ottoman Empire was deprived of the opportunity of bargaining with other European states to lower the trade barriers applied to their products. For instance, the high tariffs on Turkish wine in France and Italy, a major complaint of the OPDA, could have been made a bargaining issue, had these countries not already been granted privileges.

The second major restriction imposed by the capitulations concerned state monopolies. In most developed countries state monopolies existed in various sectors of the economy, such as salt, tobacco, alcohol, matches, playing cards, petroleum, cigarette paper, etc. and the revenues derived from these monopolies made up a considerable portion of state revenues. However, the Ottoman Empire was deprived of the right to establish monopolies in sectors other than salt and tobacco. According to Adam Block, these treaties, by preventing the establishment of monopolies, constituted a 'serious obstacle to the progress and security of the country'.[21]

Adam Block was right in addressing the fact that deprivation of the right to establish monopolies also deprived the Ottoman state of considerable revenue. Considering the state's inability to collect tax on the profits of the commercial activities of foreign subjects, this particular source of income gained more importance.

In terms of its effects on the general economy, this argument has both its pros and cons. In a country such as Turkey where capital accumulation in private hands was extremely limited, establishing state monopolies could also be considered as the only way to establish large factories that could benefit from economies of scale. However, it is also true that establishing such monopolies would impose costs on the economy by blocking private attempts at industrialization in these sectors. As we will see in the case of the Régie Company, the establishment of the tobacco monopoly had been costly for the economy by causing the emigration of cigarette producers. Some of these entrepreneurs moved to Egypt, because of the absence of such restrictions in the Egyptian tobacco sector, and later formed the backbone of Egyptian industrialization.

The final major restriction imposed on the development of state revenues was the tax privileges granted to foreign citizens. This privileged population included not only foreigners but also a number of minorities in the business world, the protégés of the European powers.[22] With the exception of real estate, these foreign subjects were exempted from direct taxation unless their governments gave consent. Only in real estate were they subject to the same status as the Ottomans, except in Hidjaz where they were not allowed to own property. Hence, foreign observers regarded the situation of the foreigner engaged in Turkey as 'highly enviable' since their fiscal privileges were allowed in no Western state.[23] As we will later discuss in detail, the increasing role of this privileged population in the economy and the gradual replacement of Muslims in business activities seriously hampered the Ottoman tax revenues as well as OPDA revenues after 1881.

Domestic borrowing and the financial monopoly of the Galata Bankers

In the second half of the eighteenth century, the Ottoman government sought new methods to broaden the base of state borrowing and reach beyond the limited numbers of large *sarrafs*, who tended to dominate the *malikane* auctions, towards a larger pool of small and medium-sized lenders.[24] For this purpose, in 1774 the Ottoman government introduced a new system of domestic borrowing called *esham*. *Eshams* were issued by the government to pay for the goods and services for which ready money could not be found, and for the repayment of short-term loans over longer terms. These securities were secured on anticipated revenues from particular sources. When the funds of the ministries were exhausted, payments were also made in *sergis*, an official promise to pay at a later date.

Another form of government paper issued for the same purpose was the *kaime*. *Kaimes* were treasury notes, the first issued in 1840 with a life term of eight years. From 1840–44 they carried interest of 12.5 percent per annum, paid half yearly. Thereafter, they bore a rate of 6 percent per annum, until maturity. These notes were issued in standard currency denominations, but initially only in very large ones. After a while, they came to be used as a medium of exchange in daily transactions. In 1852, the *kaime* was transformed into a paper currency when the government started issuing large amounts of non-interest bearing *kaimes* in low denominations. These paper currencies, unbacked by specie, were increasingly used for the payment of the official salaries. By the end of the Crimean War, the *kaime* had become the main form of currency used in İstanbul. However, the growing mistrust of the *kaime* and its depreciation was a major problem for the economy. Therefore, its withdrawal from the market and replacement by a sound metallic currency became an urgent priority both for the sake of Ottoman commerce and the restoration of the state's finances.[25]

Before the 1850s, the Porte employed exclusively native *sarrafs* (Galata Bankers) for the relatively limited financial accommodations of the Empire. These Galata Bankers – called after the financial district of Galata – were generally Greeks, Jews, Armenians and Levantines.[26] The Galata Bankers provided the Ottoman government with short-term advances, for one or two years at the most, often in return for *eshams*. The rates of interest charged by these bankers were quite high; they usually ranged between 12 percent and 18 percent, but could go considerably higher. This range not only reflected the scarcity of capital in the Empire, but also the high risks involved in lending to the government and the high transaction costs incurred in the enforcement of debt contracts; particularly due to the commissions paid to third parties within the bureaucracy to ensure the repayment of the debt. As noted by Clay, 'the government had never yet formally defaulted on its debts, but there could be little certainty about exact dates of repayment and until well within living memory individual creditors had been subject to the arbitrary confiscation of their assets and even execution'. [27]

It is hard to argue that *eshams* were as successful as originally planned in broadening the base of state borrowing beyond the large financiers. The recipients of *eshams* and *sergis* were often unwilling or unable to wait for the highly uncertain maturity date. Consequently, they cashed these papers by selling them to the Galata Bankers at a considerable discount. Through this system the government securities were gathered in the hands of this small minority of *sarrafs* who accrued substantial profits.[28] It was extremely hard for small creditors (either contractors, or state officials paid in promissory notes) to receive their payments from the government, particularly in times of hardship. The Galata Bankers were undoubtedly more powerful; not only because they were the only major source of capital the government could borrow from when needed, but also they had close ties with *Paşas* through whom they could exert some influence on the government and guarantee the repayment of their loans, at least to some degree:[29]

> A poor pensioner who has no influential contractor, or a contractor whose further services are not for the moment required, may be put off from day to day, from week to week, from month to month, and even from year to year; whereas a superior official of the Palace, an influential Pasha, a contractor who regularly supplies the troops, or a Galata banker who is

ready to make a little advance in moments of extreme difficulty, cannot be so unceremoniously treated.[30]

Hence, the beneficiaries of the growing financial instability and uncertainty in the Empire were the Galata Bankers and their collaborators in the bureaucracy. The bankers charged the holders of government securities premiums for undertaking the risk and managed to encash these papers rather easily by means of their connections. As the financial needs of the Empire grew, the Porte became more dependent on these bankers. Until the 1850s, the Galata Bankers enjoyed exceptionally high interest on their credits thanks to their unrivaled position in the domestic market and built a reputation in Europe as the 'Galata Vampires'.[31]

External borrowing and institutional reforms to improve the credit of the Empire: 1854–75

Ottoman foreign borrowing in the pre-OPDA era

Until the 1850s the Ottoman government managed to meet its budget deficits without resorting directly to foreign credit, using various means such as the debasement of the coinage and the issue of securities and banknotes. However, foreign capital hardly remained indifferent to the high interest rates offered by the government. Foreign money flooded into the country through the local intermediaries, the Galata Bankers, most of whom either had direct links with foreign banking houses in financial centers or had established their own branches in Western capitals.[32] They borrowed from abroad and lent to the government, often enjoying substantial profits for their intermediary roles. Through this system the government continued to borrow from the local bankers at higher interest rates and avoided borrowing directly from foreign creditors.

The major reason for the Porte's reluctance was the potential political costs of foreign borrowing.[33] It was not uncommon for European governments to demand political concessions from the borrower as a precondition to open their markets to their bonds. Above all, the Porte feared the possibility of foreign intervention in case of any difficulty in servicing debt. In 1850, Reşid Paşa decided to break the monopoly of the domestic bankers and signed a successful foreign loan agreement for Fr 55 million. However, shortly after agreeing the loan, Reşid Paşa was removed from power, and the contract was cancelled by the government due to these concerns.[34]

In 1854, the great treasury crisis caused by the expenses incurred during the Crimean War forced the Ottoman Empire to reconsider the borrowing opportunities in foreign markets. In the same year, with the support of its allies Britain and France, the government contracted its first official foreign loan in the European markets, in spite of all the concerns about its consequences. The original amount of the loan was £3 million; the bonds were floated in Britain at an 80 percent issue rate, carrying 6 percent interest. The loan was secured against the Egyptian tribute, which would be deposited directly by the Khedive of Egypt at the Bank of England. Thus, the collateral would be secured in the creditor country. Moreover, in the prospectus of the loan issued by the underwriting banking house in London, the approval of the British government was specifically emphasized. This, of course, did not mean a guarantee in any legal sense (as in the 1855 loan) but played a crucial role, along with the collateral, in securing better terms for the loan.[35]

Some Ottoman historians argued that the issue of the 1854 loan marked the date the Ottoman government was 'pushed' into indebtedness by the European powers.[36] This interpretation overlooks the fact that the Ottoman treasury was not left with many other alternatives. By the time a new loan was floated in the European markets, much of the money had in fact already been borrowed from the domestic market in the form of short-term advances, or would have to be borrowed in the near future in order to meet the payments on earlier loans. In this sense, the successive foreign loans were nothing more than a series of consolidation operations through which the domestic short-term loans carrying high interest rates were repaid by foreign long-term borrowing carrying considerably lower interest rates. Moreover, as argued by Clay, the complaint of the Ottoman officials was not that the European powers pushed them to borrow from abroad unnecessarily, but that they refused to lend on demand.[37]

In 1854, the government had already exhausted all its domestic borrowing alternatives. The interest rates charged by the Galata Bankers on their short-term advances had reached over 15 percent. Large issues of *kaimes* had already started causing problems. Further depreciation of the currency would bring nothing but more political unrest. On the other hand, the terms of the 1854 loan were very attractive, considering the financial difficulties of the Empire during the Crimean War. The effective interest rate on this loan was 7.9 percent, significantly below the interest asked by the local bankers. In this sense, it was the most successful foreign loan contract in the pre-OPDA era, with the exception of the guaranteed loan of 1855.

The net receipts from the 1854 loan fell far short of the accumulated expenses incurred by the Ottoman government whilst waging war in Crimea. Hence, the Ottoman government issued another loan in 1855, this time under the official guarantee of its allies who demanded that the loan be devoted to financing the war. 'The guarantee of the British and French governments', Blaisdell notes, 'brought the most conservative bankers into the field, and the price reflected this competition'.[38] The 1855 loan was the most favorable foreign loan contracted by the Ottoman government, in economic terms. The £5 million loan was issued at 102.6 percent, which simply means that the government received 2.6 percent more than the face value of the bonds, yielding 4 percent nominal interest. The loan was secured on the Egyptian tribute held by the Bank of England and the customs revenues of İzmir and Syria.

These two loans were called the Egyptian Tribute loans, secured on the most liquid and the least risky collateral the Empire had to offer. The support of the allies was without a doubt another crucial factor that contributed to the success of these loans, despite the war conditions. After the war, the government continued to borrow from foreign markets. In 1902, Morawitz noted 'There are things that are very quickly learned. The art of indebtedness is among them. As soon as the Ottoman Empire was initiated it made rapid progress in this direction.'[39] First used for meeting the demands of the war, then for retiring the progressively depreciating *kaimes*, foreign borrowing eventually became a major instrument for meeting budget deficits. However, with each loan the credibility of the Empire depreciated even further.

Contractors of the Ottoman bonds often enjoyed a large commission and/or a wide spread between the contract and issue prices (the price the government received from the contractor and the price at which the contractor offered the loan to the public) in return for the risk borne by underwriting the transaction. Also, in many contracts an option clause was introduced, according to which the issuing house, buying outright a part of the issue, reserved the right to float the remainder at a price of its choosing. On the other hand, the issuing house was liable to pay a fixed price to the government. Even though this process entailed some risk for the issuers, it almost invariably worked in their favor.[40]

Table 2.1 Ottoman foreign debt in the pre-OPDA era: 1854–77

Year	Amount of Debt (£)	Rate of Issue	Amount acquired (£)	% Acquired	Nominal Interest	Effective Interest	Allocated to	Pledges	Major Investor
1854	3,000,000	80.00%	2,286,285	76%	6.0%	7.9%	Crimean war	Egyptian tribute	B
1855	5,000,000	102.63%	5,131,250	102%	4.0%	3.9%	Crimean war	Egyptian tribute, customs-İzmir, Syria	B
1858	5,000,000	76.00%	3,687,500	74%	6.0%	8.1%	Support the exchange rate	İstanbul octroi and customs	B
1860	2,037,220	62.50%	1,273,262	62%	6.0%	9.6%	Budget deficit	Indirect contributions	F
1862	8,000,000	68.00%	5,440,000	68%	6.0%	8.8%	Withdrawal of the *kaimes*	Taxes on tobacco, salt, stamps, profits	B
1863	8,000,000	71.00%	5,680,000	71%	6.0%	8.5%	Repayment of debt	Customs, silk, olive oil, tobacco, salt tithes	F
1865/1	6,000,000	66.00%	3,960,000	66%	6.0%	9.1%	Repayment of debt and Budget deficit	Ergani mines	F
1865/2	36,363,636	50.00%	18,181,818	50%	5.0%	10.0%	Repayment of 1854 loan	General debt	F , B
1869	22,222,220	54.00%	12,000,000	54%	6.0%	11.1%	Repayment of debt and Budget deficit	Tithes from various vilayets	F
1870	31,680,001	32.13%	10,177,109	32%	3.0%	9.3%	Rumeli railway	General debt	A,G,I
1871	5,700,000	73.00%	4,161,000	73%	6.0%	8.2%	Budget deficit	Egyptian tribute	B,F
1872	11,126,200	98.50%	9,457,276	85%	9.0%	10.6%	Budget deficit	Revenues of Salonica, Edirne, Danube, sheep tax of Anatolia	B, A,G
1873/1	11,465,450	55.00%	6,306,000	55%	5.0%	9.1%	Consolidate the treasury bonds issued in 1872	General debt	F,B
1873/2	27,777,780	54.00%	15,000,000	54%	6.0%	11.1%	Budget deficit	Revenues of Aleppo, Danube and animal tax of Anatolia	F
1874	40,000,000	43.50%	17,400,000	43%	5.0%	11.5%	Floating debt	General debt	F, B
1877	5,000,000	52.00%	2,600,000	52%	5.0%	9.6%	1877 Russian War	Egyptian tribute	F

A=Austria, B=Britain, F=France, G=Germany, I=Italy. Source: Annual Reports of the CFB; Kıray, 1995; Pamuk, 1994; Suvla, 1966.

Table 2.1. illustrates the original amount of issue, the issue rate, and the nominal/effective interest rates on the Ottoman bonds issued by the government in 1854–77. As observed from the table, most Ottoman bonds were issued at significantly lower rates than their nominal value with the exception of the second loan in 1855.

As the Empire's credibility declined in the markets, the underwriters charged larger risk premiums. Thus, in some cases the amount acquired by the government fell below 50 percent of the amount of debt incurred by bond issues (in 1870 and 1874) and effective interest rates rose to around 11.5 percent. Moreover, at each loan the Ottoman government saw itself obliged to pledge the most productive of its remaining sources of revenue. The surplus of the Egyptian tribute, the sheep tax, customs revenues, the tobacco revenues, the copper mines and various other tithes, were all hypothecated one by one to the different issues.

As noted by the European press the process was very similar to 'the shifts of a ruined family, where every article of value follows each other to the pawnshop'.[41] Particularly after the 1860s the Porte had difficulty in finding acceptable securities to be pledged for new bonds, and issued treasury bonds secured on the general revenues of the Empire. These bonds could be issued in larger amounts since there was no need to pledge special revenues. However, they also carried significantly higher effective interest rates. Since the Empire had already exhausted its attractive collaterals the only alternative way to raise another loan was to improve the general credit of the treasury by creating new commitment mechanisms through new institutional arrangements.

Institutional arrangements to improve the credit of the Empire in the pre-OPDA era

There are two conditions for a state to be able to borrow from the domestic market at reasonable terms. First, national savings must reach a sufficient level and secondly, the holders of these savings must have confidence in the state. As argued before, in the Ottoman Empire neither of these conditions existed. To acquire foreign loans, on the other hand, the borrowing country must show some effective guarantees of its capacity for future repayment. In the Ottoman case, a budget system, which was part of the 1839 reform program, had not as yet been established by the Porte. The existing accounts of the treasury were unreliable and it was extremely difficult for creditors to monitor these accounts. Therefore, it was very difficult for the government to issue loans secured on the general revenues of the treasury. In other words, special revenues had to be pledged as collateral.[42] The more liquid and monitorable the collateral, the more confidence would it command in foreign markets. Moreover, the collateral had to be easily and costlessly seizable by the creditors in case of default, otherwise it would not be very credible. Hence, when the revenues of the treasury are considered, the tributes were probably the most attractive collaterals, both in terms of stability and liquidity. In this sense, the Egyptian tribute was a practical solution to these problems but it was already re-mortgaged to guarantee bond issues during the Crimean War. The customs revenues of İstanbul and İzmir were also among the attractive collaterals, but had already been used to raise the loans in 1855 and 1858. For every attempt to raise a new loan the Porte had to rely more on less attractive collaterals. This led to a reluctance amongst investors to lend money to the Porte and gave rise to high-risk premiums associated with uncertainty. Following the 1860s, the Porte initiated several institutional reforms in order to improve the credibility of the government.

Budget reform and European concerns about the reliability of the Ottoman financial records

In the 1850s very little was known in the European markets about the state of the Ottoman finances. Ambassadors sometimes reported back to their governments about the economic condition of the country. However, the information they could obtain was very limited and the reliability of the figures was often questionable. Moreover, this information hardly reached the small investors, and when it did it was usually through a couple of lines in the newspapers along with some other inaccurate information rarely substantiated with numbers.

On the other hand, with each loan the markets became more doubtful about the state of the Ottoman finances. Consequently, effective interest rates on these loans (with the exception of the 1855 Tribute loan officially guaranteed by the British and French governments) were steadily climbing. For the 1860 loan rates of the issue had plunged to 62.5 percent, and the effective interest offered by the government had reached 9.6 percent. Moreover, in the very same year the government had attempted to raise another loan, contracted by the infamous French banker Jules Mirès, which had failed because of the French government's refusal to allow the loan's quotation on the French Bourse.[43] These were all signs of the erosion of the Porte's already limited financial credibility. The first Ottoman budget was prepared under these adverse conditions by the newly appointed Grand Vezir Fuat Paşa in advance of the financial year 1860–61.[44] Fuat Paşa was convinced that to access further loans with lower interest rates the Porte had to restore its credibility in the foreign markets. He therefore initiated a series of reforms in this direction and the establishment of a budget system was at the top of the list.[45]

However, the Ottoman budget system remained short of fulfilling the expectations of foreign investors as budgets were nothing more than vague estimations of expected revenues and expenses of the state.[46] In 1862, after a long investigation, Mr Foster and Lord Hobart reported to the British Parliament that the Porte itself simply had no means of obtaining accurate information about its receipts and expenditures.[47] As late as 1885, Vincent Caillard, the president of the OPDA, wrote 'The state accounts are rarely, if ever balanced. The budgets, drawn up at the commencement of each financial year, are mere approximate estimates, never revised at the close of the year, but left to work themselves square by a kind of process of evolution.'[48]

According to Caillard, the Turkish budget system illustrated 'the evils of the financial decentralization in their most aggravated form'.[49] The Ottoman Empire was divided up for administrative purposes into 31 *vilayets* (provinces). The local budgets of these *vilayets* were prepared by the local officials. Later on, they were sent to İstanbul for the approval of the government and to be corrected if necessary. Finally, the Imperial budget was constructed from these local budgets provided by the provinces. One common principal-agent problem that arose during the preparation of budgets was the strategic reporting of the local authorities. It was habitual for the local authorities to understate their revenues and overstate their expenditures, for the following reasons. First, knowing that the Imperial Treasury would increase its demands on their revenues, they wanted to retain sufficient funds to run their administration. Second, they aimed to avoid being flooded with cash demands by the central government, and to make provisions for future calls on their resources. Hence, the government itself had no accurate data at its disposal by which trustworthy conclusions could be drawn as to the real state of the finances of the Empire.

Also, the common use of *havales* (drafts) for the repayment of loans to creditors and contractors made the system very complicated to monitor for the bondholders as well as for the Ministry of Finance. *Havales* were the payment orders delivered by ministers to pay the state bills when the ministry was short of cash. These payment orders were issued on the revenues of different provinces, and were often negotiated at a considerable discount to the recipient. Blaisdell notes that favoritism among ministers and between ministers and creditors created the gravest abuses in the *havale* system.[50] Therefore, even the Ministry of Finance found it impossible to come up with an accurate estimate of total state expenses for the coming year.

Another major complaint regarding the reliability of the Ottoman budgets was that there was virtually no control mechanism over the borrowings of the sovereign and his use of the proceeds.[51] The private budget of the Sultan was not included in the state budget. It was under the control of a minister responsible only to the Sultan and required to obey the Sultan's orders in order to maintain his post.[52]

Under these conditions of uncertainty, the Ottoman government often exaggerated its revenues and underreported its expenditures to enable it to borrow from the international markets at lower rates.[53] On the other hand, European newspapers constantly protested that the government allowed budgets to stand in place of yearly financial accounts, and pointed out that no reliance could be placed on the figures shown in the budget. As argued by the investors, the newly issued budgets were of little use without the past budgets and the final accounts for the respective years, which were required to assess the accuracy of the estimates in the budget.[54]

The National Bank Concession and the establishment of the BIO

Another item in Fuat Paşa's reform program was the national bank concession. In 1863, after three failed attempts to create a national bank, the Ottoman government granted a concession to the BIO (La Banque Impériale Ottomane).[55] The first attempt had been in 1853. The concession was granted to the Ottoman Bank, but it failed due to the Crimean War. The second one, the INBT (Imperial National Bank of Turkey) concession in 1856, collapsed due to the deterioration of the financial conditions in Europe in the winter of 1856–57 before the bank commenced its operations. The third concession was granted to an Anglo-Greek consortium, NBT (National Bank of Turkey), in 1859, which required the withdrawal of *kaimes* from the market at least three months before the bank commenced its operations. The concessionaires inserted this clause to the concession because they argued that if other forms of money remained in existence, the monopoly on the note issues, the most important privilege of the bank, would be meaningless.[56] Furthermore, withdrawal of *kaimes* required the raising of a new loan large enough to wipe out the progressively depreciating currency. However, the lack of confidence both in the domestic and foreign markets was the main reason behind the government's consent to the establishment of a national bank controlled by foreign bankers. The growing financial difficulties of the government made it impossible to withdraw *kaimes* in the following years. Instead, in 1861, after a failed attempt to raise a new loan in the foreign markets (Mirès Loan in 1860), the government again resorted to *kaimes* and issued a record amount of paper currency. Consequently, *kaimes* flooded the markets and the exchange rate against the gold lira plunged to 400 paper piastres – causing a major wave of inflation.[57] Hence the national bank concession failed once again. The Ottoman government tried to break out of this impasse with the fourth concession.

Under the Convention of 1863, the Anglo-French concessionaires were granted the privilege of establishing a state bank in the Ottoman Empire, which was to bear the name BIO. All senior officers and most shareholders of the bank were foreign. Concerned about the possibility of foreign interference, the Porte underscored that the bank was bound to operate in accordance with Ottoman law, which meant it could not enjoy capitulatory status.[58]

Government's involvement in the management of the bank was one of the major issues during negotiations. This role was to be kept to a minimum in order to command confidence in the European money markets. In other words, the 'bank could be of service to the state if it was entirely independent of the state'.[59] Hence, the Porte was obliged to accept a role for its representatives that would be little more than maintaining the appearance of an Ottoman element in the hierarchy of the bank. The government would also appoint a *nazır* (minister) for inspection purposes and a *muhasebeci* (accountant) to supervise the financial operations between the bank and the treasury, but take no part in the actual running of the bank.

The functions and privileges granted to the BIO could be summarized as follows:[60]

1- The most important privilege of the BIO, and the major reason behind the consortium's demand for the concession, was the exclusive privilege of issuing notes. Through this privilege the bank would obtain an interest-free loan from the public for the difference between the amount in circulation and the specie required to be held in reserve. Although it was often misinterpreted, only in the case of the issue of paper money was the bank granted a monopoly.[61]

2- The bank would also keep the accounts of the government in İstanbul. It was charged with handling the operations of the treasury, collecting the revenues and making the payments ordered by the Ministry of Finance. Outside the capital, where it had branches, it would collect the revenues assigned to it. However, the proportion of the government revenue handled by the bank remained far below initial expectations.

3- The BIO would also provide the government with cheaper short-term credits, through the *sergis* issued by the Ministry of Finance. This practice, the government hoped, would end the reliance on the Galata Bankers. The amount of *sergis*, previously issued by each ministry, would be fixed monthly in agreement with the bank and only be issued by the Ministry of Finance. The advances would be secured by the government revenues assigned to the bank. Since the securities against which the advances were to be provided would be unimpeachable, the credits would carry a relatively lower interest.

4- The BIO would act as the financial agent of the government both inside and outside the Empire charged with servicing domestic and foreign debt payments, and raising new loans. In return, the BIO would receive 1 percent commission on the sums handled, in addition to an annual fee of LT 20,000.

The national bank concession granted to the BIO, an Anglo-French consortium, helped the government to raise three loans in 1862–65, contracted by the bank. In 1862, the government raised a loan to withdraw the *kaimes* from the domestic market before the bank commenced its operations. The original amount of the loan was £8 million, the issue rate was 62 percent and the effective interest was 8.8 percent. In 1863 and 1865, the Porte signed two other contracts for a total of £14 million with effective interest rates of 8.5 percent and 9.1 percent respectively.[62] After the failure of the Mirès Loan in 1860, the government's reform attempts had once more provided access to the international markets. According to Eldem, 'the mere presence of this institution [the BIO] in a country that had lacked any permanent and formal representation of Western financial interests was sufficient to give a sense of security to European investors, already reassured by the success of the 1862 loan'.[63] However, the risk premiums on these loans were still considerably high. The level of spread between the yield of British consols and that of the Ottoman bonds during the period suggests that the reforms might have provided some sense of security to foreign investors, thus enabling the Porte to raise new loans. Yet, the credibility of the reforms was still being questioned in financial circles.[64]

The 1874 reform program

In 1874, the government was unable to borrow from the Galata Bankers even at interest as high as 25 percent.[65] The credit of the Empire was no better in foreign markets. So far, the coupons of various loans had usually been met at maturity. As early as 1866 the payment of general debt coupons had been deferred for two months, followed by a failure to maintain provisions for the charges on several foreign loans during 1871. Subsequently, a proportion of the coupons had remained unpaid.[66] However, rumors of bankruptcy began circulating in the European markets. It was often argued in the newspapers that the country's finances were finally exhausted, the budgets were untrustworthy, nobody knew anything about the condition of the Empire's exchequer, and the administration was corrupt and totally uncontrolled in matters of finance.[67] The credit of the Empire plunged to its lowest level so that, at one point in 1873, bonds of 6 percent had become unsellable at 46 percent of their face value.[68]

In a period characterized by mounting political problems and loss of power in the international arena, the Porte's main and immediate concern was accessing external funds on the most favorable terms in order to finance the modernization of the army. For this purpose, it initiated several reforms. However, as observed after the budget reform, instead of preparing a reliable budget that would secure the confidence of the financial circles in the long term, the government chose to overstate its revenues in order to secure loans with lower risk premiums. In the short term these budgets helped the Porte to raise additional loans, but in the long term, as more investors questioned their reliability, they contributed to the further erosion of the Porte's credibility. This generated a need for the Porte to compromise its autonomy by delegating some of its financial responsibilities to third parties who could command confidence in European financial circles. This was the main logic behind the 1874 reform program.

In 1874, desperately needing to improve its credit in the financial markets, the government resorted to drastic measures, which meant further compromising its financial autonomy. These measures included the establishment of a financial commission to control the Imperial budget and the extension of the BIO's privileges, which made the bank responsible for the supervision of the state finances.

In order to improve the credibility of the Ottoman budget, the government set up a commission to control and approve the 1874–75 budget. The commission comprised the principal functionaries of the state, bankers and directors of the leading financial establishments in İstanbul. Out of thirteen members of the commission, only three held government posts. All the rest were leading figures from İstanbul's banking community, some of whom were very well known in the European financial markets, including the General Director of the Ottoman Bank and the bank's two other directors. As far as domestic financial businesses were concerned, these were the very people who needed to be convinced that the government was going to eliminate its budget deficits. Furthermore, the government was relying on the reputation of these figures outside the Empire.[69]

The commission was well aware that the Ottoman government's bad reputation was common knowledge among European investors and posed a major obstacle to the success of any kind of economic reform. For this reason, they attached special importance to public relations. Following approval of the 1874–75 budget, the commission issued a report, to be published in major European journals. The report argued that 'successive adverse circumstances' had discredited the Empire's finances, but its negative reputation was not justified by the facts. The commission claimed that they would reveal the truth about Turkish finances and regain the confidence of European investors: 'a complete and truthful statement of the financial situation, even in its most unfavorable details, is the only means of inspiring well-founded confidence'.[70]

Another measure taken by the government for issuing a new loan was the consolidation of the BIO's privileges as a state bank. According to the convention signed between Sadık Paşa and BIO administrators on 18 May 1874, the bank would be the 'treasurer and the paymaster of the Empire'. As such, it would take over the finances of the Empire. In this context, all the tax revenues of the government both in İstanbul and the provinces would be deposited into a nearby branch of the BIO, which would extend its branch network. Likewise, the BIO was charged with making all payments on behalf of the government, including the debt service.[71]

Hence, in spite of the increasing debt burden and the risks associated with it, the Ottoman government managed to raise another loan of £40 million in the British and French markets, with the help of the new reform program.[72] The 5 percent bonds were issued at 43.5 percent of their face value on average, and the effective interest was about 11.5 percent, which was the highest rate in the history of Ottoman foreign borrowing. Still, considering the economic difficulties of the Empire, and the fact that no special hypothecations were made for the loan, the issue was interpreted as a 'success' in the European press.[73]

Although they helped the government to raise another loan, the high rate of effective interest suggests that the reforms, which entailed the establishment of an independent financial commission to control the Imperial Budget and the delegation of tax collection to the BIO, did not satisfy the European bondholders. First of all, the credibility of a commission consisting of bankers whose interests were intertwined with those of the Porte was questioned by the bondholders. After all, these bankers were the largest domestic creditors of the government and had vested interests in the issue of the new loan, which would be used mainly for the payment of the short-term domestic debt. The frequent use of this argument demonstrated the eroding confidence of the European investors in the administration of the BIO, the largest domestic creditor.[74] As the bankruptcy of the government drew near, the conflict of interest between the bank and foreign creditors became more and more apparent:

> With all respect to the English members of the Commission individually, we do not think the composition of it is in any way satisfactory. The object being to inform English creditors of the true condition of Turkish finance, it must surely be evident that certificates of soundness from a commission composed of Turkish officials, Constantinople bankers, and the directors of establishments identified justly or unjustly, in the public mind with the interests of the Turkish government, cannot be worth the paper they are written upon. If the Turkish government is to gain authority for its budgets at all, the commission appointed to report should consist of English financiers of repute, if possible with a parliamentary reputation, and above all known to be independent by the mass of English creditors of Turkey.[75]

The BIO building in Karaköy. Istanbul University (IU), *Nadir Eserler Kütüphanesi*, 90839-0043.

The convention between the government and the BIO was another factor that helped raise public expectations in Europe regarding the future of the Empire. Some newspapers welcomed the extension of the privileges of the BIO, as a bank governed by Europeans who were acquainted with European accounting techniques such as double-entry bookkeeping.[76] Moreover, the convention was regarded as a guarantee that the government was sincere in its wish for sound reform. However, authorities also warned investors to be cautious when investing in Ottoman securities. First, the BIO did not have any absolute power to check the extravagance of the government or to prevent peculation and extortion by revenue collectors.[77] Secondly, this could be just another desperate attempt by a government on the brink of bankruptcy to persuade investors to issue another loan. The proposed supervisory role of the BIO would require an extensive network of branches in the provinces, which the BIO did not have. Hence, it would take a while before the convention was put into practice, and it could be canceled after the issue of the loan. Future developments confirmed these warnings: the convention was never completely practiced as originally envisaged because of the default in 1875 and the ensuing political crisis.[78]

Ottoman borrowing during the default period: 1875–81

The unproductive use of external resources for the import of military goods or for consumption by the state bureaucracy during the 1860s resulted in a growing debt burden. As a result, in the 1870s the Ottoman state had severe debt service problems. The economic conditions of the Empire worsened further in 1875. The annual harvest had been extremely poor in several provinces and the government was compelled to provide food to prevent famine. This was followed by severe floods and an outbreak of disease in several provinces.[79] Consequently, the tithes and other tax revenues remained far below the Porte's expectations.[80] The cost of dealing with the insurrection that broke out in the Balkan provinces further aggravated the situation.

Under these circumstances, the Porte attempted to issue another loan in foreign markets. Yet, it was hard to find an acceptable security with a reliable yield not pledged to former creditors. Hence the only alternative available was to issue another loan on the general revenues of the treasury for which no special security had to be shown. Following the establishment of the BIO, the Porte had increasingly resorted to these treasury bonds, taking advantage of the credibility of the BIO in the financial markets. Still, the effective interest yields of these bonds were considerably higher than the others. After some consultations with the possible contractors, it became apparent that the issue price of the loan would be around 34 percent – a rate that had previously been refused by the government – or even less.[81]

On 6 October 1875 the Grand Vezir Mahmut Nedim Paşa issued a public statement declaring partial default on interest payments of the foreign loans: 'in the presence of a budget deficit of five million (LT), it (the Porte) has decided to pay only the half of the coupons…'.[82] In April 1876, after the partial default, the Porte declared a total default, suspending all the interest payments on the foreign loans, except the 1855 Loan guaranteed by the British government, which continued to be paid in full. By the time the government unilaterally decided to freeze interest payments, more than half of its revenues were committed to the debt service.[83]

Following the default, bondholders started to organize in order to exert pressure on the Porte through their governments. Creditor governments were quick to protest the unilateral suspension of the debt service. The default was also heavily criticized within the Empire. Several prominent figures of the time questioned the reasoning of Nedim Paşa in declaring a default unilaterally, without even attempting to renegotiate the terms of the debt contracts with creditors. Cevdet Paşa criticized the default decision, arguing that Nedim Paşa had not only isolated the Empire from Europe, but also created negative public opinion about the Ottomans in a period when the Empire was facing great military threats particularly from Russia. Hence, Cevdet Paşa argued, the default decision had alienated the former allies of the Empire and benefited no one other than Russia. Some writers went even further and accused the Grand Vezir of treachery, arguing that the Paşa was serving Russian interests, not those of the Empire.[84]

Amidst the continuing disunity among the bondholder committees, the Porte managed to borrow both from domestic and international markets, which undoubtedly enabled the country to survive the Russian War and delay debt renegotiations. The following section analyzes government borrowing in the default period resulting from the lack of coordination among the Ottoman bondholders, and aims to explain the reasoning of the relevant actors.

Foreign borrowing during the default: Tribute bondholders and the defense loan of 1877

When the Ottoman Empire declared itself bankrupt, a portion of its loans were secured on the hypothecation of special revenues while the rest were secured on the general revenues of the treasury. The Egyptian tribute loans, the loans of 1854, 1855 and 1871, represented the former case. These loans also had a peculiar advantage compared to other hypothecated loans since their security was directly deposited from Egypt to the Bank of England without passing through the Ottoman Treasury. After the default, the Khedive of Egypt continued to send the tribute to the Bank of England. To avoid any government interference, the Ottoman government continued to make payments on the 1855 loan which was guaranteed by the French and British governments. Yet, the Porte insisted that the general law that reduced the interest on all loans to one half was applicable to the bondholders of the 1854 and 1871 tribute loans. Hence, after the payment of the 1855 loan was made, the remainder of the tribute remained locked up in the Bank of England, which refused to give the money back to the Ottoman government, but also could not hand it over to the bondholders without the official order of the Ottoman ambassador.[85]

The Ottoman default raised controversy both among the tribute bondholders, and between the bondholders and the British government. The 1854 loan was issued to cover military expenses during the Crimean War. The British government of the time, as an ally of the Empire during the war, had publicly announced its favorable opinion of the loan, yet had never issued an official guarantee. The bondholders of the 1854 loan always held the government morally responsible for the issue of the loan, and maintained that they were also entitled to its support.[86] The following letter written by one of the 1854 bondholders sums up the basis of their claims.

> I am the widow of one of her Majesty's officers with four children, and I found myself in October, 1875 with the little all of my fatherless children invested in the Turkish 1854's money was placed in this loan not as a speculative investment …, but because it was considered a sound investment for the following reasons: 1. The money was raised and spent to enable the Queen's ally to keep his armies in the field against the Queen's

> enemies. 2. Lord Clarendon, the then Foreign Minister, recommended the loan to the public in an official memorandum from the Foreign Office, dated Aug.15, 1854.[87]

The 1854 bondholders, as the first mortgagees of the tribute, also argued that the holders of the 1855 loan had no right to the balance of the tribute until their payments had been fully repaid.[88] On the other hand, the 1871 bondholders contrived to place themselves on an equal footing as they also had claims to the tribute money.[89] The British government argued that its liabilities were limited to the 1855 loan that had been officially guaranteed by the government and hence rejected the requests for government interference for any other loan.

Consequently, the holders of the tributary loans of 1854 and 1871 formed the Tribute Bondholders League to start negotiations with the Ottoman government. The aim of the league was to convince the Porte to release the tribute held in the Bank of England, and secure the debt service in the future.[90] On the other hand, the Council of Foreign Bondholders (CFB), representing other Turkish loans, was pressing for a general settlement. The CFB aimed to form a committee under its leadership that would unite the interests of all classes of bonds in one body to avoid the 'possibility of any conflict or disunion'.[91] However, the holders of the tributary loans objected to a general settlement and argued that placing their interests in the hands of the CFB, which was also occupied with the general interests of all other Turkish loans, would weaken their privileged position.[92] The Tribute Bondholders League was determined to remain out of the general schedule, and to be ranked in a special category. They claimed that the attempts of the CFB to 'melt the tribute bondholders in the hotchpotch of Turkish bondholders', ignoring their privileged position, would favor the bondholders possessing no such security.[93] Hence, the tribute bondholders decided to pursue an agreement on their own.

As far as the Porte was concerned, the conditions were quite favorable for a partial settlement. Particularly after the outbreak of the Russian War in 1877, the Porte was anxious to make a new bargain with the tribute bondholders. The government had once again resorted to the issue of *kaimes* to finance the military campaign. Nevertheless, the resulting inflation had already begun to cause political disturbances. The treasury was desperately in need of new resources to finance the war, and to make some payment to the local bankers to keep them lending to the government. Therefore, the Porte aimed to get the creditors to agree to a reduction in the originally agreed terms of the loan payments and raise another foreign loan upon the security of the remainder of the tribute. Only with their consent would the Bank of England release the portion of the tribute that remained locked up. For a government in default, this was also the only way it could raise another loan in the foreign markets, since the Porte could not interfere with the payment of the Egyptian tribute.

The total amount of the tribute was £681,000, whereas the total interest and amortization charged on the tribute loans amounted to £859,000. Hence, for the full service of the loans, the government needed to find an additional £178,000 apart from the tribute.[94] The initial offer of the bondholders was to accept less than what was legally due, so that the 1855 loan could be repaid entirely out of the tribute. However, the government asked for a larger concession to have sufficient surplus in the tribute to raise another loan. In July 1877, a compromise was arrived at fairly easily between the government and the representatives of the bondholders.[95] Soon after, the Ottoman government issued a new loan secured upon the £280,623 per annum tribute released after the reduction of interest on 1854 and 1871 loans.[96]

The Ottoman Defense Loan, as it was called, was issued by the BIO and Glyn Mills, Curie and Co. in Britain and France. The original amount of the loan was LT 5 million, the issue rate was 52 percent, and the effective interest rate was 9.6 percent. The defense loan had obviously been very costly, considering that debt service had been secured in the best possible manner. However, the bond was not quoted at the stock exchange due to the continuing defaults, and bonds of a bankrupt, militarily imperiled state were not attractive enough to investors.

The agreement between tribute bondholders and the Porte infuriated the other bondholders and the British press. 'So long as Turkey is a defaulter, even to its unsecured creditors, all attempts to borrow must fail', noted a British newspaper.[97] Another added, 'though it [The Porte] ate its cake long ago, it would very much like still to have it'.[98] While some bondholders repeated their demand for government interference, others, once more, urged the bondholders of all groups to unite in an effort to achieve a resolution.[99] Obviously, the bondholders had lost a golden opportunity to force the Porte, which was in desperate need of new funds, to a favorable settlement because of the lack of coordination between the bondholders.

Domestic borrowing in the default era: Revival of the Galata Bankers

After the default, the Porte once again resorted to the notorious *kaimes* as a means for domestic borrowing. The issue of *kaimes* continued throughout the Russian war (from September 1876 to January 1878), and the government issued over LT 10 million of *kaimes*.[100] Once again, the government was faced with a precipitous decline in the value of the *kaime*. As illustrated in Figure 2.1, the exchange rate of Ottoman lira against *kaime* rose from Ps 106 in August 1876, to Ps 178 in August 1877, and to Ps 291 in August 1878. The sharp depreciation of *kaime* eroded the confidence in these banknotes.[101] *Sarrafs* refused to change the currency at the official rate, shopkeepers were reluctant to accept it, and even when they did they charged very high rates. Moreover, it led to unrest both among the civilians and the soldiers who were paid in *kaimes*. Therefore, by the summer of 1878 this alternative was simply exhausted, and no further additions were made to the circulation. With the military situation becoming increasingly grave, the government sought new alternatives.

Figure 2.1 Exchange rate of Ottoman lira against the *kaime*: 1876-78

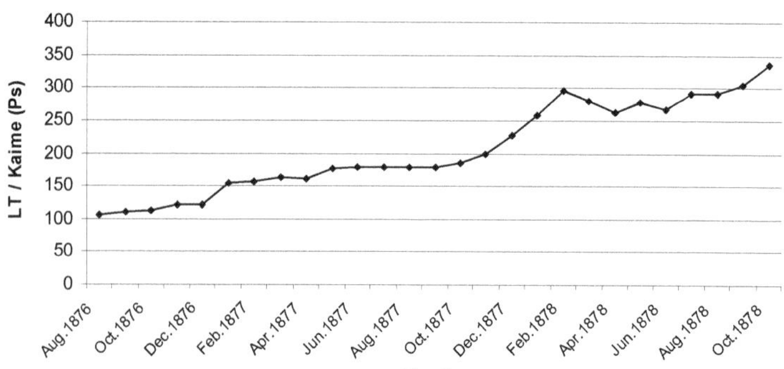

Source: Clay, 2000: 348.

During the period of foreign borrowing (1854–75), the Galata Bankers had lost their privileged position and their role in the government finances was reduced considerably, to one of furnishing the government with short-term loans between major bond issues in the European financial markets.[102] During the years of default when the Porte was excluded from the international financial markets (with the exception of the 1877 loan), the government increasingly relied on domestic borrowings from Galata Bankers and the BIO.

Pamuk points out that during the Russian war in particular these bankers 'adopted a variety of patriotic Ottomanist themes to mobilize support for their centuries-old customer during this difficult period'.[103] However, behind this patriotic discourse lay the vested interests of the Galata elite in the territorial integrity of the Empire. The risks involved in lending to a government that was already bankrupt and fighting a difficult war were clearly great. Yet these bankers were already owed a considerable amount of money and had a great deal to lose if the Empire were to be dismembered. In such a case, the interests of the bondholders might be safeguarded by the great powers during the peace settlement, but it was very unlikely that the local bankers, who were known in Europe as the 'Galata Vampires', would receive much consideration. Evidently, if they did not take further risks by lending the government they could eventually end up losing everything. Moreover, during the period, the bankers took advantage of the isolation of the Empire from the international markets and charged up to 24 percent interest on their short-term advances.[104]

Finally, as discussed before, the Islamic inheritance system hindered the development of durable and large partnerships, which meant that private enterprises in the Empire tended to remain small in comparison with their European counterparts.[105] Due to their small size, the credit needs of these enterprises were very limited. Consequently, the bankers in the Empire were almost completely specialized in dealings with the government, and as argued by Clay, they 'did not have any other form of business to fall back on'.[106]

The Bankers' Convention and the Administration of the Six Indirect Revenues

During the period of default, the loans of the bankers made it undoubtedly more difficult for the European investors to force the Ottoman government to reach a new settlement. On the other hand, the Galata Bankers not only enjoyed high returns on their advances, but also gained priorities on the debt services of the Empire.[107] In January 1878 the Ottoman Empire and Russia signed the Treaty of San Stefano, which ended the war. However, there was still a threat of a new war, this time with Greece, over the rectification of the border. The Porte sought a new loan in the domestic market for the military preparations. The Galata Bankers once again made advances to the government under very stiff terms, and the most lucrative sources of state revenue, such as customs and indirect revenues, were pledged as security. This process led to the establishment of the Administration of Six Indirect Revenues (ASIR), *Rüsumu Sitte İdaresi*, a forerunner of the OPDA.

On 22 November 1879 the Porte signed a convention with the Galata Bankers (including the BIO as the largest domestic creditor), who had made advances to the government amounting to LT 8,845,000 partly secured on the İstanbul Customs.[108] According to the convention, the bankers would make an additional advance of LT 120,000, and give up their rights on the customs revenues. Hence, they would agree to accept the reimbursement of their advances on the customs over a considerably longer period than under the existing contracts. In return, the local bankers and the BIO would be entitled to administer and collect the six indirect revenues (the revenue from salt, tobacco, spirits, and stamp taxes as well as the silk tithes of İstanbul and Bursa and fish tax of İstanbul and vicinity). Galata bankers and the BIO had the first call on LT 1,100,000 of the revenues for interest at 8 percent on these advances, and for their redemption. The remainder would be appropriated to the payment of foreign debt. The arrangement would remain in force for ten years and, being merely provisional, it was declared that the rights of the foreign bondholders would be left intact.[109]

This arrangement between the government and local financiers raised protests from European bondholder organizations, particularly from the ones representing the four loans secured on the customs and the indirect revenues (1858, 1860, 1862 and 1863 loans), who called for government intervention. The local bankers, particularly the BIO, were held responsible not only for lending to a government in default but also claiming priority over the revenues that had previously been pledged for their loans. The bondholders of the 1862 loan, which was secured on the indirect contributions, called the agreement a 'shameless act of financial dishonesty'. According to the bondholders, it was morally and legally unacceptable for the Porte to obtain advances upon the security of the 1862 loan, through the aid and cooperation of the BIO who were the agents of the 1862 loan.[110] The bondholders of the General debt also criticized the convention and argued that they were offered a 'miserable pittance' in return for their loans.[111] In March 1880, the protests of the bondholders' organizations were followed by diplomatic protests from the British and French governments.[112]

The BIO, as by far the largest domestic lender and the major shareholder of the ASIR, was at the center of protests. The BIO defended itself by arguing that the advances made by the bank had enabled the Empire to live through a period when its survival was under threat. Thus, according to BIO officials, the Banker's Convention had not violated the rights of the foreign bondholders on their collaterals or the sanctions imposed on the Ottoman Empire. On the contrary, the BIO had made a sacrifice to ensure the Porte's fulfillment of its foreign debt obligations in the future.[113]

In the meantime, foreign bondholder organizations offered alternative plans to break the convention and make a new debt settlement. In December 1879, Comte De Tocqueville, the representative of the Anglo-French bondholders Committee, arrived in İstanbul to protest the Bankers Convention and offered a large loan to break the convention and build a similar administration, the beneficiaries of which would be the foreign bondholders. However, the representative power of Tocqueville's committee was limited and lacked the support of the influential CFB and the BIO, the largest domestic creditor. The Tocqueville scheme consequently failed to produce any result.[114]

The lack of coordination among the Ottoman bondholders during the period of default

Despite the existence of an organization such as the CFB, which aimed to organize foreign bondholders to exert pressure on the defaulting sovereigns, lending to sovereigns of the periphery entailed great enforcement problems in the nineteenth century. First of all, the main focus of the CFB was the British bondholders even though it also aimed to cooperate with other bondholder organizations in different European countries. Moreover, in cases where the bondholder groups had conflicting interests, the CFB failed to coordinate these different bondholder groups even within Britain. The state of disunity and the lack of coordination among the bondholder groups was one of the major problems in the enforcement of sovereign compliance with debt contracts. The lack of coordination among the bondholders not only allowed for new loans to defaulters but also raised the risk premiums on foreign loans. Enforcement problems in lending to the Ottoman government during the pre-OPDA era can be better understood through a brief analysis of the experiences of the Ottoman bondholders during the period of default in 1875–81.

The default announcement of the Porte caught the Ottoman bondholders at a time when they were divided among different committees. All committees aimed to exert pressure on the Porte and their home governments to bring the Ottoman government to the negotiating table. However, they were divided with regard to the priority of each loan in the amortization of the Ottoman debt. The CFB, on the other hand, aimed to bring all these committees together under its roof for the purpose of a general and lasting settlement. The key part of the CFB plan was the conversion and unification of the Ottoman debt, which would reconcile the conflicting interests of the bondholders. The British press supported the CFB and warned the bondholders to put forth a 'unified effort instead of losing themselves in sectional squabbles'.[115]

> The conversion and unification of the Turkish debt will have an important effect on the political situation of the Ottoman Empire. Henceforth, the creditors of Turkey, instead of being split up into little coteries with diverse views and interests, will be a compact and homogenous body with one mind and one purpose.[116]

Despite the warnings of the press and the efforts of the CFB to unify the different bondholder groups, the process that led to the Decree of *Muharrem* proved to be a fairly complicated one, due to the difficulties that the bondholder organizations had in taking collective action. The main reason behind the lack of coordination was that the interests of all the bondholders were not identical because of the different characteristics of different bonds and, in some cases, conflicted with each other. Then again, unless they reached an agreement among themselves it would be hard to reach a satisfactory settlement with the Porte. The disunity among the bondholders not only enabled the Porte to play one group off against another but also provided the government with an excuse to do nothing at all.[117]

A major conflict of interest arose between the bondholders regarding the priority of each group of bonds in the rescheduling of debt service. As illustrated in Table 2.1, some portions of the Ottoman loans were secured on different collaterals, while the rest were secured on the general revenues of the treasury; thus, no special hypothecation was made. The collaterals comprised more liquid, more profitable, relatively easily monitorable and/or administrable revenues of the Porte, such as the Egyptian tribute, customs revenues, mines and the monopoly revenues. The holders of the bonds that were secured on these special revenues did not want to share their collateral with other bondholders. Each group asked to be ranked in a special category as opposed to the holders of the 'General Debt' bonds. The ongoing discussions between the bondholders of the 1858 and 1862 loans – secured on the customs and the indirect revenues – and the General Debt bondholders is the most significant example, which also led to a major schism among British bondholders. The disagreement between these bondholders could not be resolved until after the signing of the Decree of *Muharrem*.

Similar disagreements also arose among holders of the hypothecated loans. For instance, bondholders with relatively easy access to the collateral pursued separate negotiations with the Ottoman government, such as the British holders of the bonds secured by the Egyptian tribute (1854, 1855 and 1871 bonds), which was routinely channeled through London.[118] The tribute bondholders knew that the Ottoman government would avoid a general settlement, particularly while preparing for a major war. Moreover, even if the government was brought to the negotiating table, a general settlement would require them to make concessions from their easily seizable collateral in favor of other bondholders, particularly those of the General Debt, whose bonds were not secured on any specific revenue.

Another conflict of interest was among the bondholders whose bonds were secured on the same collateral.[119] As one bond issue followed another, the Porte found it harder to find new collaterals that would command confidence in the foreign markets and, therefore, pledged the same revenues over and over again as security for different issues.[120] Some attractive revenues, including the customs duties and the indirect contributions, were overstated in the budgets to convince the investors for a second mortgage. The most salient example of this kind of conflict took place among the tribute bondholders. After the default, representatives of each group had agreed on the distinctive character of their collateral and decided to negotiate with the Porte as the tribute bondholders' committee apart from the rest of the European bondholders. However, to start the negotiations with the government, certain concessions had to be made by the bondholders. Conflicts arose between the bondholders regarding the priority of each group of bonds in the amortization process and the amount of reduction to be applied to each group. Nevertheless, the tribute bondholders eventually found common ground and made a new arrangement with the Porte, at the expense of other bondholders. The 1877 Defense Loan was issued after the partial debt settlement agreed with the tribute bondholders, upon the security of the remainder of the Egyptian tribute. The CFB and other bondholders managed to block the government's access to the London Stock Exchange or Paris Bourse, but the attractiveness of the collateral enabled the Porte to raise another loan in Britain and France. The British and French governments were reluctant to intervene during this process due to the strategic position held by the Ottoman Empire in restraining Russian expansion.

Aside from the unity of the European bondholders, successful implementation of the sanctions required the cooperation of the local actors, the Galata Bankers and the BIO. However, these bankers had strong incentives in lending to the government. Now that the borrowing alternatives of the Empire were much more limited, these bankers could charge higher interests for their short-term advances than they did before the period of foreign borrowing. Obviously, lending to a government in default entailed greater risks as compared to the former period, but also gave the local bankers an opportunity to impose additional conditions on their loans. Thus, as these bankers continued to lend to the government they also gained rights on the collection and administration of the revenues that had previously been mortgaged for the foreign loans. As mentioned before, these bankers (including the BIO, an Anglo-French consortium) had offices in financial centers of Europe and often borrowed from abroad to lend to the government. Had foreign bondholders coordinated their efforts, they could have imposed costs on these bankers (such as damaging their reputation in the European markets) and consequently increased the cost of default for the Ottoman government.

In November 1879, when the Porte issued the decree announcing the establishment of the ASIR, and granted the local bankers the right to collect and administer the 'indirect revenues' previously assigned to foreign bondholders, the foreign bondholders were divided into different organizations.

Around 70 percent of the total outstanding Ottoman foreign debt in the pre-OPDA era belonged to either British or French investors.[121] Despite the existence of an organization such as the CFB in Britain, the cooperation between the bondholders was achieved fairly easily in France, as compared to Britain. There were several reasons for this. First of all, a significant proportion of the General Debt bonds, which were issued in 1865–1874 without any special hypothecations, were held in France. From the beginning the holders of these bonds, which made up 43 percent of the outstanding Ottoman debt after the default, argued in favor of a general settlement.[122] Had the bondholders of the hypothecated loans pursued partial settlements and gained possession of their collaterals, almost all the liquid and easily administrable revenues of the Empire would be taken over by these creditors. Moreover, even though the proportion is not definite, it is understood that in France the banks held a considerable portion of the Ottoman bonds. Most of these banks held both secured and unsecured loans; therefore, it was not difficult to reconcile the interests of these bondholders.[123]

On the other hand, in Britain the situation was more complicated. Despite the early efforts of the CFB to unify the bondholders of all groups, the bondholders were divided between organizations representing the conflicting interests of the different groups of bondholders. The first one was the Tribute Bondholders' League, which had already reached a settlement with the Porte. The Khedive of Egypt, politically controlled by the British government, would continue to send the tribute directly to the Bank of England, and the Porte had given up all its rights on the tribute until the amortization of the bonds. Since their payment was secured in the most effective way possible in 1877, tribute bondholders had no interest in being part of a general settlement.

The second organization was the CFB representing the 1858 and 1862 bondholders. Their bonds were secured on the revenue of the customs and the 'indirect revenues', which were assigned to the Galata Bankers under the November 1879 Convention. Another important feature of these bonds was that they were almost exclusively issued and held in Britain. These bondholders asked for a special treatment for their special securities and protested at being ranked equally with the General Debt bondholders. The CFB, while arguing in favor of a general settlement in line with its original mission, also insisted on the protection of the privileges of the hypothecated bondholders. This led to division among the British bondholders.

The third bondholders' organization was the General Committee of the Turkish Bondholders, mainly representing the holders of the General

Debt that was not secured on any special revenues. Since no securities were involved in any of these bonds, they found common cause with their French counterparts on the Anglo-French committee. This committee backed the unsuccessful Tocqueville scheme. Upon the conclusion of the November Convention between the bankers and the Porte, and the failure of the Tocqueville scheme, they again sought cooperation with the CFB and the bondholders of the 1858 and 1862 loans. 'The various classes must see the inutility of continued selfishness, and resign themselves to equitable ideas', Guedella, the chairman of the committee argued in his report.[124] According to Guedella, the securities of the 1858 and 1862 loans should not have been a matter of argument since 'not one of the dividends of the various loans had ever been paid out of the special securities hypothecated'. The debt payments for all loans were made entirely out of the general revenue or borrowed money. Furthermore, their 'vaunted securities' had been mortgaged over and over again for new loans. It was precisely by the mortgaging of these securities that the BIO and the Galata Bankers had made their advances to the government.[125] The bondholders of the General Debt agreed with the CFB on the importance of forming a unified front to prevent the Porte from making further partial or special arrangements; and argued that 'it was time for Turkey to make a comprehensive arrangement embracing the whole of the creditors'.[126] However, while they argued for equal treatment of all issues, the CFB insisted on the protection of the privileges of the hypothecated loans.

Ottoman debt settlement and the Decree of *Muharrem*

The Ottoman default was followed by the hardships of the Russian war in 1877–78. As a defaulting government, the Porte had difficulty in borrowing from abroad, and with the exception of the 1877 loan, could not raise another loan from Europe. The government, desperately in need of new financial sources, once more turned to local bankers. The notorious Galata Bankers agreed to new loans under very tight conditions and very high interest rates. Nevertheless, considering the high interest rates and the limited financial resources in the domestic economy this borrowing pattern was unsustainable in the long run.

On the other hand, diplomatic pressures from the creditor countries had intensified after the adverse outcome of the Russian war. Subsequent to the signing of the armistice between Russia and the Ottoman Empire, foreign bondholders were concerned that the territorial losses of the Empire in the Balkans and the war indemnity demanded by Russia would make it impossible for the Porte to resume the debt service. Diplomatic pressure on the Porte reached its peak after the Berlin Congress that was called by the European powers to reconsider the terms of the Treaty of San Stefano, which Russia had forced on the Ottoman Empire. According to the terms of the Treaty of Berlin, the newly independent Balkan states would be responsible for a proportionate share of the debt. Moreover, it was agreed by the Russian delegation that the prewar foreign debt of the Empire would have priority over the war indemnity demanded by Russia. Finally, the conference recommended to the Porte the establishment of an international committee that would supervise the resources of the Empire assigned to debt service. Thus, after the Treaty of Berlin, the Porte was concerned that unless a deal was struck with the bondholders, matters might be taken out of their hands and an international commission might be imposed upon them. The proposed commission would consist of representatives of the European powers and bring a definitive end to the fiscal and political sovereignty of the Empire.

From this perspective, the signing of the November Convention, which partially resumed the foreign debt service, was an attempt to escape from the proposed international commission. However, the arrangements made with the local bankers including the partial repayment of the coupons did not satisfy the foreign bondholder organizations. By the terms of the November Convention, local bankers had been granted an administrative role over the resources previously assigned to foreign loans as well as a priority in debt service. This was unacceptable for the foreign bondholders who protested the convention and lobbied for the implementation of the recommendations of the Treaty of Berlin.

Under these circumstances, the Porte's concerns to reach larger credit markets and political pressure from the European governments led to debt renegotiations with foreign bondholders. At the invitation of the Ottoman government, negotiations between the Porte and the representatives of the Dutch, English, French, Austrian, German and Italian bondholders commenced in September 1881 in İstanbul. The negotiations covered all foreign loans apart from the guaranteed loan of 1855, and the Egyptian tribute loans of 1854, 1871, and 1877, the repayment of which had been guaranteed by previous arrangements. The negotiations also included the Ramazan certificates, delivered in exchange for the bonds drawn under the stipulations of the Decree of 6 October 1875. Including the lottery bonds, the outstanding amount in default was

£252,801,885 before the settlement. To give an idea of the magnitude of the debt, total estimated revenue of the treasury in 1874–75 made up around 9 percent of this amount, according to official statements.[127]

The crucial issue during the negotiations was the debt reduction, which was an essential requirement for a sustainable outcome. Even before the war the Empire had severe financial problems. After the Russian-Turkish war circumstances had worsened. The loss of territory and population, in Europe alone, was estimated at 82,000 square miles and 4.5 million respectively, and the loss of annual revenue in consequence was around £4.75 million.[128] Moreover, there was the issue of war indemnity. According to the terms of the Treaty of San Stefano the Ottoman government had agreed to pay LT 350,000 to Russia as war indemnity.

Under these circumstances, a reduction in the principal of the debt was indispensable and this was recognized by the creditors even before the start of the negotiations. The issue of disagreement was the extent of reduction.[129] After long negotiations, the mean between the proposals of the bondholders and the government was adopted and the principal was reduced to £96,768,278. To this amount, 10 percent of the reduced capital was added as interest arrears, making the total of the new debt £106,437,204 or LT 117,080,957. Thus, a considerable reduction would be made in the outstanding debt of the Empire. The details of the reduction are illustrated in Table 2.2.[130]

The negotiations carried on in İstanbul between the Porte and its creditors were concluded on 20 December 1881, by the issue of the Decree of *Muharrem*. The decree sanctioned the establishment of a council of administration charged with the collection and administration of revenues assigned for the service of the foreign loans and the priority debt (loans of the Galata Bankers and the BIO). Under these terms, the revenue from the salt and tobacco monopolies, the stamp and spirits taxes, the fish tax, and the silk tithe in certain districts as well as the Bulgaria tribute, the revenue from Eastern Rumelia and the surplus of the Cyprus revenue were irrevocably ceded to the OPDA, until the debt was liquidated.

Table 2.2 Ottoman foreign debt before and after the Decree of Muharrem

Series	Loan	Outstanding principal including Ramazan bonds (£)	Arrears of interest including Ramazan certificates (£)	Total debt in default (£)	Total debt after the Decree (£)	Reduction in total debt (%)
A	1858	3,684,750	1,345,410	5,030,160	3,445,316	31.51%
	1862	4,999,650	1,876,125	6,875,775	3,738,556	45.63%
B	1860	1,654,030	620,406	2,274,436	1,044,201	54.09%
	1863-64	5,188,750	1,946,999	7,135,749	3,973,682	44.31%
	1872	4,820,200	2,759,312	7,579,512	5,223,165	31.09%
C	1865	4,098,500	1,537,897	5,636,397	2,920,713	48.18%
	1869	20,650,000	7,743,750	28,393,750	12,885,600	54.62%
	1873	27,196,740	10,198,777	37,395,517	15,026,198	59.82%
D	General debt	87,197,360	27,040,279	114,237,639	43,968,396	61.51%
	Lottery bonds	31,508,000	6,734,950	38,242,950	14,211,407	62.84%
Total		190,997,980	61,803,905	252,801,885	106,437,234	57.90%

Source: Annual Reports of the CFB.

According to the terms of the settlement, revenues obtained from the sources that were ceded to the OPDA would be applied entirely to the payment of interest and to the redemption of loans subject to the negotiations. The first obligation of the administration was the payment of the annuity amounting to LT 590,000 for the priority bonds held by the Galata Bankers. The balance of receipts was to be devoted to the service of the bond series, with 80 percent apportioned to interest and 20 percent to the redemption of the debt, on condition that at least 1 percent interest on the diminished capital was distributed to the bondholders. Moreover, the maximum rate of interest was fixed at 4 percent, and the maximum rate of redemption was fixed at 1 percent. If the conceded revenues ever yielded more than 5 percent of the principal, the surplus would go to the treasury.[131] For purposes of amortization, the ten loans in default were divided into four groups based on the respective securities on which they had been floated. Group A consisted of the 1858 and 1862 loans; group B consisted of the loans of 1860, 1863–4, and 1872; and group C of the loans of 1865, 1869, and 1873. Finally, group D consisted of bonds without any special hypothecations, those of the General Debt and the Treasury Loan. The sinking fund of up to 0.25 percent would be applied exclusively to the redemption of the first group. If a surplus remained up to 0.5 percent would be applied to the redemption of the second group. If a surplus remained, it would be applied, up to 75 percent, to the redemption of the third group, and lastly if there was still a surplus it would be applied, up to 1 percent, to the redemption of the last group.

Hence, the Ottoman state had compromised its domestic autonomy by giving up more than one-third of state revenues that were ceded to the control of the administration. As argued by historians, the establishment of the OPDA constituted 'a severe blow to Ottoman pride and sovereignty'.[132] One major question that merits an answer is why the Ottoman government agreed to a debt settlement, which in a way meant compromising both its political and financial sovereignty? First of all, after the loss of the Russian war and in the face of escalating pressure from the creditor countries for a debt settlement, the Porte was not left with many other options. In this context, the establishment of the OPDA was an imposition of the European powers rather than a choice of the Porte itself. At the time, the primary concern of the Porte was to escape from the international commission recommended by the Treaty of Berlin. It sought a new deal that would not only satisfy the foreign bondholders but also eliminate the possibility of a takeover of a greater part of Turkish finances by foreign governments. As argued by Blaisdell, 'it [the establishment of the OPDA] was less of an evil than would have been the establishment of an official political organization for the accomplishment of the same object'.[133]

Even though it is often overlooked, there were substantial differences between the recommendations of the Treaty of Berlin and the organizational structure of the OPDA, which made the latter more tolerable for the Ottoman government. As opposed to the international financial commission recommended by the Treaty of Berlin, the OPDA did not enjoy the official protection of the powers whose nationals were represented in the council. According to Protocol 18 of the Treaty of Berlin, the members of the commission would be appointed by the creditor governments, and thus would be responsible to their governments in the first place.[134] In the case of the OPDA, the members of the council were directly appointed by the bondholder organizations of the respective countries, and were responsible first to the bondholders. There is no doubt that these representatives were under the influence of their governments, and sometimes even handpicked by them. But on many occasions they also conflicted with the general policies of their governments in protecting their bondholders' interests, which were closely tied to the performance of the Ottoman economy.

Besides the fear of foreign military intervention, other concerns might also have played a role in shaping the Porte's decision. In many ways, the establishment of the OPDA can be viewed as a natural outcome of the increasing dependency of the central bureaucracy on outside resources to finance its recurring budget deficits. As observed from the repeated failed attempts at reformation, the state bureaucracy lacked the organizational and administrative skills to reform its finances. On the other hand, under the existing circumstances, cutting back expenses was no longer an option for the treasury. The Empire was in no position to get back on its feet through its own means. In the early months of 1881, the financial situation of the Empire was as critical as ever. According to a report sent to the Crèdit Lyonnais, the June receipts for the current year were estimated at below LT 10 million, leaving a budget deficit of at least LT 13 million. The palace had serious difficulties in paying the wages of its employees and even the palace cooks were striking on account of their unpaid wages.[135] Therefore, another concern of the Porte, though not as critical as the first one, was to regain access to international markets. By the terms of the decree, the Porte had lowered the outstanding debt of the Empire to a relatively more reasonable level by making a strong commitment, and thereby rebuilding the credit of the Empire. In this sense, the OPDA also functioned as a commitment mechanism and became instrumental in underwriting the government's credit and ensuring that it obtained loans on much more favorable terms than in the days before the bankruptcy.

Finally, the Ottoman central authority was not as concerned about the erosion of its fiscal sovereignty by the decree as so far argued by some historians. After all, the handling of certain state revenues by the OPDA was not that different from the very common practice of tax farming. As mentioned earlier, tax farming was employed in a large part of the Ottoman Empire, because the state simply did not have the ability or the administrative capacity to collect taxes through its own means in a more effective manner.[136] Moreover, the widespread corruption in bureaucracy and the escalation of smuggling activities posed great challenges. Besides, heavy taxation of the already impoverished population could further erode the Sultan's authority. By the delegation of tax collection and the handling of other state revenues to a third party, the Sultan could avoid direct confrontation with his people and remain a respected figure or the final executer of justice. The delegation of authority allowed the Sultan to distance himself from the highly unpopular tobacco monopoly in fighting against smugglers. Thus, it was not the Sultan but the Régie officials that were the target of the widespread protests by tobacco producers.

Furthermore, even though many writers point to the Decree of *Muharrem* in 1881 as the date when the Ottomans lost their fiscal sovereignty to the Europeans, the practice of handing state revenues to foreigners was not something new. As mentioned before, a couple of years earlier, the same sources of revenue (with the exception of some minor additions in the Decree of *Muharrem*) had been ceded to the Galata Bankers and the BIO. Here it is important to note that the BIO was by far the largest shareholder in the administration.

Another important aspect of the debt renegotiations was the BIO's active role in the process, both as a creditor and as a mediator between the government and the foreign bondholders. As the major organization controlling the ASIR, the debt settlement would deprive the BIO of its privileges granted by the November Convention. So why did the BIO consent to the signing of the Decree of *Muharrem*?

The November Convention had raised numerous protests from bondholders' organizations all over Europe. Faced with the growing enmity of the foreign bondholders and diplomatic protests by the creditor governments, the BIO officials realized that the existing structure of the ASIR was not sustainable over the long term. The hostility of the bondholders could be diffused by making certain concessions from the November Convention. The initial plan of the BIO administration, and also their most favorable solution, was giving the foreign bondholders a larger share of the revenues collected by the ASIR.[137] Such an arrangement would not only allow the BIO to maintain its control over the administration, but also enable the bank, this time backed by European bondholders, to expand its economic and political power over the economy. However, the European bondholders had already lost confidence in the bank after the signing of the November Convention. Consequently, they refused outright to leave the BIO in control of the indirect contributions, and demanded the abolishment of the ASIR. Under these circumstances, the BIO could either initiate a new arrangement involving the representatives of foreign bondholders or side with the Porte and stay out of the debt renegotiation efforts of the European financial circles in order to continue its unrivaled position in the ASIR. The BIO chose the former, and initiated the international debt renegotiations that resulted in the Decree of *Muharrem*.

Several factors might have played a role in the BIO's decision to bring the government to the negotiating table, even though it meant compromising the bank's privileged position in the existing administration. One major factor was the reputational concerns of the BIO administration. As mentioned before, the BIO was a consortium of British and French bankers, and held branches both in London and Paris. Moreover, the participants in the consortium and members of the bank's general committee were well respected, influential figures in the European financial markets and the domestic politics of their respective countries.[138] After the reactions to the Banker's Convention, we might presume that they were increasingly concerned that not only the bank's reputation, but also their reputation in Europe, could be damaged in the long run.

Furthermore, the BIO administration was also concerned that, with the increasing financial needs of the treasury, the argument it formerly deployed to defend its lending on the securities that were already mortgaged to foreign creditors could be turned against itself. That is, the

Porte could offer the administration of the indirect revenues to the foreign bondholders as security for a new loan, discarding the existing agreement with the domestic creditors. Hence, the BIO and the local bankers were concerned that they would not only lose their priorities in the debt service, but they would also lose their role in the administration of the revenues. If the Porte sought a new settlement with the creditors, they would rather be involved than remain out of the process.

Another concern of the BIO was the weakness of the enforcement mechanisms behind the November Convention. These concerns were confirmed during the early months of 1881, when the Porte threatened the BIO with canceling the agreement unless they advance an additional LT 1 million to finance military preparations against Greece.[139] The government could cancel the convention unilaterally at any time, and now that the BIO had also lost the support of the other foreign creditors and governments, they had no credible threat mechanism at their disposal other than denying further credits to the government. Therefore, the existing pattern of domestic lending was unsustainable in the long term. Each time the government was in need, it would turn to the BIO for a new loan and the BIO would be forced to accept its demands to avoid risking the repayment of its existing loans. As the total amount of the loans grew, the BIO would be more and more trapped into financing the recurring budget deficits of the government.

When revenues of the Administration of the Six Indirect Contributions were ceded to the OPDA, the BIO and the local bankers became the first mortgagees on the ceded revenues, while their debt (to be extinguished in 22 years) became marketable by permission granted to them for the issue of bonds, known as the priority bonds. The agreement reached with the Decree of *Muharrem*, as opposed to the arrangements under the November Convention, was hardly reversible. The agreement was signed by the representatives of bondholders from all major European powers. Their governments, although not directly involved in the negotiations, gave their unofficial support. With the decree, the BIO administration compromised its privileged role in the ASIR and consented to a reduction in its outstanding loans. In return, the settlement put the repayment of more than LT 4 million owed by the government on a basis that commanded wider international approval.[140] The bank also convinced the representatives of bondholders to farm out the tobacco monopoly, the most attractive source of state revenues, to a consortium headed by the BIO.

As far as the foreign bondholders were concerned, their incentives for signing the agreement should be analyzed under two subgroups. The bondholders of the hypothecated loans gained privileges in the amortization of their debt and the coupon payments, in return for a reduction in the principal and the interest on their loans and surrendering their rights on their collaterals to the OPDA, which was liable for the debt service in general. The uncertainty about the future of their loans was significantly reduced by the establishment of the OPDA, and their bonds became marketable once again.

As for the bondholders of the General Debt, at first glance this group might seem the most disadvantaged since they were ranked the lowest in amortization. Moreover, by the terms of the agreement, a larger reduction was made on their loans. However, these bonds had no collateral, the main reason for their profitability at the time. By the decree, holders of these bonds managed to grab a share in the revenues previously assigned to other bondholders in return for their concessions.

Despite the major advantages offered by the decree, it did not go unopposed in the European press. The representatives were heavily criticized for making a great concession.[141] Nevertheless, in few years, as the OPDA gained the confidence of foreign investors, the agreement proved to be very profitable for bondholders, since the risk assigned to the government was significantly reduced by the establishment of the OPDA. Figure 2.2 illustrates the trend in the market values of Ottoman bonds on the Paris Bourse from 1885–1903, before the unification of the debt. The figure does not show the group A bonds that were amortized as early as 1897. As illustrated in the figure, even group D bonds, which were considered to be the least secure, increased their value by more than 100 percent within the period.

Figure 2.2 Market value of the Ottoman bonds in Paris: 1885–1903

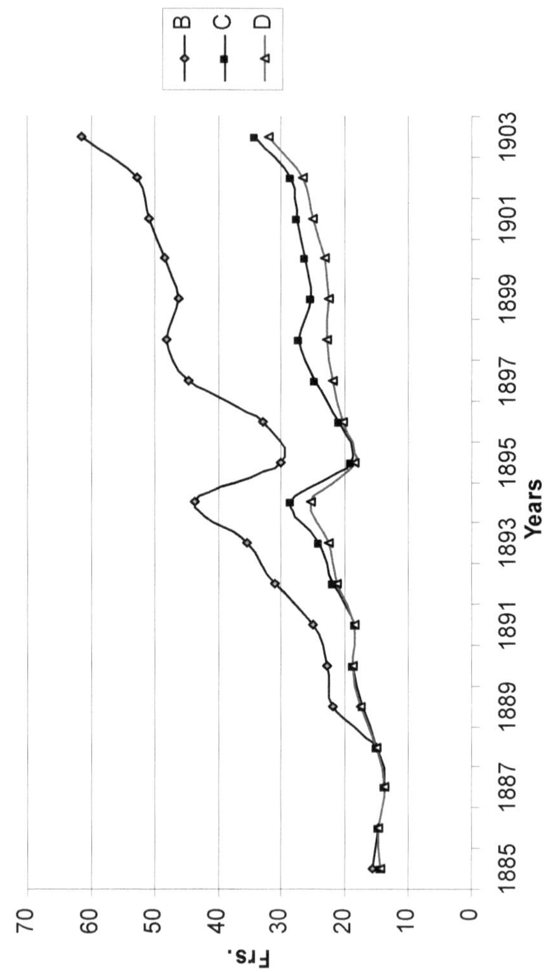

Source: Kazgan, 1985: 691.

3

COORDINATION, COMMITMENT AND ENFORCEMENT: MAKING SENSE OF THE OPDA

Debt contracts between private creditors and foreign sovereigns represent some of the oldest and most pervasive forms of cross-border commitments in international relations. However, they are often accompanied by problems of monitoring and enforcement of sovereign compliance. Historical evidence shows that in the absence of international enforcement mechanisms, mistrust between the creditors and the debtor countries limits the cross-border credit flow and damages both sides in credit markets. Hence, each party seeks to develop a mechanism to overcome this problem. On the supply side, the creditors seek to develop credible threats. The principal penalty available to creditors is to block the defaulters' access to outside sources. However, the enforcement of this penalty requires coordination among private creditors and their home governments. On the demand side, debtor countries seek to develop commitment mechanisms to further their access to foreign credits with lower interest rates.

This chapter analyzes the establishment of the Ottoman Public Debt Administration (OPDA) in 1881, by expounding on the reasoning of the main actors (creditors and the Ottoman government) that led to this process. As we shall see, two major dimensions of the organization stand out. For the creditors, the OPDA represented a cooperative effort to secure the repayment of foreign loans and to develop a monitoring and enforcement mechanism for future direct or indirect investments in the

Empire. As for the Ottoman Empire, the establishment of the OPDA provided an instrument for committing credibly to the terms specified in the debt contracts and to the protection of foreign investment in the Empire. This commitment enabled the Ottoman government to gain further access to foreign capital markets at lower interest rates and encouraged foreign direct investment in the country.

The debtor's dilemma and mechanisms for compliance

A debt contract is a voluntary exchange of money over time; therefore, it is vulnerable to problems of time inconsistency. When a government borrows from private creditors via international markets, it promises to repay the principal with interest during subsequent periods as specified by the loan contract. However, once the loan has been received, the sovereign may feel tempted to violate the contract by refusing to service and amortize it as agreed. To illustrate the 'debtor's dilemma' as coined by Tomz, let us introduce a simple bilateral two-stage game between a private creditor and a debtor foreign government.[1]

Figure 3.1 Debtor's dilemma

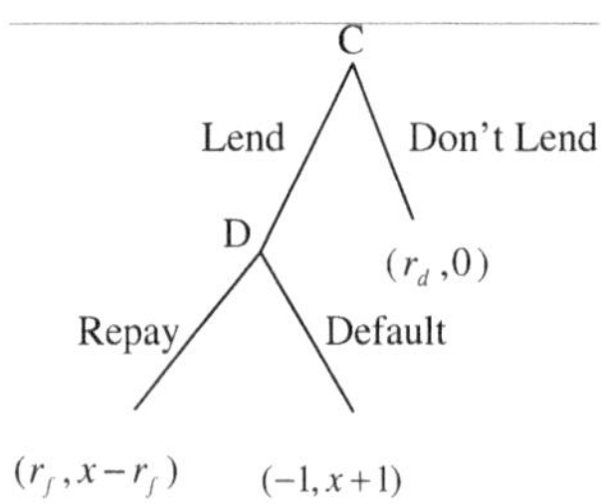

The creditor (C) makes the first move and decides whether to lend $1 for one year at a positive interest rate r_f ,which is necessarily greater than the domestic interest rate r_d in the creditor's country: $r_f > r_d > 0$. The underlying logic is that lending to a foreign sovereign often entails considerable enforcement problems. Thus, the interest on foreign loan entails a risk premium. Moreover, based on the optimal borrowing assumption, we assume that a creditor that accepts the terms of the lending contract makes an investment that yields $x > r_f$. At the end of one year, the debtor (D) has to make a decision whether to repay the principal and the interest or default. In real life, defaults range from the most extreme form that occurs when a government repudiates both interest and principal, to less severe forms, such as temporary suspension of payments, permanent reductions in outstanding principal or interest rates and extensions of the maturity date. Here, for simplicity, it is assumed that the government defaults on both the principal and the interest. So in case of default, the creditor loses the principal at $t+1$. On the other hand, the debtor receives x as the return on investment and the principal itself. Thus, the debtor's payoff in case of default is $x+1$.

Assuming that each player has complete information about the payoff structure, we can find the subgame perfect equilibrium of the game by backward induction. As an income maximizing agent, the debtor country would obviously choose to default at this terminal node since, $x+1 > x-r_f$. Knowing this, the creditor would never lend in the first place, and invest the money in the domestic economy, because under all circumstances $r_d > -1$.

Enforcement mechanisms for sovereign compliance

Self-enforcement mechanisms

As illustrated, if governments could default with impunity, no international lending would take place. However, lending occurs frequently as a matter of routine, and governments often repay their debts. This suggests the existence of mechanisms that defer default and afford the creditors the confidence to lend. One major explanation is that reputational concerns often act as a powerful self-enforcement mechanism for sovereign compliance.[2] The basic intuition of reputational models in the economics literature can be explained as follows. If the debtor government and its foreign creditors play the two-stage game repeatedly under conditions of imperfect information, and political leaders care enough about future borrowing, then debtor governments will have a strong incentive to build a good reputation by repaying their foreign debt. This way they can gain further access to foreign funds with lower risk premiums. When supported by a high level of reputational concerns, interest rates on foreign lending are expected to converge to domestic interest rates in the creditor economies.

However, under certain circumstances, such as in times of war or during economic or political crisis leaders might heavily discount the future. Empirical evidence shows that it is these times when governments are more likely to default on their financial obligations.[3] On the other hand, it is also true that at such crucial times countries desperately seek new foreign funds. The increasing possibility of default leads to higher risk premiums, which then make matters worse for those already troubled countries. This generates an especially pressing need for the debtors to build commitment mechanisms, in many cases restricting the sovereign's control over the appropriation of the economic surplus or legal supremacy to assure the lenders that the country is committed to its debt service under all circumstances.[4] It is important to make the commitment credible and essentially irreversible; otherwise, its effect on the creditworthiness of the sovereign might be fairly limited. Transfer of the collateral to a consortium of lenders, as in the case of the OPDA, might be considered as the most extreme form of the aforementioned commitment.

In the economics literature, reputational explanations of sovereign lending have not gone unchallenged. In their seminal paper, Bulow and Rogoff argued that any contract based solely on reputation must have some state of nature in which the country will default, and by doing so it would have strictly higher consumption in each future period by using short-term state contingent 'cash in advance' insurance contracts.[5] Hence, the authors pointed out that repayment is driven by sanctions rather than by purely reputational concerns. In order to give some credibility to the promise to repay, foreign lending must be supported by direct costs that lenders can impose on the debtor in the event of a default. Bulow and Rogoff did not specify the precise nature of sanctions. Possible penalties suggested in the paper are to impede the debtor's trade or seize its financial assets abroad.

Bulow and Rogoff's critique inspired further works on reputational models. In an effort to revive the reputational explanations, Cole and Kehoe emphasized the role of reputational spillovers. The authors developed a model of general reputation as opposed to previous partial reputation models and argued that a country's poor debt performance tarnishes its reputation not only in international credit markets, but in other areas as well.[6] In this context, a government that violates the contract rights of the creditors would be viewed as a government that has a greater tendency to violate its contracts in other areas. The authors argued that reputational spillovers would increase the cost of default by eroding confidence in the government as a whole, leading to a decrease in foreign direct investment and raising the cost of domestic loans and public works contracted to third parties. While sovereign debt is subject to default risk, foreign direct investment is subject to the risk not only of expropriation, but of other government actions such as modifications in tax laws and regulations that shift the surplus away from investors. Particularly in the case of foreign direct investment, investors are expected to be very sensitive to default, which they might view not only as a signal of dishonesty but also an indicator of instability that might drive the government to expropriate a larger share of their surplus. Under these circumstances, the size of foreign direct investment in the debtor country emerges as another major determinant of the repayment decision.

Punishment mechanisms and the need for coordination among creditors

When a sovereign heavily discounts the future, self-enforcement mechanisms cease to work. This generates a need for an international institutional framework to enforce sovereign compliance through punishment mechanisms.

In case of default, the principal penalty available to creditors is to deny the defaulter the ability to borrow again and block its access to outside resources. For this threat to be credible, financial markets must coordinate in refusing to lend to a debtor in default. Hence, enforcement of the contract depends upon the level of coordination among the creditors, or the 'coalitional stability' of the creditors.[7] The threat of exclusion from financial markets can be considered as a good example of Hirschleifer's weakest link sort of public good, where the credibility of threat is determined by the weakest partner's willingness to deny further credit in case of a default.[8] In this case, narrowing opportunities for the defaulter in international financial markets enable the creditors who refrain from cooperation with other creditors to charge significantly higher interest rates for new loans to these countries and gain certain privileges or priorities in the repayment schedule. Defaulting countries still incur significant costs due to dramatic increases in interest rates; however, the severity of the punishment is much less than if the government had no access at all to international markets. This makes it harder for creditors to impose an advantageous rescheduling agreement.

A major confusion in the literature is whether exclusion of the defaulting country from international financial markets is a direct result of the sovereign's bad reputation or a sanction, which requires an additional effort on behalf of the creditors. As Eaton and Fernandez pointed out, while the desire to maintain reputation can be interpreted as different from exclusion from the world markets, the two are often confused.[9] The exclusion from future lending is of course a penalty. However, distinction is often difficult since the exclusion of the defaulter from world capital markets is rarely an 'all or nothing' process. While a default naturally leads to an increase in the risk premium by increasing the possibility of default on other bonds issued by the debtor, the level of exclusion determines the availability of credits and contributes to the widening spread.

Following the works of Bulow and Rogoff, the sovereign debt literature witnessed a surge in empirical research on the role of various punishment mechanisms that might have helped to deter default.[10] One mechanism suggested by Bulow and Rogoff was trade sanctions. Analyzing sovereign defaults over the last 40 years, Rose found that the bilateral trade between the creditor and the debtor country declines significantly after a default, and suggested that trade sanctions might have played a role as an enforcement mechanism during the period.[11] Martinez and Sandleriz, on the other hand, using the same data set, found no significant decline in the total volume of trade of the defaulting country, and pointed out the ineffectiveness of trade sanctions during the same period.[12] In another recent paper, Mitchener and Weidenmier found that trade sanctions had been effective in the 1870–1914 era only when accompanied by 'supersanctions' such as gunboat diplomacy.[13]

As in the case of reputational mechanisms, the effectiveness of financial embargoes or trade sanctions depends on the debtor's level of integration into the global economy, such as the volume of its foreign trade or investments. Therefore, default is a very costly option for a developed economy. In the case of peripheral economies, on the other hand, these most commonly referred punishment mechanisms might be insufficient to support sovereign lending. Historical studies confirm this view and suggest that a broader range of sanctions were employed during earlier episodes of peripheral lending ranging from political pressures on the defaulter to military interventions by the creditor governments.[14] Some earlier works in the literature treated sanctions of a military or political nature as rare and isolated instances.[15] Kaletsky, on the other hand, pointed out the effectiveness of 'gunboat diplomacy' in the nineteenth century.[16] In a more recent work, Mitchener and Weidenmier claim that the use of political or military power functioned as a major deterrent during the classical gold standard era. They find that, in 1870–1914, the probability that a defaulting country would be 'supersanctioned' was greater than 30 percent.[17]

In case of a default, one possible response of the lenders was to seize the defaulter's assets held in their own countries. This penalty mechanism was obviously attractive to the creditors, since these assets could be seized relatively easily without imposing huge costs on the debtor. The debtor's foreign assets functioned as a major support for the issue of certain loans, as in the case of the 1854, 1855, 1871 and 1877 Ottoman loans, which were mortgaged on the Egyptian tribute held by the Bank of England. Yet, for most cases of peripheral lending, this penalty was not an option. Historical evidence shows that governments with large assets abroad were unlikely to borrow heavily, and for most debtor countries their assets abroad were vastly outweighed by their liabilities.[18] Another punitive measure available to creditors was military intervention by their home governments and the seizure of the debtors' most liquid revenues. Particularly before the First World War, military interventions provided some assurance for the lenders.[19]

However, military intervention might be very costly, particularly in cases where the defaulter is capable of putting up strong military resistance. Also, in the presence of various hegemonic powers, the military intervention of one power could trigger a response by another. Hence, creditor governments often seek to base their intervention on legitimate grounds. Moreover, in most cases of default there are several creditor countries all of which might have conflicting interests on the debtor. Hence military intervention not only requires legitimate ground but also some degree of coordination among the creditors. Even though their function has often been overlooked, 'hypothecated loans' played a major role in many bond issues before 1914. In the presence of an attractive collateral, these bonds were often issued at very low risk premiums since the existence of the collateral provided the creditor government with some legitimacy for the seizure of that particular source of revenue, besides enabling the holders of these bonds to avoid coordination problems with other creditors during the liquidation of the debt. Our findings from the history of Ottoman borrowing suggest that the presence and nature of collateral had powerful effects on the way creditors assessed risk.

Analytical framework: The debtor's dilemma reconsidered

In the light of theoretical contributions and the empirical evidence offered by previous studies in the sovereign debt literature, we can extend the simple debtor's dilemma game into a debt game where the creditor can enforce sovereign compliance by punishment mechanisms. This will not only help us to understand the dynamics of sovereign lending before the First World War but also to analyze different punishment mechanisms and their effects on the risk assessments of the creditors.

Figure 3.2. illustrates a game where the creditor threatens the debtor with punishment, Φ_d , in case of a default. It is assumed that when the punishment occurs the creditor derives certain benefits from its action, denoted by β, but also inflicts a cost upon itself, Φ_c. The country will repay its debt if its utility from doing so is greater than its utility from default, i.e. $U_R > U_D$, where U_R stands for the country's utility from repayment and U_D stands for its utility from default. For simplicity, we assume that both actors are risk neutral, and there is no future discounting. The latter assumption implies that each actor's time preference rate is nil, i.e., $\delta_c = \delta_d = 0$.

Punishments can be in the form of exclusion of the debtor from future borrowing in the world markets or trade embargoes, where the only benefit the creditor derives is building a reputation for future loan contracts, or the ones already in force. Benefits from such punishment will naturally be larger for a creditor holding different bonds issued by a variety of debtors and negligible for the small investor. Here we assume that the creditor derives no direct benefit from such punishment. If excluded from world markets, the sovereign can only borrow from the domestic markets. Each loan, L, is made at r_L, the local interest rate in the capital-scarce debtor country, which is assumed to be greater than r_f due to the paucity of capital in the peripheral economy. In this case, the cost of exclusion from world capital markets to debtor can be defined as

$$\phi_e = \sum_{s=t+2}^{\infty} \frac{L_s(r_L - r_f)}{(1+\delta)^{s-t}}. \qquad (1)$$

The level of coordination among the creditors, and the level of the debtor country's integration into international financial markets, determine the severity of the punishment. If coordination between the creditors is loose, they might seek partial settlement in return for new advances to the debtor. In this case, the debtor can still borrow from abroad at rates lower than the local interest rate.

Figure 3.2 Sequential debt game with perfect information

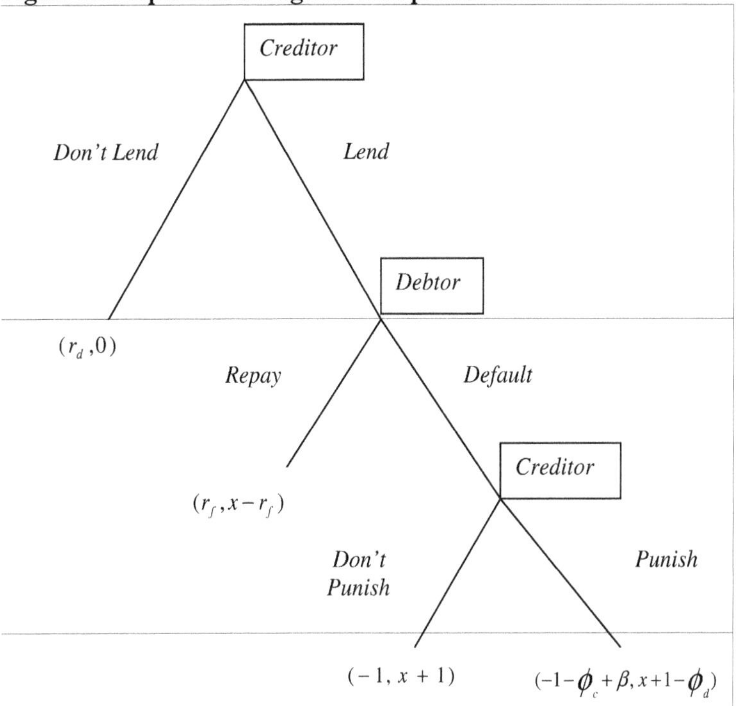

Punishment can also occur in the form of the seizure of the debtor's assets abroad at period *t+2*, following the default at *t+1*, or the seizure of an income stream such as the seizure of exports, custom house revenues, or as in the Ottoman case, seizure of tributes collected from different parts of the Empire. If the creditor punishes the debtor by seizing its assets, or revenues, denoted by Φ_s, it not only inflicts a cost on the debtor but also derives a benefit, denoted by β. In most instances punishments imposed on the debtor encompass several of the above-mentioned forms. Here we simply define the cost of punishment to the debtor as $\Phi_d = \Phi_e + \Phi_s$.

In this game, assuming that the debtor is liquid enough to repay its debts, the occurrence of lending-repayment equilibrium requires two conditions. If the punishments imposed on the debtor are greater than the benefits of the default then the debtor would choose to repay its debt,

$\Phi_d - (1+r_f) > 0$. However, this requirement by itself is not sufficient to support the lending decision. As pointed out by Eaton and Fernandez, in the absence of a commitment mechanism on the part of the creditors, either to withholding the carrot or applying the stick, the repayment of the loan crucially depends on the precise strategic environment.[20] Formally put, the repayment equilibrium depends on whether the strategies are subgame perfect, i.e. in the absence of a commitment mechanism whether the creditors would find it in their interest to punish the debtor in default at period $t+2$. If the costs of punishment exceed the benefits from punishment then the threat is not credible. Knowing this the debtor would default at $t+1$. Hence, credible threat also requires that $\beta - \Phi_c > 0$.

So far, we have assumed that the creditors themselves can directly inflict a punishment on the debtor. However, certain penalties such as the seizure of the debtor's assets often require the intervention of creditor governments. If the creditor is a government, then the punishment mechanisms are readily available. However, if the creditors are banks or individual bondholders then punishment of the debtor requires the intervention of a third actor, the creditor government. The creditor government has its own economic and political priorities. Therefore, it takes action only if its own net benefits of intervention are greater than for non-intervention. In the case of government intervention, creditors can seize the debtor's assets or revenues without direct costs on themselves.

The sequential debt game under full information explains why creditors lend to foreign sovereigns, but does not allow for the occurrence of default. In the absence of the required enforcement mechanisms, the creditor would reject any loan demand regardless of the interest rate offered by the sovereign. To allow for the possibility of default we should relax the assumption of perfect information. For this purpose, let us now assume that there is imperfect information in the financial markets, and the type of the debtor is unknown to the creditor. In this game, as illustrated in Figure 3.3., we introduce two types of debtors: stable and unstable debtors. The creditor assigns a probability to the debtor; p is the probability that the debtor is of stable type and $1-p$ is the probability that the debtor is unstable. The unstable debtor heavily discounts the future and hence has a greater time preference rate, δ. For simplicity we assume that time preference rate of the stable type is zero. Payoff structures of the creditor, the stable and the unstable debtors are assumed to be common knowledge.

Figure 3.3 Sequential debt game with asymmetric information

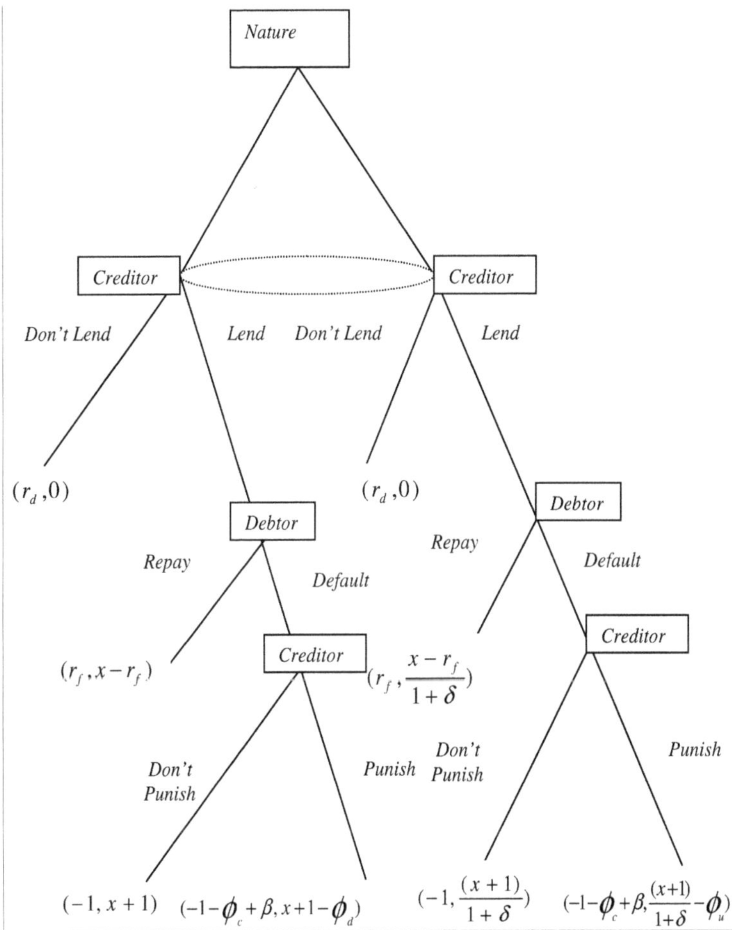

As in other economic models, we assume that the sovereign always has the ability to repay its debt. It is rather its willingness to pay that determines whether repayment is the equilibrium outcome.[21] Under instability a sovereign heavily discounts the future and might choose to default even if it is undesirable for a stable type. Instability occurs when the sovereign's revenues fall below the minimum amount required for the sovereign to continue its rule. The reasons for instability might be domestic or international political threats, which might require the expansion of military expenses or economic reasons. For instance, in an agricultural economy such as the Ottoman economy, national income might fall drastically due to unfavorable climatic conditions during the year. This not only diminishes the taxes collected by the sovereign but also requires the sovereign to redistribute some of its revenues to its citizens in order to avoid civil unrest. Due to random shocks on the economy or unfavorable political developments, a sovereign that is stable before the loan contract can face instability after the loan is made.

Time preferences capture an actor's subjective level of impatience. An unstable actor would be very impatient and place very little value on what happens in the future, whereas a stable actor would be patient and give more weight to future costs and benefits. Time preference rate for the unstable type, δ, is set such that the cost of default for the unstable type is smaller than its benefits. Hence, an unstable sovereign heavily discounts the future and chooses to default regardless of its consequences. For the stable type, on the other hand, the cost of default exceeds its benefits, otherwise the creditor does not lend in the first place.

Φ_d = Cost of default for a stable sovereign.

Φ_u = Cost of default for an unstable sovereign,

$\Phi_d > \Phi_u$, $\Phi_u < 1+r_f/1+\delta$ and $\Phi_d > 1+r_f$.

Thus, the debtor will choose to default at t+1 if unstable and repay the loan, if stable. Hence, if the creditor has the means to implement the sanctions, expected utility of the creditor from lending is

$$E(U_c) = pr_f + 1\text{-}p\,(-1-\Phi_c+\beta). \qquad (2)$$

As a risk-neutral investor, the creditor will be indifferent between investing in the domestic market and lending abroad if

$$pr_f + 1\text{-}p\,(-1-\Phi_c+\beta) = r_d. \qquad (3)$$

As previously mentioned, sovereign borrowing in the nineteenth century often worked through government bonds. Most of the time the creditors were either banks or small bondholders who needed government intervention for the implementation of sanctions that would not only harm the defaulter, but also recover a part of the loss suffered by the bondholders, such as the seizure of the debtor's assets. Previously, under perfect information, we assumed that the creditors and the debtor had full knowledge of the creditor government's potential costs and benefits from an intervention. In real life, cost and benefit assessments of a government are much more complicated and very difficult for third parties to grasp in detail. Under imperfect information, the creditors and the debtor assign a probability to government intervention. Creditor government intervenes with a probability γ on behalf of the creditors and seizes the assets or revenues of the debtor. The creditor, on the other hand, receives $\beta \leq 1+r_f$ from the intervention. Hence, under imperfect information a risk-neutral investor will be indifferent between investing in the domestic market and lending abroad, if

$$pr_f + 1\text{-}p(\text{-}1+\gamma\beta) = r_d \qquad (4)$$

Implications of the model

Costs of asymmetric information in the financial markets

The sequential debt game under asymmetric information helps us to clarify the major dynamics behind the trend in the risk premiums – the spread between the foreign lending rate and the risk-free domestic investment – charged on Ottoman bonds. As illustrated in the model, an essential determinant of the risk premium charged on loans is the level of uncertainty about the debtor's type. Formally, as p increases, the risk premium on foreign borrowing tends to diminish. The debtor seeks to minimize the risk premium on the credits and therefore employs different commitment and signaling mechanisms to increase the perceived probability of being a stable type.

As Goodhart notes, 'financial markets are markets in information'.[22] In the second half of the nineteenth century, one major limitation on the expanding global financial markets was the asymmetric distribution of information and high monitoring costs. In the absence of a system to provide information on public finances, such as the IMF's data dissemination system, sovereign rating agencies or credit departments (first established in Credit Lyonnais bank at the end of the nineteenth century), many investors relied on the information about foreign market conditions sent back to their native countries by recent immigrants.[23] In this context, it is not surprising that British foreign investment often went to countries with bank branch networks capable of gathering information on local market conditions. This was one of the main reasons behind the tendency, now dubbed the 'the Lucas Paradox', of foreign capital to flow to relatively advanced high-income countries.[24]

Asymmetric information and high monitoring costs were among the major factors determining the sectoral composition of foreign investment within countries. Empirical evidence shows that foreign investment usually went to railway bonds or mining companies, which had tangible assets that were relatively straightforward to monitor. Therefore, it is hardly surprising that six out of every seven pounds of portfolio investment were in securities of debtors with tangible and transparent assets.[25]

One major problem a foreign investor faced in the peripheral economies of the nineteenth century was that the financial records of states were not easily accessible by private creditors and in many cases they were not accurate.[26] Before the issue of bonds, the debtors often chose to reveal selective information regarding their economic performance, and exaggerated their net revenues.[27] This often contributed to the reluctance of investors to lend to these countries and led to high risk premiums associated with uncertainty. In most peripheral countries, including the Ottoman Empire, the issue of yearly budgets was not yet properly established. Some debtors chose to issue budgets as a means to gain the confidence of the international financial markets. Nevertheless, these budgets were often regarded with suspicion, because of monitoring problems. Hence, some countries, like the Ottoman government, initiated reforms in their state finances to bring credibility to the financial information declared by the government.

Coordination among the creditors and the enforcement of debt contracts

As illustrated in the model, another determinant of the risk premium is the lender's expected net benefits from punishment in case of default. The availability of various punishment mechanisms, which not only inflict cost on the debtor but also benefit the lender, drives down the risk premium on foreign loans. Accordingly, the lower the seizable assets or revenues of the debtor, the greater will be the risk premium. In addition, the perceived probability of government intervention, γ, plays a key role in the risk assessment of the creditors. The risk premium on foreign loans will be considerably lower as the perceived probability of government intervention increases.

The creditor country's military and political capacity was a major enforcement mechanism for peripheral lending throughout the nineteenth century. If the creditor government is a major military power, the creditors will feel safer investing in the peripheral economies. Hegemonic powers are more likely to intervene to further their political interests in the debtor countries. Historical evidence shows that even when controlled for discrepancies in wealth across core economies, creditors from the hegemonic powers tended to lend more to the sovereigns in the periphery. Another factor, which is at least as important as the creditor government's political or military capacity, is that of the debtor country. If the debtor has considerable military power, military intervention might be very costly, not only in economic terms but in political terms as well. Alternatively, even if the debtor is weak in terms of political or military capacity, intervention by a creditor government might raise objections from other governments. In the presence of multiple creditor governments, each government claims rights on the debtors' assets; hence unilateral intervention might trigger responses from other governments. This was the exact situation in the Ottoman Empire in the pre-OPDA period:

> When a single government is subjected to diplomatic influences springing from a number of sources, these impulses can usually be made to counteract with each other, leaving practically a free hand to the supposedly 'weak' government. A comparable situation existed at Constantinople during this period (pre-default period). And what the Turks consented to give with their right hand was frequently taken away with the left.[28]

Furthermore, hegemonic powers might have conflicting interests on the debtor country. In particular, intervention of one hegemonic power, in a way that extends its political control over the debtor country, might disturb another power even if it is in no position to claim rights to the debtor's assets. Hence, while the strategic importance of the debtor for the creditor government increases the probability of intervention, an increase in the expected costs of intervention in the international arena makes it less likely.[29] By contrast, cooperation among creditor governments or the legitimacy of the claims as perceived by the international community increases the possibility of intervention. This final point is critical to understanding the nature of hypothecated loans and their effect on the creditors' risk assessments. The issuing of 'hypothecated bonds' was a common borrowing mechanism used by sovereigns of the periphery in the nineteenth century. Typically, the most liquid, easily monitored, administrable and seizable state revenues were mortgaged in return for these loans. When a loan is secured through collateral, the management of default is simplified, for assets can be seized relatively easily. In the absence of collateral, the default might cause coordination problems and legitimacy problems among creditors, and among governments having conflicting interests on the debtor country. Subsequently, as opposed to general loans, the probability of government intervention (on behalf of the creditor), γ, increases in the case of hypothecated loans. Therefore, bonds with collaterals often bear lower risk premiums. Risk premiums also vary depending on the attractiveness of the collateral. For instance, the more liquid and administrable the collateral, the lower will be the risk premium.

Another important factor is the political costs of non-intervention for the creditor government. The level of coordination among the creditors plays an important role in the creditor government's policy. A coordinated body of lenders makes non-intervention costly for their home government. A good example is the Corporation of Foreign Bondholders (CFB) set up by British bondholders in the 1860s. As argued by historians, in cases when the debtor violated the terms of the contract the CFB often pressurized the British government for political or military intervention.[30] To persuade the government to support the bondholders' claims, the corporation not only used its connections within the government but also lobbied through the media and aimed to create favorable public opinion regarding intervention. The greater the coalitional stability among lenders, the more likely is government intervention; hence the risk premium on foreign bonds tends to be lower.

Enforcement of debt contracts before the OPDA: Understanding the role of the CFB

In the second half of the nineteenth century, after the major wave of defaults, creditors sought different solutions to overcome the aforementioned coordination problems. The CFB (Corporation of Foreign Bondholders), set up in 1868 to protect the interests of the British bondholders, was a byproduct of this effort.[31] During the period, one major weakness of the financial markets was the lack of information about the borrowing countries, particularly those with underdeveloped economies. This was the major reason behind the reluctance of European bondholders to invest in these 'gambling stocks', and the high risk premiums on these bonds associated with the lack of accurate information about the issuer. Hence one key function of the CFB was providing the investors with information regarding the countries whose bonds were contracted in London.[32] The CFB not only helped the bondholders to make more accurate risk assessments regarding their future investments, but also enabled the issuers of relatively more secure bonds to borrow at lower rates.

An equally important function of the CFB was the enforcement of cooperation among bondholders in blocking defaulting countries' access to international markets. By providing information on whether the countries had defaulted, which might not otherwise have been easily available to all investors, it facilitated the reputational mechanisms and helped to reduce the likelihood of other creditors extending credit to a defaulting country.[33] Furthermore, it cooperated with the London Stock Exchange, which blocked the quotation of the new bonds of the defaulting countries. Finally, it enforced collective action among creditors by disseminating information on creditors (to harm the reputation of the creditors) who defected and lent to a defaulting country while it was embargoed.[34]

Establishing the CFB was an important step in the direction of enforcing cooperation among British bondholders and coordinating their negotiations with debtor governments. However, it only represented the British bondholders (and not necessarily all of them), and blocking the defaulting countries' access to global markets requires international cooperation. It is true that in some cases the CFB managed to establish coordination with the bondholders and stock exchanges in other countries and prevented access of the defaulting sovereigns to these markets. Nevertheless, these were often temporary solutions and because of either the attractive returns on bonds or the political rivalries between the European powers, defaulting sovereigns managed to borrow in other financial markets.[35] In this respect, the Decree of *Muharrem* that led to the establishment of the OPDA exemplifies a more permanent solution, through which financial cooperation was achieved among major colonialist powers that were engaged in a harsh rivalry over the exploitation of the resources of the Ottoman Empire.

Enforcement of debt contracts after the OPDA

A major function of the OPDA was the maintenance of coordination among the Ottoman bondholders, which also created an important enforcement mechanism by creating wider international consensus on the legitimacy of the OPDA. Hence, as the perceived probability of government intervention in case of default increased, expected returns from lending to the Ottoman government rose considerably. This lowered the risk premium charged on loans to the government.

One important measure taken with the Decree of *Muharrem* was the unification of the Ottoman debt. By the decree, Ottoman bonds were unified under four categories to reconcile the interests of different claim holders. Another important measure taken in this direction was the removal of the allocations stipulated in the debt agreements.[36] All revenues allocated to debt service, including the loans taken after the establishment of the administration, would be pooled in the OPDA and debt services would be made from this single source. Thus, the agreement left no space for different bondholder groups to pursue negotiations separately from the others and to seek priorities in the repayment process, and tied their interests to those of the administration. More importantly, the decree was recognized and enforced by all major European powers; therefore, any measure taken against the OPDA could bring harsher sanctions. Hence, once the commitment had been made, it was very costly for the Ottoman government to go back and abolish the OPDA. The potential costs of such an action were noted by a French member of the Council, M. de la Bouliniere:

> Although the Administration of the Debt is Ottoman, the presence at its head of an independent Council composed of foreign delegates is sufficient to keep Turkey from violating its engagements; the potential menace of the provisions of the Congress of Berlin … could likewise, if necessary, encourage it to respect an institution, which Turkey has created in order to escape the commission provided for in the Protocol. Moreover, if it is true that the powers have no cause to intervene to insure the normal working of the prescriptions of the Decree of Mouharrem (*Muharrem*), and if it is the role of the Debt Council to do so, it is no less certain that Turkey had to notify the powers of the same Decree, and that any infraction of its provisions or any violation of the obligations undertaken would justify the

> immediate intervention of the interested powers, to which the delegates and the bondholders' syndicates would certainly appeal.[37]

Despite the disagreements over whether the decree prepared the ground for military intervention in the case of a violation, the bondholders believed their governments would support the OPDA if trouble came.[38] The enforcement power of the decree was also acknowledged by historians. A major reason for this consensus was the commitment of the Ottoman government to the decree, in spite of the political and international hardships it experienced during the OPDA period. As Blaisdell notes:

> For over forty years, the Ottoman Government made no formal attempt to disengage itself of the obligations assumed under the Decree of 1881. Even in times of stress, unless it was during the Great War, the attitude of the Government was satisfactory. During these forty years the Empire fought five different wars, experienced three revolutions, and on numerous occasions was disturbed by internal difficulties. Under these varied circumstances, the sanctions of the decree must be recognized as having possessed considerable force.[39]

Another important factor behind the lower risk premiums on foreign loans in the OPDA period was the reliability of the financial accounts declared by the administration. In the previous period, the risk premiums remained very high despite solid hypothecations in some loans due to the fact that financial statements of the Ottoman government lacked the confidence of the European financial circles. The same lack of confidence was observed in the reactions to the attempted reforms of the government, particularly made before the issue of new loans. One such example was published in the *Stock Exchange Review* as a critique of the financial reform program announced in 1874:

> It may be laid down as the rule that the government and their agents omit no opportunity of playing scurvy tricks for unfair gain where it can be done without exciting attention abroad.[40]

From the articles in the European press it is apparent that initially the OPDA suffered from the same trust issues as did the Ottoman government. The members of the council were assigned their seats by bank consortiums that held a considerable amount of bonds; hence they had an incentive to manipulate the investors by disseminating favorable information about the Ottoman economy and the assigned revenues in particular in order to raise the market value of the existing bonds:

> What they are striving to create is a market for the large masses of Turkish stocks at present held by them. If by means of this scheme they can induce the public to relieve them of their holdings, their object will be attained, and after that the collapse of Turkish credit will be a matter of comparative indifference to them ... No matter what the present bondholders may do, until the ability of Turkey to live within her diminished income is clearly demonstrated, new investments in Turkish stocks ought to be more sedulously avoided than ever.[41]

As can be understood from this article, published a month after the establishment of the OPDA, confidence in the service of Ottoman public debt had not yet been restored in European financial circles. Many suspected that the main concern of the council was to provide a market for their holdings and realize their profit before the inevitable collapse of the new scheme. Nevertheless, the members of the council and the bondholder syndicates they represented pursued larger profits over the longer term and gave priority to regaining the confidence of the investors.

In a country with a default in its recent history and a government with a reputation for deceitful manipulation of financial statements, further uncertainty would only bring the worst presuppositions to mind.[42] On the other hand, the council was convinced that revenues ceded to the administration would create an income stream that would surely cover the debt service. Consequently, the main priority of the OPDA would be to lift the 'veil of secrecy' that the government had deliberately thrown over its financial position to persuade the public that the administration was capable of carrying on the debt service. In this context, the OPDA introduced international standards in accounting and auditing, provided transparency and standardization in the financial records and helped the creditors to monitor the financial status of the administration with more accurate risk assessments.[43] At the end of each financial year the OPDA issued annual reports with detailed information regarding the administration of each revenue source ceded to its control. In contrast to the Porte's financial reports, which lacked comparison with previous years, the reports of the OPDA not only included the past year's accounts but also the estimations for the upcoming financial year, as well as the reasons for the expected increase or decrease in any particular source of revenue. Consequently, one major factor behind the declining risk premium on foreign loans was lowering of risk associated with uncertainty. The probability of repayment assigned by the creditors increased due to the confidence in accuracy of financial information revealed by the administration.

Another factor that increased uncertainty in the pre-OPDA era was the complex system of hypothecations. Since trust in the government had been lost, hypothecations gained special importance for the investor's risk assessments. Nevertheless, information on each particular source of revenue was scarce and not easily obtainable.[44] This caused the public credit to depreciate further even when this depreciation was not justified:

> The complicated system of loans each loan hypothecated on a different source of revenue, requires too much information, depreciates public credit even when carefully examined the security may be found very satisfactory.[45]

During the OPDA era the hypothecated revenues for all bond issues guaranteed by the administration were gathered under the control of the OPDA and payments were made from this single source. On many occasions, the OPDA's surplus was pledged as security. The investors bought these bonds because of their confidence in the administration, regardless of the pledges. The revenues hypothecated for other bond issues were again collected either by the Régie or the OPDA in the name of the government, such as the state's share of the Régie's profits and the tobacco tithe. Once again, these revenues could be easily monitored by foreign investors through the annual reports of the Régie or the OPDA.

Another factor that reduced the probability of default was the constraints placed on the sovereign. By the decree, the sources allocated to the debt service would be directly administered by a council assigned by the bondholders. The revenues would be collected without government interference directly from the taxpayers, and would be applied to the debt service again without passing from the hands of the government. Under these terms, even if the sovereign faced economic or political instability which shortened his time horizon and created an incentive for default, the funds apportioned to the debt service would not be under his disposal. The administration would also have the power to introduce reforms as long as they did not impose new burdens on the people or conflict with the existing laws of the Empire.[46] As admitted by the representative of the British, Dutch and Belgian bondholders: 'There is no instance in which powers so extended have been granted to a foreign organization in a sovereign state.'[47] Hence, in Bourke's words, the revenues of the bondholders were 'secured in the most effective way possible'.[48]

A further cause of the Empire's eroding credibility was the lack of confidence in the government's performance. Shortly before the default, a European newspaper had noted that 'it is not sufficient for the Turks to be honest; the European public has a right to demand an intelligent administration of public expenditure'.[49] This of course required substantial institutional improvements in public administration. In this context, the OPDA was welcomed 'as a more stable guarantee of efficient and trustworthy stewardship of capital than existed in the Ottoman Government'.[50]

The establishment of the OPDA assured debt payments despite the recurrence of heavy budget deficits and boosted confidence in the Ottoman bonds. As noted by Blaisdell, until the First World War the credit of the Empire rested largely on the prestige of the OPDA:

> As in the days prior to 1882, European confidence rested on the Ottoman Bank, so in later years, foreign investors placed their confidence in the Administration of the Public Debt as a European-controlled institution rather than the government. … The credit of the Empire undoubtedly profited from the prestige of the Public Debt; likewise the security of foreign capital was increased, risks reduced and profits enhanced.[51]

Unable to command confidence in the financial markets by its own means, the government aimed to benefit from the credibility of the OPDA. Therefore, when necessary the government voluntarily transferred more sectors to the control of the OPDA in order to raise new loans at more favorable terms. Hence, in a manner that echoes the argument developed by North and Weingast in their seminal paper on the economic consequences of the Glorious Revolution, the constraints on the sovereign enabled the Ottoman government to regain access to foreign capital markets with lower risk premiums and helped to finance the modernization of the administrative system.[52] However, one notable difference was that in Britain these constraints were imposed by the internal dynamics of the country, whilst in the case of the Imperial

Ottomans they were imposed from outside nearly 200 years later, which made the country, in the 'age of high imperialism', even more vulnerable to the political and economic exploitation of the European powers.[53] The reason why the Ottoman Empire could not develop a similar set of institutions as in Britain is beyond the scope of this work. However, it surely is crucial in understanding the Empire's future subordination to the European powers.

Ottoman foreign borrowing in the OPDA era

By signing the Decree of *Muharrem*, the Porte had greatly compromised its financial and political autonomy. Yet, the decree also helped to solve the Porte's short-term liquidity problems as the Ottoman government regained access to European financial markets at significantly lower interest rates than ever before. As mentioned in the previous chapter, Ottoman borrowing in the pre-OPDA period was marked by several reforms aimed at restoring eroding confidence in the Ottoman government. During the OPDA period, confidence was restored through the constraints placed on the sovereignty of the government and the extension of the OPDA's control over the Ottoman economy. Lending to the Ottoman government was no longer a matter of trust in the government itself; rather it was trust in an international commission established for the liquidation of the foreign debt. Figure 3.4 illustrates the downwards trend of the nominal interest rates on Ottoman bonds after 1881.

Yet, this figure fails to capture the overall drastic change in the market conditions in favor of the Ottoman bonds. Before the OPDA, most Ottoman bonds were issued at significantly lower rates than their face value, with the exception of the second loan in 1855.[54] Occasionally, the government also paid considerable amount of commission to different banks or bankers for the issue of bonds. Thus, in some cases the amount acquired by the government fell below 50 percent of the amount of debt resulting from the issue of bonds (in 1870 and 1874 loans) and effective interest rates rose to around 12 percent. To capture this dimension, the effective interest rate for each loan in 1854–1914 has been recalculated. As illustrated in Figure 3.5, the establishment of the OPDA brought a 5 percent fall on average in the effective interest rates.

Figure 3.4 Nominal interest rates on Ottoman bonds: 1854–1914

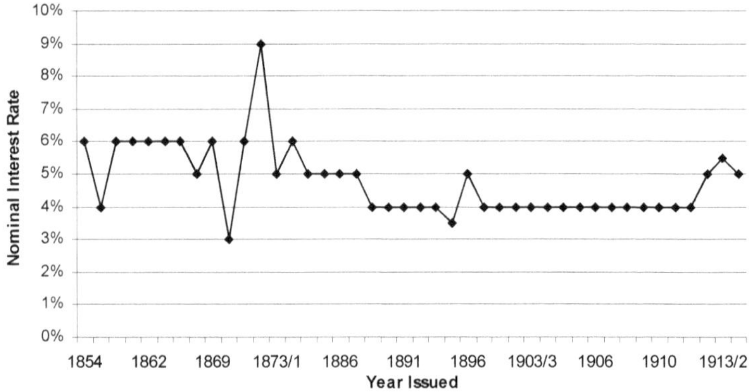

Source: Annual Reports of the CFB; Yeniay, 1964; Suvla, 1966; Kıray, 1991.

Figure 3.5 Effective interest rates on Ottoman bonds: 1854–1914

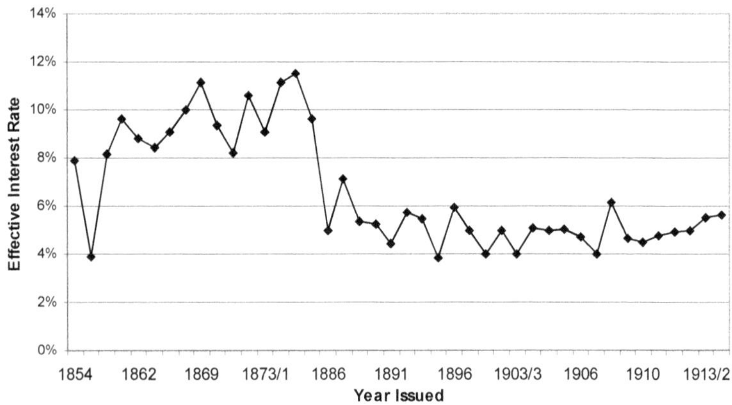

Source: Annual Reports of the CFB; Yeniay, 1964; Suvla, 1966; Kıray, 1991.

Finally, one might argue that the reason behind the decline in the effective interest rates on Ottoman bonds could also be the declining interest rates in the core economies, which might lead to a cheaper capital outflow. In the sequential debt game, this aspect was accounted for by the introduction of the risk premium, which was defined as the spread between the foreign lending rate and the rate of return on risk-free domestic investment. To illustrate the trend in the risk premium on Ottoman loans, the 2.5 percent British consols have been chosen as an indicator of the returns on risk-free domestic investment in core economies, and the spread between the yields of the Ottoman bonds and the risk-free British consols has been calculated.[55]

As illustrated in Figure 3.6, after the 1854 and 1855 loans, which were secured against the Egyptian tribute, the risk premium on Ottoman loans always remained above the 5 percent level, and rose to 8 percent in 1877. After the establishment of the OPDA, the risk premium fell dramatically and always remained below the 3.5 percent level. The average risk premium on Ottoman bonds in this period was 2.1 percent, as opposed to 5.7 percent in the pre-OPDA period.

Figure 3.6 Ottoman bonds' spread over UK consols before and after OPDA

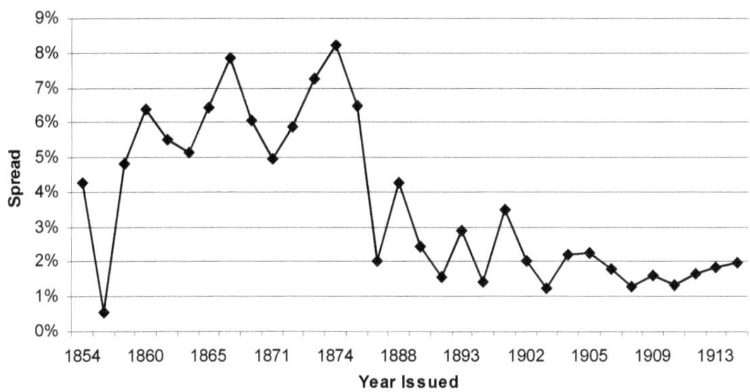

Source: Annual Reports of the CFB; Yeniay,1964; Suvla,1966; Kıray,1991; GFD.

Finally, the declining interest rates after the Young Turk revolution of 1908 should be noted. Contrary to expectations, the nationalist government pursued a more cooperative policy towards foreign investment, until the outbreak of the First World War. After the proclamation of the constitution in July 1908, Monsieur Laurent, an eminent French expert, was assigned to the Ministry of Finance to help come up with measures for financial reform, ascertain the amount of floating debt and frame a budget for the coming year.[56] For the first time, in the fiscal year 1909–10, a reliable budget was prepared and published; the confidence in the government and the reliability of the budget enabled the Porte to raise another loan for LT 7,000,000 at very favorable terms.[57]

Table 3.1 Ottoman foreign debt after the OPDA: 1881—1914

Year	Amount of debt (£)	Rate of issue	Amount acquired (£)	Rate of amount acquired	Nominal interest	Effective interest	Allocated to	Pledges	Major inv.
1886	5,909,091	100.0%	5,909,091	100.00%	5.0%	5.0%	Debt consolidation, Treasury	Customs, Régie share	F
1888	1,470,588	70.00%	1,029,411	70.00%	5.0%	7.1%	Munitions from Germany	Fisheries (OPDA)	G
1890/1	7,827,240	75.00%	5,870,527	75.00%	4.0%	5.3%	1881 privileged bonds		
1890/2	4,541,364	76.00%	3,451,436	76.00%	4.0%	5.3%	Settlement of the floating debt	Cereal tithes from various *vilayets* (OPDA)	F, B
1891	6,316,920	90.00%	5,685,227	90.00%	4.0%	4.4%	Conversion of 1877 loan, Treasury	Egyptian tribute (OPDA)	B, F
1893	909,091	70.00%	636,364	70.00%	4.0%	5.7%	Budget deficit	Tobacco tithe	F
1894/1	1,600,000	73.50%	1,176,000	73.50%	4.0%	5.4%	Debt from Eastern Railways, Treasury	Remainder of revenues (OPDA)	G,F
1894/2	8,212,340	91.00%	7,473,229	91.00%	3.5%	3.8%	Debt consolidation (1854, 1871 loans)	Egyptian tribute (OPDA)	F,B
1896	2,975,200	84.00%	2,499,167	84.00%	5.0%	6.0%	BIO, Military expenses, Rumeli Railway, Treasury	Sheep taxes and tithes (OPDA)	F
1902	7,818,200	80.00%	6,254,560	80.00%	4.0%	5.0%	Repayment of the 1886 loan, Treasury	Customs and intermediary taxes	F
1903/1	2,160,000	100.00%	2,160,000	100.00%	4.0%	4.0%	Baghdad Railway	Various crop tithes	G,F,B
1903/2	2,400,000	80.00%	1,920,000	80.00%	4.0%	5.0%	Debt consolidation and exchange of bonds (1888 loan)	Fishery revenues (OPDA)	G
1903/3	29,762,520	100.00%	29,762,520	100.00%	4.0%	4.0%	Debt consolidation, Exchange of B,C,D series bonds	Remainder of revenues (OPDA)	F
1904/1	2,500,000	78.50%	1,962,500	78.50%	4.0%	5.1%	Budget deficit	Remainder of revenues (OPDA)	F
1904/2	4,824,240	80.00%	3,862,665	80.07%	4.0%	5.0%	Repayment to the BIO	Remainder of customs (OPDA)	F

Table 3.1 Ottoman foreign debt after the OPDA: 1881—1914 (continued)

Year	Amount of debt (£)	Rate of issue	Amount acquired (£)	Rate of amount acquired	Nominal interest	Effective interest	Allocated to	Pledges	Major inv.
1905	2,400,000	79.50%	1,908,000	79.50%	4.0%	5.0%	Military equipment	6% addition to OPDA revenues, customs rev. (OPDA)	G
1906	8,670,000	85.50%	7,412,850	85.50%	4.0%	4.7%	Exchange of 1890 privileged bonds, Treasury	Remainder of OPDA revenues (OPDA)	F,B
1908/1	9,080,000	100.00%	9,080,000	100.00%	4.0%	4.0%	Plan 2 and 3 of Baghdad Railway	Remainder of revenues (OPDA)	G,F,B
1908/2	4,282,840	82.50%	2,790,414	65.15%	4.0%	6.1%	Budget deficit	Customs, remainder of revenues (OPDA)	F
1909	6,363,640	86.00%	5,456,821	85.75%	4.0%	4.7%	Budget deficit	Aleppo sheep tax.	F
1910	1,556,640	89.00%	1,385,409	89.00%	4.0%	4.5%	Soma-Bandırma Railway	Revenues of the railway, İzmir-Kasaba Railway (OPDA)	F
1911/1	909,100	84.00%	763,644	84.00%	4.0%	4.8%	Hudida-San'a, Extension Railway	Customs revenues of Hudaida and Jabana (OPDA)	F
1911/2	6,400,000	81.50%	5,216,000	81.50%	4.0%	4.9%	To pay back some advances, Budget deficit	Customs revenues of İstanbul.	G
1913/1	744,518	100.00%	744,518	100.00%	5.0%	5.0%	Debt from Konya plain irrigation project	Revenues from drained and sold lands, tithes of Konya (OPDA)	
1913/2	1,350,000	100.00%	1,350,000	100.00%	5.5%	5.5%	Construction of the docks, maritime arsenal	Tithes of Sivas (OPDA)	B
1914	20,000,000	88.75%	17,750,000	88.75%	5.0%	5.6%	Floating debt resulting from the Libyan and Balkan Wars	Remainder of OPDA rev. the subsidy tithes and customs (OPDA)	F

A=Austria, B=Britain, F=France, G=Germany, I=Italy. Sources: CFB; Kıray, 1995; Pamuk, 1994; Suvla, 1966.

In the pre-OPDA period, the total amount of foreign loans was £228,372,507. However, the Ottoman government received only £122,741,500, which made up just 53.7 percent of the outstanding debt. During the OPDA era, on the other hand, the total foreign loans amounted to £150,983,532. The government received £133,510,354, which made up 88.4 percent of the total foreign debt contracted during this period. Out of 25 loans contracted during the OPDA period, in 18 of them the OPDA was directly involved in the supervision of the resources pledged to the service of debt. For these loans often the surplus of the OPDA revenue was pledged as security along with custom duties and tithes from different districts.[58] In other loan operations, easily observable and trustable pledges were chosen, such as the government's share in the Régie or the tobacco tithe, which was again collected in the Régie's warehouses. Details of the Ottoman loans in the 1881–1914 period are shown in Table 3.1.

From the annual reports of the CFB we understand that the administration was initially reluctant to lend its name to further loans:

> It is a question for anxious and careful consideration whether the Council of Administration should any further lend its name to loans, the security for which stands on a different footing from that of the Ottoman Public Debt, for the administration of which it was originally constituted, and whether in any case it is politic to facilitate the pledging of present revenues by the Government, which as matters already stand, has some difficulty in making the two ends meet. Under the special circumstances of the present case neither the Council of Foreign Bondholders nor the English Delegate considered that it would be wise to withhold their consent. But the question as to the future is not being fully discussed, and the Council of Foreign Bondholders has placed itself in communication with the various Foreign 'Syndicates' in regard to it.[59]

One possible factor behind the reluctance of the administration was the bondholders' concern about the depreciation of the credit of the administration, which would also depreciate the market value of their bonds. On the other hand, the extension of the OPDA's control over the Ottoman economy was also an attractive opportunity for the diplomatic missions, which aimed to increase their political and economic influence on the government, and large European firms seeking new investment opportunities throughout the country, mainly the railway companies that relied on the OPDA's cooperation. Many members of the council also occupied key positions at these companies and, hence, had direct interests in maintaining the security of these investment contracts. As can be observed from Table 3.1, a considerable proportion of the loans approved by the council were used to pay for the government's liabilities to these foreign contractors.

Consequently, the OPDA's control of resources expanded far beyond the assignments of the Decree of *Muharrem.* In 1898, revenues collected outside the Decree surpassed the revenues collected by virtue of the Decree's functions by over £1 million. According to a recapitulation on 1 March 1923, 'Hors Décret' loans administered by the OPDA amounted to over LT 56 million, while Decree Loans amounted to at least LT 10 million less than this figure. The Ottoman government, on the other hand, administrated a total loan of LT 25 million.[60]

The extension of the OPDA's control over the Ottoman economy was surely of concern to the government, but it was so in need of short-term liquidity that it often resorted to foreign loans, despite the fact that each loan agreement brought more constraints on the economic sovereignty of the Porte. Some historians interpreted Ottoman borrowing in this period as evidence of the continuing irresponsibility of the bureaucracy and its lack of foresight. As noted by Suvla,

> The establishment of the Administration and its infraction upon the state's independence and dignity were not sufficient to teach the Ottoman government a lesson. As soon as there was an opportunity, additional loans were taken from abroad, without considering the pressure of increasing stipulations.[61]

Here it is important to note that, as opposed to the loans in the pre-OPDA period, a substantial part of which were allocated to the extravagant expenditures of the palace and budget deficits, a significant portion of the loans in the OPDA period were allocated to rebuilding the infrastructure of the Empire.[62] Out of 25 loans contracted in this period, six were allocated to railway construction, and one to the construction of docks. These investments developed the means of communication between the Porte and distant regions and strengthened the central authority. They also facilitated economic growth by improving the means of transportation. Another loan contracted in 1913 paid for the Konya plain irrigation project, which was considered the single greatest agricultural improvement initiated by the Ottoman government.[63]

There is no doubt that all these projects were in line with the interests of the foreign bondholders and the foreign powers represented in the council. Under the guarantee of the OPDA, the railway projects in the Empire had always been a profitable source of business for European capitalists. Moreover, they enabled European merchandise to reach the interior. The Konya project was originally proposed by the German Baghdad Railway Company, which expected to increase its tax revenues collected from the region. Nevertheless, it is also true that these investments benefited the Empire as well.[64]

Foreign direct investment after the Decree of *Muharrem*

The establishment of the OPDA and the subsequent financial reforms initiated by the administration encouraged not only foreign lending but also foreign direct investment in the Empire. The OPDA, initially set up to watch over the interests of the pre-decree bondholders, gradually grew into a 'watchdog' of foreign capital in the country.[65]

Particularly after the default, foreign capitalists had little or no confidence in the integrity of the government. The default not only created reluctance among investors to do business with the government, but also imposed huge transaction costs and made it extremely expensive. The contractors who thought they would have to spend a great deal of time and money obtaining payment from the government, or were at considerable risk of obtaining no payment at all, added large profit margins to their contracts. Under these circumstances, the government, often paid contractors around 20 percent more than the regular market price, which included the costs of insurance and/or the costs of obtaining the money, such as *bahşiş* (bribe), or the commissions paid to intermediaries. If the contract was based on the regular market price, the costs of insurance and *bahşiş* would be covered by reducing the quality of the service.[66]

Before the establishment of the OPDA, European investors in the Ottoman Empire experienced many difficulties with the government over tariffs, securities, and the protection of their property.[67] Besides the difficulty in receiving payments from the treasury, many investors complained about the arbitrary bureaucratic procedures that prevailed in the Empire. Such complaints were often voiced by the European press. For instance, a shareholder of the Metropolitan Railway of

Constantinople, operating between Galata and Pera (Beyoğlu), complained that after the expropriation of the land from the price settled by the jury, the government officials had demanded 60 percent in excess of the amount already paid. The company, under protest, had paid the money. However, the shareholder noted that immediately after the payment had been made the government officials had asked for a further deposit of LT 9,000. When the company's officials resisted payment, the operations of the company were stopped by the government.[68] Similar concerns were pointed out in the American journals along with the need for institutional reforms in order to attract foreign capital into the country:

> The best and the most necessary guarantee and the most efficacious attraction, which Turkey could offer to the capitalists of Europe and America is the organization of what it most needs: a good administration, an independent and impartial judicature, and the most absolute security for human life and property.[69]

Nevertheless, under the prevailing circumstances, FDI did not gain significance until after the establishment of the OPDA and the consolidation of its position as an economic factor in the Empire. The OPDA not only restored but also drastically improved the credibility of the Empire as compared to the era before the default. As noted by Blaisdell,

> The Administration of the Public Debt was, in fact, admirably fitted to perform the functions which foreign promoters found lacking in the government itself. The two primary demands were: an agency in which perfect trust could be reposed, and the cooperation of an administration which was capable and efficient. In the opinion of foreign investors the government possessed neither of these attributes. But the Public Debt, also from the viewpoint of Western Europe, did possess them; its support and cooperation were therefore necessary.[70]

Figure 3.7 illustrates the trend in five-year moving averages of FDI in the Ottoman Empire in 1859–1913. As shown in the figure, foreign direct investment into the Empire began as early as in 1860s, but it only became significant during the OPDA era, particularly after the 1890s. Based on Pamuk's calculations, the estimated total net capital inflow arising from

FDI (after the deduction of the repatriated capital) in the 1859–81 period amounted to £12.607 million, averaging around £548,000 annually. On the other hand, in the 1882–1913 period following the establishment of the OPDA, total net capital inflow arising from FDI amounted to £63.684 million, averaging around £1.996 million annually.[71] The major wave of FDI was in 1888–96, which made up around 40 percent of the total amount invested in the Empire until 1913. The most important component of the investment boom consisted of the railway investments under the supervision of the OPDA.

Figure 3.7 Capital flow arising from foreign direct investment: 1859–1913

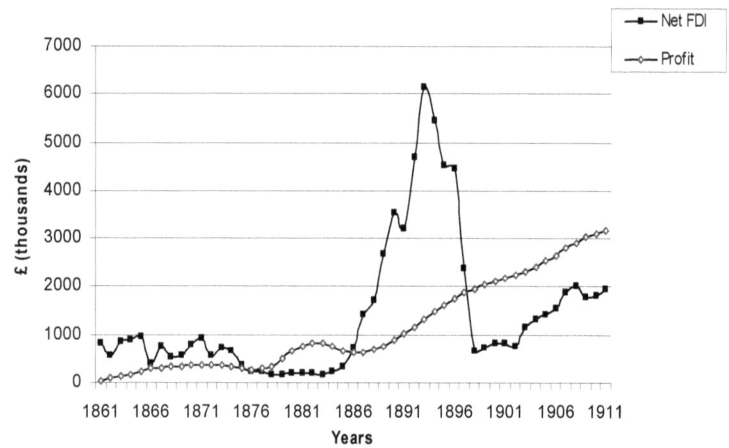

Source: Pamuk, 1994: 197–200.

Note that in 1876–87 and in 1897–1913 there was a net capital outflow arising from foreign direct investment. The first phase of capital outflow can be explained by the reputational spillovers of default, which discouraged FDI in the Empire and led to the withdrawal of foreign capital until the credibility of the government had been restored. The second phase was due to the high level of repatriated profits following a major wave of investment. This trend partly overlaps with the capital outflow arising from foreign indirect investment in the OPDA period, particularly until 1911, and lends support to the imperialism theories and the arguments of the dependency school. They argue that the OPDA functioned as a post of Western imperialism, assuring the transfer of resources from periphery to core and contributing to the further impoverishment of the peripheral economy.[72]

The impact of the OPDA on FDI can also be observed from Figure 3.8, which illustrates the five-year moving averages of the number of foreign joint-stock companies established in the Empire in 1854–1914. Before the Decree of *Muharrem*, in the 1849–1881 period, 19 foreign joint-stock companies had been established in the Empire. By 1908, this number had increased to 83, and in 1914 it reached 213, the largest being the Tobacco Règie. In 1882–1913, Toprak reports a net capital inflow of £64 million from these foreign companies and a subsequent profit repatriation of £54 million.[73]

Figure 3.8 Foreign joint-stock companies established in the Ottoman Empire: 1849–1914 (5-year moving averages)

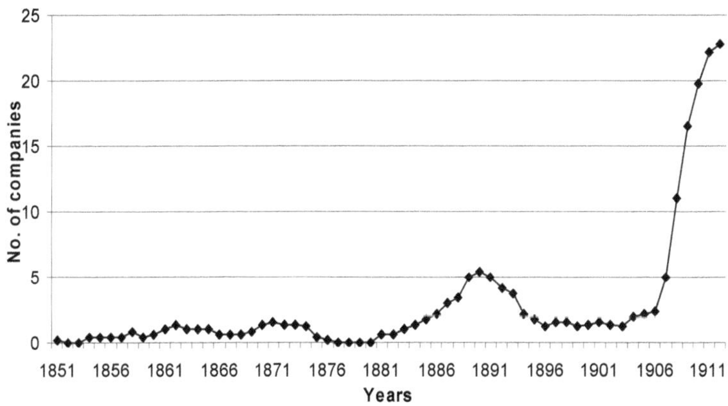

Source: Based on the data provided by Toprak, 1995: 115.

An analysis of foreign investment in the Ottoman Empire in 1888–1914 shows that investment in Ottoman foreign loans always remained above FDI figures. However, in the 1888–1914 period, FDI grew faster than foreign loans, and from one-seventh of foreign loans in 1888 it climbed to half the total amount of foreign loans in 1914.[74] As can be observed from Figure 3.9, which illustrates the sectoral breakdown of FDI by 1914, only around 5.3 percent of FDI went to industry. The rest went mostly to the ports and railways, promoting the flow of goods within the Empire as well as between Europe and Middle East. A portion of the investment in banking and insurance can also be included under this category. Railways held 63 percent of the total, and was by far the most attractive field of investment for foreign entrepreneurs. The direct involvement of the OPDA in a considerable number of railway projects demonstrates, once again, the crucial role played by the OPDA in directing the inward flow of capital.

Figure 3.9 Sectoral distribution of foreign direct investment by 1914

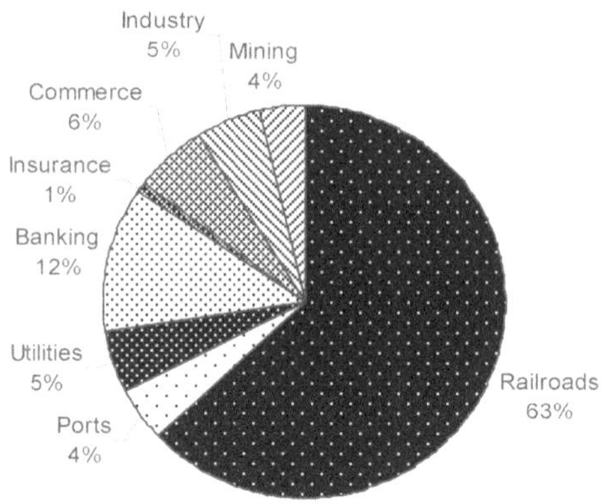

Source: Based on Pamuk, 1994: 74.

Towns in the interior of the Ottoman Empire were poorly connected with each other and the seaports. The lack of means for rapid communication not only retarded economic development, but also added greatly to the difficulty of defending the Empire.[75] Hence, the development of an extensive railway system was regarded by both the Ottoman government and by most foreign authorities as the key to the country's economic progress. However, the Turkish government had neither the financial nor the technical resources to undertake the projects itself. After the two remaining government-owned lines were sold off to European companies in the early 1890s, the only major railway project undertaken by the government was the Hijaz railway from Damascus to Medina, and even this project required an extraordinary effort to raise the necessary resources.[76] Under these circumstances there was no other option for the government but to allow foreign companies to build the new lines themselves. Hence the Ottoman railway system was financed almost entirely from outside as were irrigation work, port and bridge construction, mineral exploitation, and municipal public utilities.[77]

The OPDA played a crucial role in the railway investments. European capitalists who sought profits amid the disorder that prevailed in the country often asked for the protection or the cooperation of the OPDA. The involvement of the administration in the railway projects secured their investments to a large degree, minimized their risks and enabled them to enjoy handsome profits. Based on his detailed account of the relationship between the OPDA and the railway companies, Blaisdell confirms this view:

> It is a question whether any of these enterprises would have been undertaken had it not been for the existence of the Administration of the Public Debt.[78]

The fact that the OPDA was able to act in concert with the railway companies as well as providing the government with financial and technical assistance placed them in a strong position to obtain favorable terms for their protégés. Two issues in particular became the subjects of controversy. The first was the granting of a variety of ancillary rights to the railway companies, such as the ownership of any mineral deposits, including oil, that could be found within 20 kilometers on either side of the Baghdad railway line from Konya to the Iraqi provinces. These concessions, granted to foreign companies, often formed the basis for huge concessionaire claims presented to the successors of the Ottoman Empire after the First World War. The second issue was the kilometric guarantees given to railway companies by the government. The railway company would run a certain number of trains over a particular piece of track, and in return the government promised to make up for any shortfall in gross receipts up to a certain amount, usually somewhere between Fr 13,000 and Fr 18,000 per kilometer. However, the government's promise was not enough for the railway companies. As additional security, these companies demanded that the government set aside a portion of its revenues to meet the guarantee.[79] Moreover, these pledged revenues, often the tithes or sheep tax collected from the districts along the railway, would be placed under the supervision of a trusted and 'neutral' third party, the OPDA.

The practice of kilometric guarantees was bound to raise disputes between the government and the railway companies. In these disputes the OPDA generally sided with the latter, since their interests often coincided. As previously mentioned, the members of the council were closely linked with, and sometimes handpicked by, their own governments, which were often ready to act forcefully in support of enterprises managed by their fellow countrymen. This could sometimes take the form of direct pressure on İstanbul, such as a refusal to permit the flotation of a particular loan until some claim had been met or a further concession granted. Hence, it is almost impossible to assume that the members of the council would remain impartial in disputes concerning the interests of investors from their own country.[80] Also, personal interests cannot be overlooked; several delegates of the council were simultaneously members of the directing boards of these railway companies.[81]

Figure 3.10 *Öşür* revenues after the railways: 1889–1914

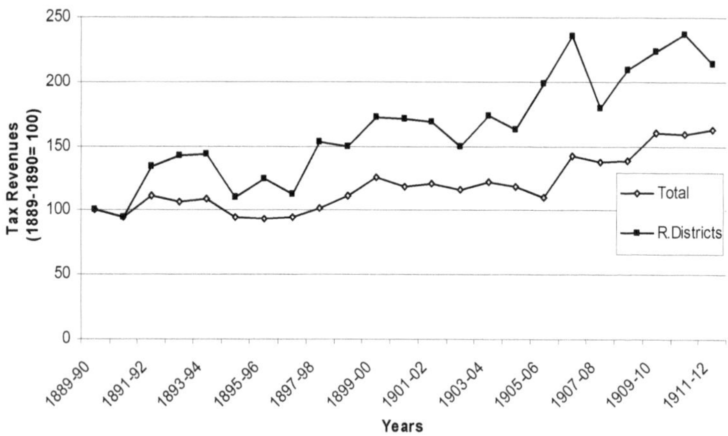

Source: Based on the data provided by Eldem, 1994: 93.

The construction of the railway system increased the productivity of the regions traversed by the lines, assuring the natives a means of transportation for all production beyond local requirements. In 1889 the total value of the tithes in the region traversed by the Anatolian Railway was LT 145,378; it rose to LT 215,470 in 1898 and LT 291,919 in 1909.[82] As illustrated in Figure 3.10, in 1889–1914 the increase in *öşür* revenues in districts of İzmit, Ertuğrul, Kütahya, and Ankara that were traversed by the Anatolian railway was 114 percent, while the general increase in *öşür* revenues collected in the Empire remained at 63 percent overall.

There is no consensus in the literature regarding the economic benefits of the railways to the government. Based on the data on payments made to the Anatolian Railway Company in 1893–1909, some argue that the payment made by the government for the kilometric guarantees outweighed the increases in tax revenues; hence the treasury did benefit from these investments in economic terms.[83] Eldem, on the other hand, looking at the data from 1889–1914, argues that the railway system brought an increase of Ps 254.51 million in taxes collected by the government, Ps 60.16 million above the payments made to the Anatolian Railway Company.[84]

As far as the OPDA was concerned, the administration benefited greatly from the construction of the railways without incurring any costs. It experienced a rapid increase in revenues as transportation was made easier and further markets were opened by a network of railways. Moreover, by the transfer of pledged revenues to the supervision of the administration, it gradually extended its control over the economy. These investments also benefited European capitalists in general as they created considerable demand for European iron and steel, and more importantly enabled the penetration of European goods into the interior parts of the country.

The OPDA's role in foreign investment in the Ottoman Empire

This chapter has laid out the institutional basis of foreign investment in the Ottoman Empire during the OPDA period. Through a game theoretical model, we explained how foreign investors made their risk assignments and how the risk premiums on individual loan issues were determined in the international markets, and investigated the sources of decline in the risk premiums on loans issued in the OPDA era. As illustrated in the model, the constraints placed on the sovereignty of the Porte by the Decree of *Muharrem* enabled the government to borrow at lower risk premiums from international markets. There were basically two main factors that affected the risk assignments of the creditors. The first was the higher perceived probability of debt service in the OPDA era. The reliability and the monitorability of the financial accounts of the OPDA reduced uncertainty regarding the repayment of debt and brought about a considerable fall in the risk premiums. The second was the increase in expected net returns in case of insolvency. The key function of the OPDA was the maintenance of coordination among the Ottoman bondholders. The coalitional stability of the creditors formed an important enforcement mechanism by creating a wider international consensus on the legitimacy of the OPDA. As the perceived probability of government intervention in case of default increased, expected returns from lending to the Ottoman government rose considerably. This lowered the risk premium charged on loans issued by the Ottomans.

The OPDA not only encouraged foreign lending but also foreign direct investment into the Empire at an unprecedented rate. A considerable amount of the FDI in this period went to the railway schemes, which not only facilitated domestic economic activities but also enabled the penetration of Western goods into the interior. The construction of the railways was one of the major dynamics behind the integration of Ottoman provinces into the world economy. The OPDA played a crucial role in the railway investments. European capitalists who sought profits amid the disorder that prevailed in the country often asked for the protection or the cooperation of the OPDA. The involvement of the administration in the railway projects secured their investments to a large degree, minimized their risks and enabled them to enjoy large profit.

Railway workers on the 232nd km. of the Hijaz railway (1903). IU *Nadir Eserler Kütüphanesi*, 90590-003.

A view from the 232nd km. of the Hijaz railway (1903). IU *Nadir Eserler Kütüphanesi*, 90590-0032.

4

ORGANIZATIONAL STRUCTURE OF THE OPDA AND THE ADMINISTRATION OF THE INDIRECT REVENUES

Organizational structure of the OPDA

The OPDA was not a typical example of foreign financial control established over several peripheral economies in the latter half of the nineteenth century. Its organic statute was not backed by an international treaty or a diplomatic act. Moreover, in contrast with the financial commission established for Greece and the Egyptian *Caisse de la Dette* that was composed of official representatives from foreign governments, the Ottoman Council of Foreign Debt was ostensibly private in spite of the close ties between its members and their home governments. The council consisted of two members from France, one each from Germany, Austria, Italy, and the Ottoman government itself, and one representing both Britain and Holland. The foreign members of the council were selected by the bondholders or banks or, in the case of Italy, by the Rome Chamber of Commerce. The council established the Ottoman Public Debt Administration (OPDA).

The Decree of *Muharrem* entrusted to the OPDA the direct administration, receipt, and encashment, by means of agents acting under its authority, of the revenues and other sources ceded to the service of debt. It had the power to appoint and dismiss its employees, who were considered as functionaries of the state in the performance of their duties.

The government was also bound to give the OPDA, in the exercise of its administration, all the general assistance compatible with the existing institutions, and to afford the military protection indispensable for the security of its principal seats and of its local services. The administration was largely independent from the Ottoman government. The government was entitled to send a commissioner to the regular meetings of the administration and examine its books. However, beyond this point it had no right to interfere with its operations. In case of a disagreement between the government and the council, an arbitration panel consisting of four members (two appointed by the council, two by the government and a fifth chosen by the arbitrators if necessary) would be formed to resolve the matter.

Under the terms of the Decree, the revenues from the salt and tobacco monopolies, the stamp and spirits taxes, the fish tax, and the silk tithe from certain districts as well as the Bulgaria tribute, the revenues of Eastern Rumelia and the surplus of the Cyprus revenue were irrevocably ceded to the OPDA, until the debt was liquidated. In 1903–4, the gross receipts of the administration from the assignments of the decree made up around 13 percent of the total treasury revenues of the Empire, including the revenues ceded to the OPDA; by 1911 it reached 17 percent.[1] Moreover, as the Ottoman government continued to borrow from abroad, the control of the administration over the resources of the Ottoman economy extended far beyond the assignments of the decree.[2] As a result, by 1912, the OPDA had more employees than the Ottoman Ministry of Finance.[3]

According to Blaisdell, the OPDA, while functioning as an outpost of European Imperialism, also gave a good example of the best features of European financial management. The administrative system introduced by the OPDA, in many aspects, formed a great contrast to the financial administration of the Ottoman government:

> Adjudication of the tithes took place on schedule; accounts were closed on time; coupons on the consolidated debt were met at maturity. Within its own ranks, the Administration never condoned dilatory methods; in its business with Government the Council was continually pressing matters for solution. Salaries of native officials and laborers employed in the P.D.A (OPDA) were adequate, and were paid when due. On no occasion did the number Europeans employed in the Administration exceed seven or eight percent of the total. The policy of regular payment

> of sufficient salaries practically wiped out, within the Administration's ranks, the abuses of baksheesh (bribery) and of retention of collected receipts by local revenue agents, two vices which had sorely troubled the Imperial Government in attempts to reform its financial administration. Indeed, to become an employee of the Administration was the ambition of many a Turk and Ottoman Christian.[4]

Hence, reasonable salaries offered by the new administration not only created an attractive employment opportunity, but also helped prevent the sort of corruption that prevailed in all ranks of the Ottoman bureaucracy. The Annual Report of the OPDA in 1883 elaborated on this point by contrasting the operations of the OPDA with the working of the Ottoman bureaucracy:

> The Oriental System is to give an official a mere pittance paid irregularly, and to allow him to rob. If you stop his robbing you must increase his pay and give him a sufficient sum to live upon in decency and comfort. Meanwhile the regularity with which our officials receive their salaries proved a sufficient attraction to enable us to select our employees from a large number of candidates. There are, I should estimate, some fifty applications for every vacant post at Constantinople.[5]

One major aspect of the OPDA's employment policy was to leave the provincial executive in the hands of the locals, and to entrust only the duty of control and supervision to foreign officials. In the first year of the OPDA, 5704 officers were employed by the administration in 15 different *nezarets*. Out of these officers only 88 were of foreign nationality.[6] As noted by Edgar Vincent, the representative of the English, Dutch and Belgian bondholders in the Council of Public Debt, it would be a mistake to import European executives to implement European methods they had been taught to regard as perfect in a different country with a different population. Through such a policy, the foreign officers and the administration would gradually alienate themselves from the local populace. Instead, Vincent defended keeping the old lines, but with Western precision and regularity. Hence, the foreign officers were ordered not to meddle in executive business, but to report any irregularities immediately to the council, and to give assistance to Turkish directors when needed. The reasoning behind this policy was nicely summarized by Edgar Vincent:

> In a country like Turkey, there can be nothing more dangerous to the permanence of a system of collection than to levy heavy taxes by means of foreigners….We have seen an example of this in Egypt: the reasons which gave popularity to the late rising there, would operate with far greater force in Turkey.[7]

Thus, while making several institutional reforms in the sectors ceded to the administration, the OPDA pursued a careful policy of 'keeping the old lines' whenever possible in order to avoid widespread public opposition. Only in case of the tobacco monopoly did a radical change take place with the establishment of the Régie Company. The company displaced the existing cigarette producers. The details of the Régie will be discussed in detail later. Still, it should be noted that the enforcement unit of the monopoly, the *kolcus*, was drawn from the local population.

The OPDA introduced new technologies to the relevant sectors under its responsibility, improved the regulations and made the necessary legislative changes concerning the development of its revenues. Improvements in the revenues under its control and the introduction of new institutions in the relevant sectors also created positive externalities for other sectors of the economy.

Figure 4.1 illustrates the trend in the revenues obtained from the indirect contributions – salt monopoly, silk tithes, stamps, spirits and fishery taxes – under the ASIR and the OPDA. As shown in the figure, the OPDA's administrative policies yielded significant increases in the revenues obtained from the indirect contributions as they increased by 176 percent over the 30 years following its establishment. In the same period, the total gross receipts of the administration from the assignments of the decree increased by 160 percent.[8] Until 1907–8, the increase in gross receipts remained considerably below the increase in the indirect contributions.[9] This was mainly due to the so-called 'permanent assignments' of the decree and the fixed annuity paid by the Régie, which remained stable over time and held back the rate of increase in gross receipts.[10] This trend was reversed after 1907, when gross receipts of the administration rose drastically due to the 3 percent customs surtax arising from the revision of commercial treaties made with foreign powers. After the revision of treaties the custom duties on imports were raised from 8 percent to 11 percent *ad valorem*.[11]

Figure 4.1 The revenues from the indirect contributions: 1879–1914

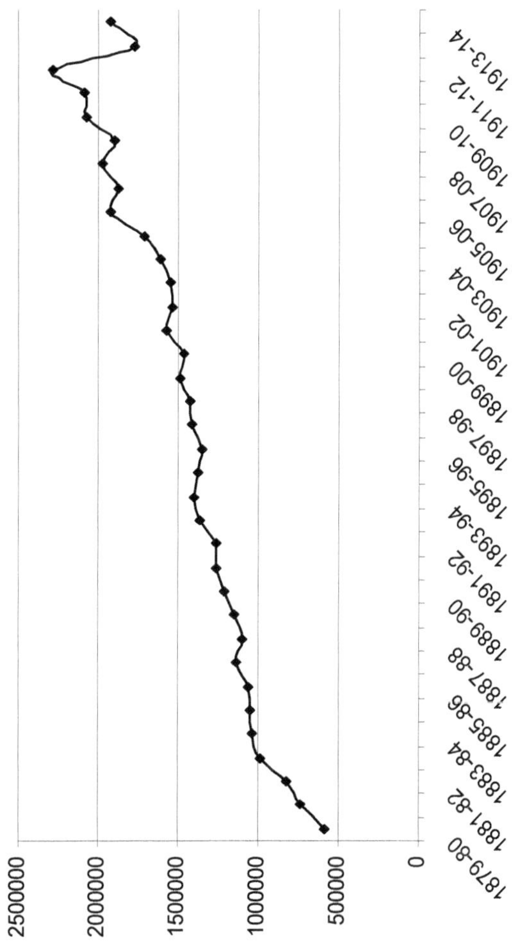

Sources: Fane, 1892; Roumani, 1927; Kazgan, 1985; Annual Reports of the CFB.

Finally, the international treaties imposed on the Porte by the European powers also restricted the administration's ability to improve its revenues.[12] In several contexts, including the stamp law, wine duties, and patent law, OPDA officials complained about the unfair conditions imposed by these treaties and asked for revisions. The following section provides an in-depth analysis of the administration of the indirect contributions under the OPDA, tracks the sources of increase in these revenues and outlines the obstacles encountered by the administration.

Administration of the five indirect contributions under the OPDA

Administration of the salt monopoly under the OPDA

In terms of income, the salt monopoly was the most important revenue ceded to the bondholders. In 1862, the government had created this monopoly during the negotiations for a loan contract and it had formed part of the security for the loan. The Ottoman Empire was particularly rich in salt, both in rock form and from salt marshes. However, the administration and the development of the monopoly presented certain difficulties. One major obstacle was the prevalence of contraband salt, which, according to some estimates, made up around 50 percent of salt sold by the government and seriously limited the government's revenues obtained from the monopoly.[13] The extensive coastline made it difficult to prevent the penetration of smuggled salt from overseas.

Another issue was the security of the salt works within the Empire. Due to the large size of the salt works it was hard to establish proper control over them and guard them from smugglers.[14] Besides, the absence of railroads or an extensive system of highways impeded the transportation of salt. High transportation costs raised its price in regions distant from salt works.[15] Not surprisingly, contraband was more pervasive in these districts. Moreover, due to the interruptions in supply shortages of salt, a household necessity, were not uncommon in these districts; therefore peasants were accustomed to purchase their yearly supply of salt all at once, which made it a serious burden on their budget so that the purchase of contraband salt became even more attractive.[16]

There were two main components of the OPDA's supervision policy in the salt sector. First was the prevention of smuggling in order to strengthen the monopoly of the OPDA in the domestic market. Second was to extend the market for salt by reaching external markets and encouraging the development of other domestic sectors that required large supplies of salt, such as fisheries.

From the early days of its establishment the administration pursued a determined policy to eradicate contraband salt from the market. To this end, the administration initially moved to reduce the sale prices where contraband was sold on a large scale and took measures to maintain a better supply in regions where contraband was facilitated by the lack of salt, rather than by monopoly prices.[17] Furthermore, the OPDA rented the salt works in Sisam and Crete, both of which, until then, served as bases for the contraband salt smuggled into the Empire.[18]

Nevertheless, until the 1890s, the reports of the OPDA show that despite some significant improvements, contraband was still common in some districts where the OPDA was unable to gain full control. On the sea coast, the monopoly had to compete against daring smugglers who brought in salt from the salt pans of Cyprus and Crimea.[19] In some interior regions, such as Aleppo and Yemen, the salt works were exposed to incessant depredation by nomad tribes due to the proximity of the desert. Particularly in Yemen, the revenue had almost entirely disappeared.[20]

In the Black Sea region, the OPDA itself assumed responsibility for the transportation of salt from İzmir to reduce its price in the region and wipe out the contraband.[21] However, it failed to compete with the Crimean salt smuggled into the region and asked for the government's cooperation to guard the sea coast. The government often ignored the smuggling activities until 1892, when the Porte was forced to establish a sanitary cordon along the Black Sea coast due to the prevalence of cholera in Russian Black Sea ports. To enforce the quarantine cruisers were sent to patrol the open sea. The Annual Report of the CFB in 1892 notes that 'the smugglers were unable to elude the vigilance of the cruisers or break through the sanitary cordon'. As a result, the OPDA's salt revenue in the Black Sea Region increased by approximately 50 percent within a year.[22] This dramatic increase also illustrated the magnitude of smuggling activities in the region. In the following years, the pressure exerted by the OPDA on the government yielded a result and the government purchased two coastguard vessels for the Black Sea coast, which increased the ability of the administration to combat contraband.[23]

Even more gratifying results were achieved following the construction of railways under the guarantee of the OPDA. The administration made agreements with the railway companies for the cheap transportation of salt and established sales depots near the train stations where salt was sold at a 25 percent discount.[24] The close cooperation between the OPDA and the railway companies not only reduced the price of salt but also made it readily available. Hence, the expansion of the railways within the Empire prepared the ground for wiping out the contraband salt trade and played a crucial role increasing salt revenues.

In the first decade of the 1900s, a significant part of the increase in salt revenue was due to the new markets created for salt.[25] From the beginning, the OPDA sought external export markets.[26] However, the contribution of exports to total sales revenues remained insignificant until after 1892, when the administration stopped focusing purely on anti-smuggling activities and adopted the policy of developing the export trade. For this purpose, the administration opened the salt works at Salif on the Red Sea coast, and constructed a port for direct shipments to the purchasers. On account of its geographical proximity and market size, India was chosen as the target market. The OPDA made the necessary contacts for the export of salt from Salif on the Red Sea to Bombay, Calcutta, Rangoon and Singapore in addition to seeking markets in Japan and Australia.[27] Shipments were also made to the Balkans.[28] Consequently the export revenue, which was negligible in 1890s, reached LT 100,000 in 1908–9.[29]

Besides searching for external markets, the OPDA also aimed to develop other uses for salt in order to increase its sale in the domestic market. The fishing industry and the cultivation of olives required large amounts of salt and offered good opportunities for the development of domestic consumption.[30] Significant increases were noted in 1914 due to the olive crop and fishing.[31]

Figure 4.2 illustrates the annual revenue from the salt monopoly during the administrations of the ASIR and OPDA. As the figure shows, salt revenues rose steadily after the establishment of the ASIR. This trend gained pace, first after 1902 due to the export-oriented policies of the OPDA and then after 1908, due to the increasing cooperation of the government against smugglers. The fall in 1912–13 can be explained by the mobilization of the army during the Balkan War and the subsequent territorial losses of the Empire.

Figure 4.2 The administration of the salt monopoly: 1879–1914

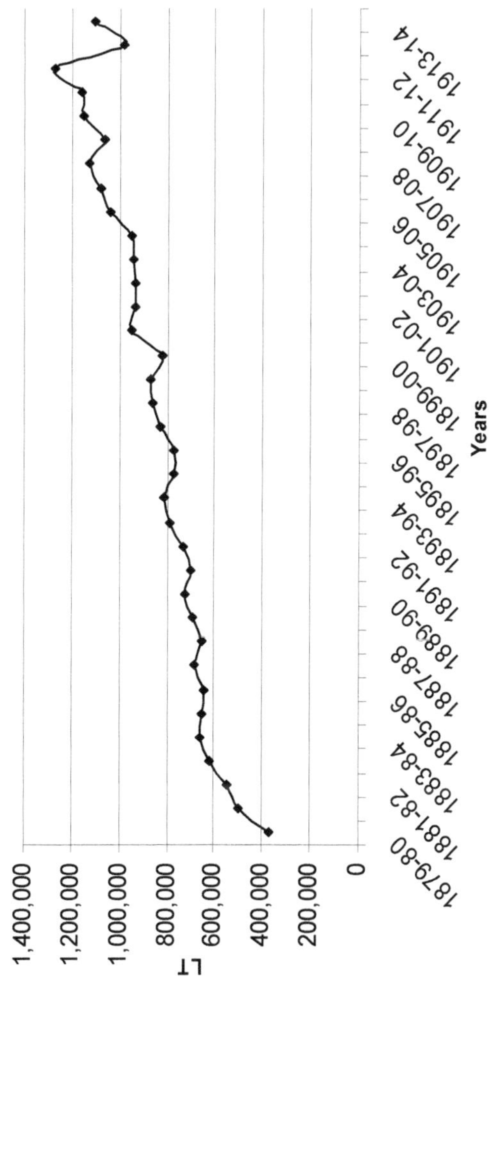

Sources: Fane 1892; Roumani 1927; Kazgan 1985; Annual Reports of the CFB.

Administration of the silk tithe under the OPDA

Sericulture was introduced to Anatolia in the sixth century, when two Nestorian monks smuggled silkworm eggs out of China, and subsequently the Byzantine Empire had a flourishing silk industry.[32] However, by the eleventh century the main source of raw silk for the Anatolian industry had become Northern Iran. This trade was frequently interrupted during the Turco-Iranian wars in the sixteenth and seventeenth centuries. In this period, the Ottoman government encouraged domestic production of silk, and by 1587 silk was being grown in Bursa, which later became the silk center of the Empire. The collapse of Iranian silk production in the eighteenth century and the rising world demand for silk in the early nineteenth century generated a further impetus for the expansion of Ottoman silk production. In the 1850s the increase in the output and exports was accelerated by the ravages caused by the pebrine disease in Europe. Until the 1860s silk production of the Empire continued to grow by 15–20 percent a year.[33]

Nevertheless, the golden era of Ottoman silk production did not last long. In the 1860s silk production in the Empire faced a serious decline caused by the silkworm disease that had also ravaged Europe. All counter-measures, such as the government's efforts to introduce Japanese silkworms that were immune to the disease, or the individual efforts of some merchants and silkraisers in Bursa to import the Pasteur techniques from France, failed.[34] Moreover, after the opening of the Suez Canal, East Asian silk products flooded the European markets, making matters even worse for Ottoman silk producers and the silk industry.[35] The Annual Report of the OPDA in 1884 summarized the adverse conditions of Ottoman silk production in the pre-OPDA era:

> An unscientific and promiscuous importation and combination of various sorts of eggs, a faulty method of feeding the worms, and the absence of any kind of proper silk worming nurseries' had caused a deterioration in the silk enabling other countries to displace Turkey from her position as the producer of the 'finest known quality of silk'; and the competition thus set up with countries more advantageously placed, and possessing more capital and more mechanical resource, has well ruined what was, only thirty years ago, one of the most flourishing industries in the Ottoman Empire.[36]

Following the transfer of the silk tithe revenue of certain districts to the OPDA, the priority of the administration became the prevention of the silkworm disease in order to develop silk production and increase its tax revenues.[37] In this context, the newly established administration contacted Pasteur in person and upon his recommendations invited Kevork Torkomyan, an Ottoman Armenian and a graduate of the French Montpelier Agricultural School, to eliminate the disease and restore the industry. For the same purpose, the OPDA established a silk-raising institute to teach the Pasteur technique to the producers and help them raise disease-free silkworm eggs.[38] The institute had three instructors, including Torkomyan himself. The OPDA enforced participation in this program by making it obligatory to receive a license for silk-raising. By 1908 the diploma of the institute had been granted to 919 students, and around 500 silk growers had passed through the course of instruction. When sent home, these instructors spread their knowledge and accelerated the diffusion of modern methods in silk culture.[39] Another important measure taken by the OPDA was the introduction of a tight screening procedure for the silkworm egg sales. Due to the contagious nature of the pebrine disease, it was crucial to eliminate the diseased eggs and establish a quality control mechanism in order to prevent the outbreak of a new disease. This was also one of the reasons why in the pre-OPDA era individual efforts in the prevention of the disease had failed.

In few years following the establishment of the OPDA, the administration had considerable success in fighting the disease, and revived the silk culture in the Empire through an institutionalized effort. The European press praised the success of the OPDA policies:

> The result of this applied science has been remarkable. Silk culture in Bursa, which a few years ago threatening to become extinct, is now flourishing more than it has ever been before.[40]

As a result of the OPDA policies, in the 1890s cultivation of silk was spreading steadily across the Empire. These measures enabled the Ottoman producers to take advantage of booming world demand for raw silk. Another reason for the widespread cultivation of silk was the high European tariffs on Turkish wine. Profit margins on Turkish wines had shrunk so much that in many places peasants took to replacing their vineyards with mulberry plantations.[41] In 1890–1910, around 60 million mulberry trees were planted in the Empire.[42] Consequently, the raw silk production in Bursa more than tripled between the late 1880s and 1914; similar impressive results were achieved in silkworm egg and cocoon outputs.[43]

In the latter part of the 1880s, favorable silk-raising conditions prompted other technological improvements. The OPDA played an active role in the diffusion of the new technology and in the establishment of factories. For this purpose, the administration established a silkworm nursery in Bursa to serve as a prototype. The nursery used the Dorr model equipment in silk reeling which was used to kill the worms with steam and hot air. The equipment used in this nursery was imitated by other silk-raising centers in the Empire. Over time, it gradually replaced the oven technique, which damaged the cocoons. The OPDA also aimed to introduce the silk industry into new regions. One successful example was in Salonica where the administration established a model filature (silk-reeling plant) equipped with the latest technology in order to attract local investment to the industry.[44] A few years later a consortium of local merchants and bankers established a large factory in Salonica following the example set by the OPDA.[45]

Other technological transfers in the silk industry centered on silk weaving. For a long time, in contrast to raw silk production, European states had a negative attitude towards the mechanization of silk cloth production in peripheral economies because it was seen as a threat to local silk cloth producers. This attitude changed in the latter part of the nineteenth century as the European industry increasingly emphasized the production of capital equipment and thus stood to gain from the mechanization of textile production abroad.[46] Hence, Ottoman silk cloth production, particularly in Bursa region, staged an important comeback as it mounted sharply towards the end of the nineteenth century.

Figure 4.3 illustrates the development of the silk tithe revenues of İstanbul, Bursa, Samsun and Edirne that were ceded first to the ASIR and then to the OPDA. As a result of the radical improvements in the silk industry, the OPDA's silk tithe revenue increased sharply under the new administration and reached LT 131,217 in 1907–8 from LT 13,219 in 1881–82. After 1911, the silk revenue started to decline due to the territorial losses of the Empire in the subsequent wars and fell to LT 82,497 in 1913–14.[47]

Figure 4.3 The administration of the silk revenue: 1879–1914

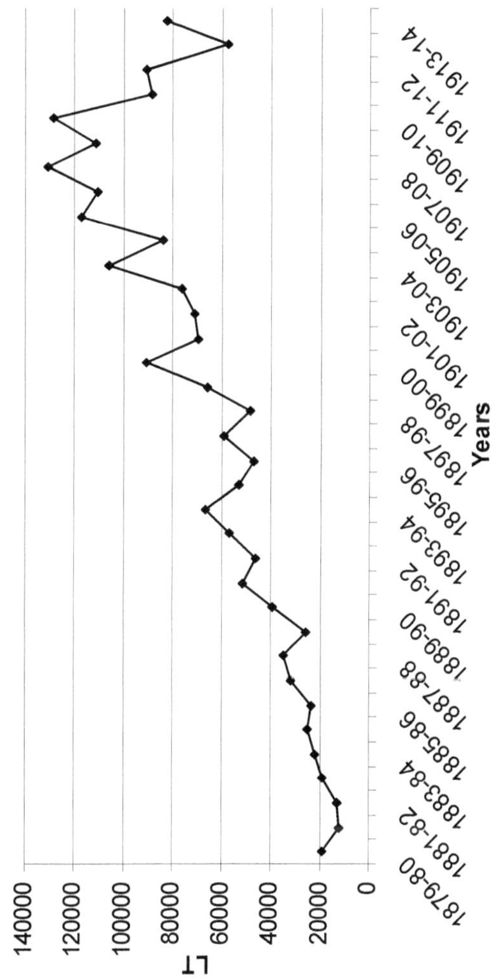

Sources: Fane, 1892; Roumani, 1927; Kazgan, 1985; Annual Reports of the CFB.

The stimulus created by the OPDA in the silk industry was not limited to the region under its responsibility, and it generated positive externalities for the Ottoman silk industry as a whole. Hence, similar increases in silk tithe were observed in other regions not administered by the OPDA as the total revenue from silk tithes increased from LT 20,000 to LT 276,000 in the abovementioned period.[48]

Finally, the adoption of the new set of regulations introduced by the OPDA, even though they were proven to improve the quality of the local production, were rejected because of opposition by the local merchants in other silk centers of the Empire that remained outside the coverage of the OPDA, such as Beirut.[49] As the efforts of the Pasteur Institute had shown, domestic production had great advantage over foreign competitors both in terms of cost and higher yield as a result of better acclimatization to local conditions. However, the Beiruti merchants, the importers of foreign silkworm eggs, opposed the establishment of a Pasteur institute in Beirut on the grounds that it would introduce a tight system of rules and regulations governing egg sales and act as a restraint on their trade. This powerful lobby managed to prevent the establishment of the institute in the region and held back the development of local production.[50]

Administration of the stamp revenue under the OPDA

One of the most fruitful sources of government revenue created during the Tanzimat period, levied to finance reforms, was the stamp tax applicable to all commercial and governmental business documents. Initially, the *sheriat* (Islamic law) court proclamations were exempted from tax. This exemption was ended in 1861 by Fuad Paşa, who reorganized the administration of stamp tax revenue and established a separate stamp tax (*damga vergisi*) department in the treasury to organize the printing and distribution of the stamps and supervise the enforcement of new regulations. Under the new regulations, transactions requiring the use of stamped documents were divided into four categories for rate purposes.[51]

1- Contracts and receipts for loans, commercial transactions, the organization of companies and insurance, and all documents presented to state courts and administrative councils.

2- Contracts, receipts, petitions, and other documents presented to the treasury, other government departments, to individual or administrative officials.

3- Documents presented to *sheriat* courts.

4- Documents issued by legislative, judicial, and administrative councils, trade courts, or other government departments giving decisions on particular matters. The individual had to pay for the stamp in order to receive the decision.

For commercial documents involving money or value a relative tax was applied starting at Pr 20 and adding Ps 1 for every Ps 2,500 of value; for other matters a specific tax was applied depending on the document ranging from Pr 20 to Ps 10. If a commercial paper or contract was presented on a document that was not stamped properly, a penalty of three times the required stamp duty was applied prior to its legalization.[52]

In 1873, the coverage of the stamp law was broadened to include all commercial activities requiring notarization as well as stock shares issued by corporations, bank checks and receipts, newspapers and public broadsides. Penalty provisions were also broadened to include not only the person who offered a document without a stamp but also the person who accepted it.

When the stamp revenue was ceded to the OPDA in 1881, it was seen as one of the most promising sources of revenue. However, in the following years the development of this revenue presented unusual difficulties, causing conflicts between the OPDA, foreign embassies and the Ottoman government. One major problem was the systematic evasion of stamps in contracts between individuals.[53] Among themselves, Muslims rarely resorted to a written contract to finalize an agreement. Only with Greeks and Armenians was something more than a verbal contract used.[54] Written contracts were mostly used among the religious minorities and almost only in cities.

On the other hand, due to the capitulations granted to foreign powers, the citizens of states possessing extraterritorial rights were exempted from tax. This privileged population included not only foreigners but also a considerable portion of the minorities. These protégés, who could enjoy the tax privileges granted to foreign subjects, controlled a vast proportion of commercial activities, as well as the modern economic sectors such as banking and insurance.[55] Hence, the enforcement of stamp law was seriously hampered by the privileges granted to foreign subjects through the capitulations.[56]

Figure 4.4 The administration of the stamp revenue: 1879–1914

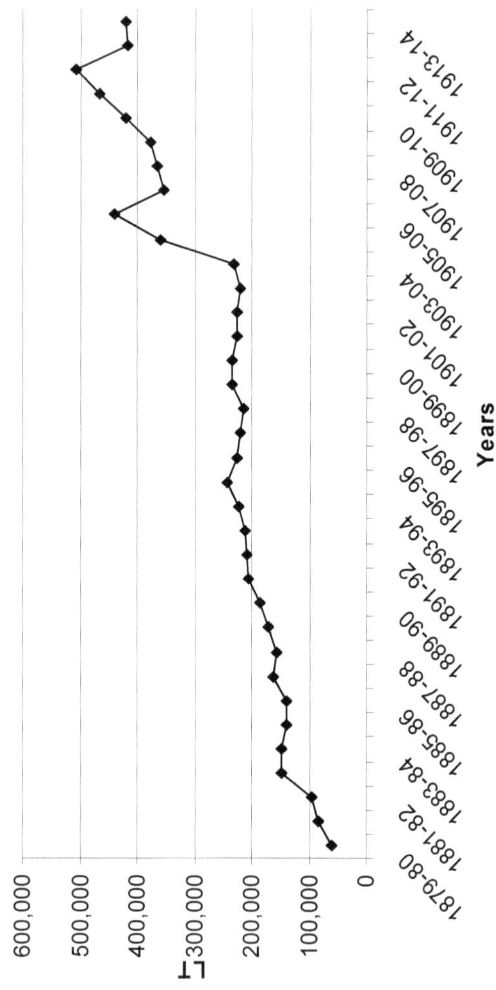

Sources: Fane, 1892; Roumani, 1927; Kazgan, 1985; Annual Reports of the CFB.

Besides the exemption of foreign subjects from the stamp law, the OPDA also complained that the old stamp law imposed such ridiculously high charges upon all classes of commercial business that it was systematically evaded. Hence the new administration agreed upon a new law, which was actually prepared during the administration of the ASIR.[57] By the new law, the administration not only aimed to reduce the charges to a more reasonable level but also to extend the coverage of the law, including foreign nationalities. In addition, foreign exchange, payroll and accounting receipts were also taxed for the first time.

Figure 4.4 illustrates the trend in stamp revenue under the ASIR and the OPDA. As shown in the figure, the new administration achieved around a 77 percent increase in its first years due to the new regulations and the stricter enforcement of the law. Nevertheless, the increase was still far below the OPDA's expectations as a result of the opposition of the foreign missions to the new stamp law.[58] Foreign subjects and their commercial establishments continued to exempt themselves from the payment of stamp tax in their operations.[59] It was only after 1904 that the new stamp law could be enforced for all residents in the Empire without exception.[60] As can be observed from the graph, in 1904–5, following the end of exemption granted to foreign subjects, the stamp revenues increased by 54 percent and reached LT 59,791.

Significantly, the limitations on the privileges of foreign subjects were brought about through the efforts of an organization controlled by the bondholders of the very countries that enjoyed these privileges. This example, along with several others, shows that the OPDA did not simply act as an official agent of foreign powers. On some occasions it sided with the Porte when its interests conflicted with those of the major powers and coincided with those of the Porte or the Ottoman economy in general. After all, the decision makers, the members of the Council of Public Debt, were appointed to those seats by the bondholders whose interests were in many cases tied to those of the Ottoman economy. This fact has often been overlooked by historians.[61]

The Ottoman government, on the other hand, received protests from the OPDA on two issues regarding the stamp tax. The first issue concerned the stamps on newspapers. By an order issued by the Ottoman government, İstanbul newspapers had been exempt from the obligation of affixing a stamp to each copy of their newspapers. The loss to the OPDA due to this exemption was estimated to be around LT 10,000 a year. The

OPDA officials argued that according to the Decree of *Muharrem*, the Ottoman government had no right to authorize exemptions without previous agreement with the OPDA.[62] Nevertheless, despite the OPDA's objections, İstanbul newspapers continued to be exempt from the tax.

Another source of contention between the government and the OPDA involved the refugee stamp (*muhacirin ianesi*), created to aid the Muslim refugees from Crete and elsewhere. The stamp was to be affixed to a large number of documents that were subject also to ordinary stamps whose revenue went to the OPDA. The government defended the refugee stamp on two grounds: first, it was provisional and second, it was a voluntary contribution, not a tax. For the OPDA, this distinction was illusionary since it served as an additional tax levied on the same documents that were subject to the stamp tax, the proceeds of which were ceded to the administration; thus it had to be withdrawn to prevent further diminution of the OPDA's revenues.[63] In this case, as in the former disagreement, the OPDA failed to reverse the government's actions or obtain any compensation to cover its loss.[64]

Another conflict with the government occurred in 1885–86, when the duties on passports and permits of circulation (*mururiye tezkereleri*), which were collected by the OPDA up to that time, were withdrawn from the administration and transferred to the police department. Furthermore, the OPDA was held liable to restore the sums it had already encashed from these duties.[65] This time, the problem was resolved in favor of the OPDA. In 1888, the duties were once again ceded to the OPDA and the administration was also compensated for its loss.[66]

Finally, it should be noted that the sharp fall in revenues in 1906–7 was due to the census operations in 1905–6, which caused a temporary spike in the use of stamps.[67] In the years that followed, the stamp revenues climbed steadily until the Balkan War. Particularly after the Young Turk revolution, it was reported that the government worked closely with the administration. Hence, a large part of the increase after the revolution was due to the stricter enforcement of the stamp law, public compliance and the formation of new companies whose bonds were subject to the stamp tax.[68] Overall, under the OPDA, the stamp revenues increased by 334 percent and reached LT 419,241 in 1914, despite the territorial losses of the Empire and the war conditions.

Administration of the spirits revenue under the OPDA

Since spirits were legally prohibited by the *sheriat*, there were no official taxes on their consumption in the early days of the Empire. Instead, the holders of the tax farms (*mültezims*) collected a grape juice tax (*şire resmi*) from the growers of wine grapes after they ripened and were pressed into wine. In the seventeenth century an official spirits tax (*müskürat resmi*) was imposed on non-Muslims who, thus, were officially allowed to consume alcohol for the first time. But soon thereafter this permission was rescinded and the tax was abolished in order to avoid any official sanction of actions that were legally prohibited for both Muslims and non-Muslims.[69]

The spirits tax was introduced once again in the *Tanzimat* era and a single tax of 20 percent was applied in place of the myriad taxes developed during the eighteenth century.[70] In 1861, the taxes levied on spirits were lowered to 10 percent, and the sellers of these beverages were held liable to purchase annual shop permits at a fee of 15 percent. No permits were granted for locations within Muslim quarters or within 200 yards of mosques or *tekkes*. In 1867, the regulations were revised and the license tax was raised to 25 percent, but the shops were allowed to locate within 100 yards of religious buildings. Hotels and restaurants selling drinks to their customers at mealtimes were exempted from this tax, but if they sold spirits at other times, the tax was levied according to the proportion of spirit revenues in their total business receipts. The final revision to the spirits tax was made soon after the accession of Abdülhamid II when it was raised from 10 percent to 15 percent.[71]

In 1881, along with other revenues, the spirits tax revenue was turned over to the OPDA. As can be observed from Figure 4.5, in 1881–1912 the OPDA achieved a 138 percent increase in this revenue. As with other indirect contributions, this revenue fell sharply after 1912 due to territorial losses and war conditions. Nevertheless, the increase in this revenue remained far below the increases achieved in other sources. One obvious reason was the Islamic belief in abstention from alcoholic consumption. Even though alcohol consumption among Muslims was not uncommon, average consumption figures were considerably below the European states.[72] Backed by the legal arrangements discouraging alcohol consumption by Muslims, religious concerns restricted the increase in this revenue.

Figure 4.5 The administration of the spirits revenue: 1879–1914

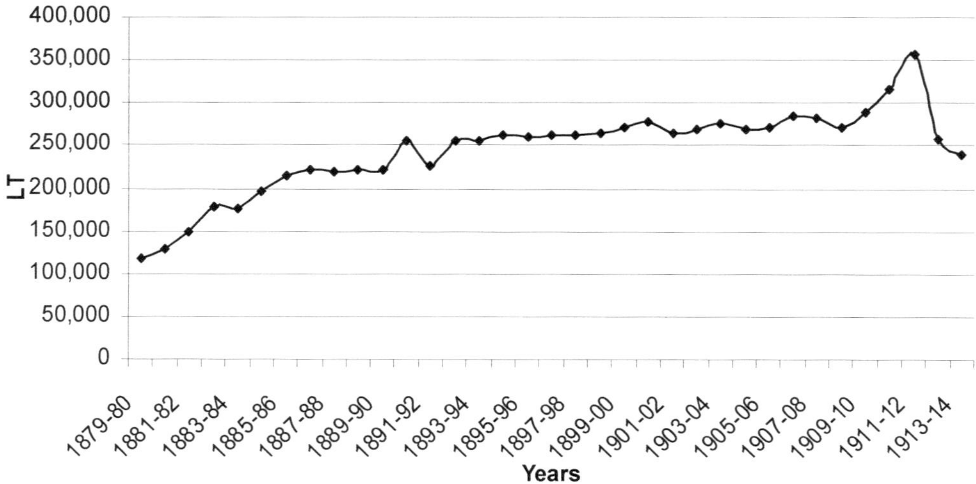

Sources: Fane, 1892; Roumani, 1927; Kazgan, 1985; Annual Reports of the CFB.

Other major obstacles in the development of this revenue were posed by the capitulations and the privileges granted to the import of wines, beers and other alcoholic beverages of foreign origin. Due to the disadvantages created by these legal arrangements the importer of wine paid 8 percent import tax whereas the domestic producer had to pay a 15 percent *ad valorem* tax to the government. Once again, the OPDA complained about the international agreements imposed on the Porte and made considerable efforts to change these terms, but to no avail. The disincentives for domestic production limited the extension of vine growing and the development of the domestic alcohol industry throughout the OPDA era.

Due to the restraints on the expansion of domestic consumption, the OPDA also worked to improve the quality of Turkish wines and increase their exportation. During the first years of the administration one major problem faced by vine growers was phylloxera, a disease that had destructive effects on the vineyards. The administration gave assistance to the vine growers and achieved significant improvements.[73] These efforts paid off and by the 1890s the quality and price of Turkish wines reached levels that made them competitive with famous French wines, even in the French market. Around 25 percent of the wines produced in the country were exported. However, the French government did not hesitate to impose additional import duties on foreign wines in order to protect domestic producers.[74] Italy, another important market for Turkish wines, followed the French example by increasing import duties, causing a serious fall in Turkish exports.[75] The OPDA reports consistently complained about the unfairness of European policies towards Turkey and argued that the Turkish vintner had to face exceptional difficulties owing to the low level of tariff levied on alcohol imported into Turkey, while exported Turkish wine was subject to very heavy duties. In some parts of the country the cultivation of the vine was being replaced by that of the mulberry tree. In the annual report, the OPDA officials noted, 'While these conditions continue, it is difficult to see how the decay of the wine industry can be averted'.[76]

In order to compensate for the decline of the wine industry, the OPDA aimed to develop a domestic beer industry, which did not exist in the pre-OPDA era. For this purpose, the administration granted tax privileges to beer producers in 1896, which served as the major stimulus for native production.[77] Consequently, the same year, the first native beer factory was established in Bomonti, followed by three others located in İstanbul and İzmir. The sharp increase in the revenues in 1910–12 was mainly due to the growth in the manufacture of domestic beer and its increasing popularity among consumers.[78]

Administration of the fishery revenue under the OPDA

Another source of revenue ceded to the OPDA was the tax on fishing in İstanbul and its suburbs.[79] The taxation of fishery revenues worked in the following manner. Fishermen brought their fish to the market where they were sold at an auction directed by an OPDA agent. On the amount realized by this sale, 20 percent fishing tax was levied for the council and an additional 3 percent to meet expenses.[80]

Among the indirect contributions taken over by the OPDA, the fishery revenue was the least troublesome to administer. The receipts of the administration were largely dependent on the migration of fish through the straits of İstanbul and climatic conditions.[81] In order to improve the productivity of the fishermen, the OPDA brought scientists from Europe to investigate the existing species and the alternative methods of fishing. The results of these investigations were published as pamphlets and books; in addition lectures were given to the fishermen.[82]

Figure 4.6 illustrates the trend in the fishery revenues under the ASIR and OPDA. Analyzing the early years of the administration, the technical assistance given to the fishermen and the establishment of a more efficient tax collection system stand out as the major factors behind the increase in the fishery revenues. After 1888, there was a slight increase due to the expansion of the area taxed by the OPDA. The fishery revenues followed a considerably smooth trend until after 1906, when once again the revenues jumped as a result of the stringent checks placed on contraband and the growing export of salted fish.[83] Being also the supervisor of the salt monopoly, the OPDA encouraged the use of salt in the fishing industry. Besides increasing the salt revenue, this policy also helped to develop the export of fish, which lasted for about a year when salted. An annual report of the CFB noted that, thanks to the growing quantities of exports, a fall in prices had been prevented even when fish were abundant.[84]

Figure 4.6 The administration of the fishery revenues: 1879–1914

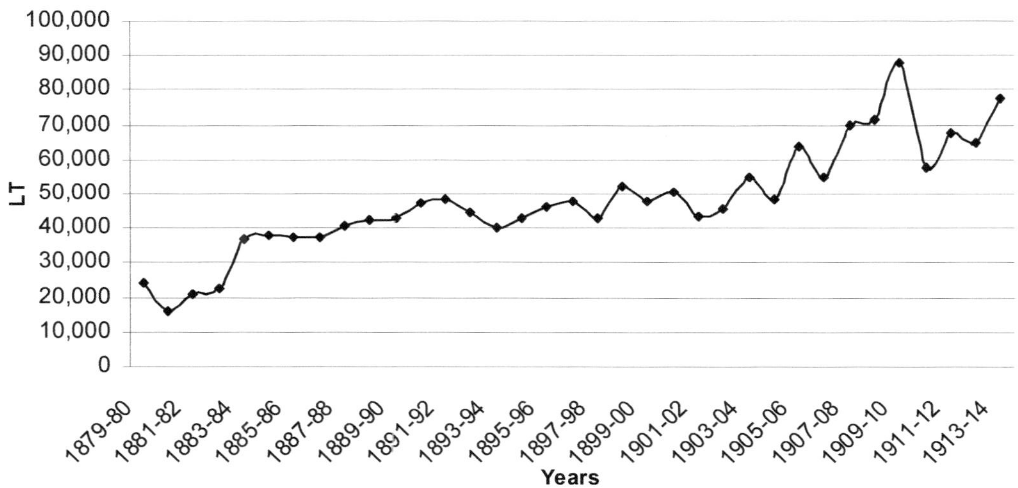

Sources: Fane, 1892; Roumani, 1927; Kazgan, 1985; Annual Reports of the CFB.

An assessment of the OPDA's economic performance

This chapter has provided an in-depth analysis of the administration of the revenues under the OPDA, tracking the sources of increase in these revenues and the obstacles encountered by the administration. The OPDA, considered as 'the outpost of European Imperialism', also gave a good example of the best features of European financial management. The administrative system introduced by the OPDA, in many aspects, formed a great contrast to the financial administration of the Ottoman government. The OPDA introduced new technologies to the relevant sectors under its responsibility, improved the regulations and made the necessary legislative changes concerning the development of its revenues. Improvements in the revenues under its control and the introduction of new institutions in the relevant sectors also created positive externalities for other sectors of the economy.

By the same token, the international treaties imposed on the Porte by the European powers also restricted the administration's ability to improve its revenues. In several instances, such as in the case of the stamp law, wine duties or the patent law, the OPDA officials complained that the conditions imposed by these treaties were unfair and requested their revision. Hence, though it was widely seen as the 'outpost of European Imperialism' in the Empire, the OPDA also suffered from the impositions of the hegemonic powers. These examples also serve to illustrate the nature of disagreements among European capitalists having conflicting interests in the Empire, such as the bondholders or other investors whose interests were tied to those of the Ottoman economy and European merchants who pushed for less protectionism and more privileges, regardless of the consequences on the overall condition of the economy.

Main entrance of the OPDA building in İstanbul. Ottoman Bank Archives, AINDP001-002.

5

THE TOBACCO SECTOR AND THE RÉGIE COMPANY

The history of tobacco in the Ottoman Empire

Tobacco, one of the most prominent crops of Turkish agriculture in the nineteenth century, was introduced to the Ottoman Empire by European merchants in the sixteenth century. In a short period of time, tobacco plantation and its consumption became increasingly popular within the Empire. In the first half of the seventeenth century, there had been several attempts to forbid smoking, especially under the reign of Murat IV when many thousands of men were sent 'to the abode of nothingness'.[1] These efforts were often supported by *fatwas* of the religious authorities condemning smoking as an evil habit causing dizziness. Despite all these attempts, both tobacco use and plantation continued to prosper. In 1646, tobacco consumption was legalized by a fatwa from *Bahai Efendi*, the newly appointed *Şeyhülislam*, himself an addict.[2] Subsequently, the tobacco sector became one of the richest sectors in Ottoman agriculture. Accordingly, it became an attractive source of revenue, first for the government, then for domestic creditors and, finally, for the OPDA and the Régie company.

Before the introduction of cigarettes in the nineteenth century, there were two smoking devices in the Ottoman society. The *Çubuk* (pipe) was adopted first when the Ottomans began to use tobacco; it remained the most popular device until cigarettes appeared on the market. The other device was the *nargile* (water pipe), a Persian invention used to facilitate the consumption of *tömbeki*, an especially strong Persian tobacco. In addition to smoking tobaccos, the Ottomans also used snuff and chewing tobacco.

There is no agreement among historians regarding the origin of cigarettes. Some argue that they were introduced to Middle East by the French; others maintain that they originated in the Middle East.[3] What is uncontested is that, once introduced, the cigarette spread quickly among the Ottomans and replaced the previous consumption patterns, becoming the prevalent form of tobacco usage due to its practical nature. The expansion of cigarette smoking throughout Europe, as well as in America, was through Turkish cigarettes. In the 1850s, during the Crimean War, British soldiers were introduced to the hand-rolled cigarettes preferred by their Turkish allies as a more practical way of smoking. The cigarettes, known as 'Papirossi' or the 'Crimean Fad', were brought back to England in large numbers and were popular among the veterans. In 1856, the first cigarette factory was opened in Walworth, England by Robert Golag, a veteran of the Crimean War.[4] The cigarette found its way to North America through Britain and became increasingly popular particularly among soldiers during the Civil War.[5]

Hence, from the early 1870s onward, the growing domestic and global potential for Turkish tobacco made the Ottoman tobacco monopoly the most attractive source of revenue for foreign investors. Two major developments contributed to this process. The first was the invention of cigarettes, which created a larger domestic market for tobacco consumption as well as a global market for the mild Turkish tobacco and hand-rolled cigarettes. Secondly, the American Civil War in 1860s had two important effects on Turkish tobacco exports. First, when tobacco growing was seriously curtailed by the war, European tobacco importers turned to Turkish tobacco as an alternative. During this period, European consumers developed a taste for mild Turkish tobacco. Secondly, by the introduction of the oriental handmade cigarettes to a larger number of Americans during the war, it created a market particularly among the American elite for imported Turkish tobacco.[6]

Administration of the tobacco revenues before the Régie system

After several attempts to tax tobacco production and sale, the Ottoman government established the first tobacco monopoly, *İdare-i İnhisarıyeyi Duhan*, in 1873. The monopoly was based on a banderole system under which only the products bearing the state-issued stamps could be sold legally in the market. Banderoles were sold by the government to the manufacturers to be wrapped around packets of cigars, cigarettes and cigarette papers prior to their distribution for sale. Under this system, government control was limited to the enforcement of the sale of banderoled tobacco. There were virtually no restrictions on its cultivation. After the establishment of the Administration of the Six Revenues (*Rüsumu Sitte İdaresi*) in 1879, following the bankruptcy of the Ottoman government, the tobacco revenue was one of the six revenues handed over to the administration. With the Decree of *Muharrem* in 1881, the tobacco tithe and the monopoly rights were turned over to the OPDA. Until the establishment of the Régie in 1883, all tobacco revenues, which made up around 35 percent of the total revenues of the OPDA, were collected by the administration itself. During this period, tobacco revenues of the monopoly comprised the following taxes:[7]

1- The *Müruriyye*: A duty of Ps 5 per okka was paid when the tobacco was first sold by the cultivator. It was imposed on all tobacco except that destined for export. After this tax had been paid, the tobacco could be transported in leaf to any part of the Empire.

2- The banderole duty: Around 430 manufacturers in the Empire were granted the right of cutting up the tobacco and preparing it for local consumption. A minimum volume of production had to be guaranteed before permission was granted to open a factory. The banderoles were of five different classes ranging from Ps 45 per okka to Ps 15. They were made by the administration and sold to the manufacturers through its various agencies.

3-The *Beyiye* (license tax): Only those who were licensed by the OPDA were allowed to sell tobacco in their shops. All tobacco shops had to pay the license tax on a yearly basis. The rate of the tax was not specified in the annual reports of the OPDA.

Establishment of the Régie Company

By the Decree of *Muharrem*, the OPDA was also granted the right to hand over its monopoly rights on salt and tobacco revenues to a third party approved by the government.[8] The OPDA chose to keep the salt revenue under its control but to farm out the tobacco monopoly.

In January 1883, the OPDA and the Ottoman government started negotiations for a 30-year concession for the tobacco monopoly with the Imperial Ottoman Bank, Crédit Anstalt of Vienna and Berlin Bleichröder Bank groups.[9] As a result, the *Societe de la Régie cointeéressée des Tabacs de l'Empire Ottoman (Mamalik-i Şahane Dühanları Müşterekül Menfaa Reji İdaresi)*, publicly known as the Régie Company, was established. The Régie

Company, whose capital made up 23 percent of total foreign direct investments in the Ottoman Empire in 1881–1914, held the tobacco monopoly for 42 years, from 1883–1913 with the first concession and from 1913 until the contract was terminated in 1925, two years after the foundation of the Turkish Republic.[10]

There were two major reasons behind the consortium's demand for the concession. The most important determinant was the high expectations from the domestic market. As Quataert notes, the Régie Company was established in the expectation of vast profits based on the high rates of tobacco consumption per capita. These expectations were based on compelling facts. 'At the Ramazan cannon, they said, Muslim workers broke their fast first by lighting up a cigarette. Men, women, and children alike smoked and per capita estimates ranged from 937 to 1,500 grams per year.'[11] Secondly, especially after the American Civil War, the growing popularity of Turkish tobacco and hand-rolled cigarettes created a global market for Turkish tobacco. The company would not have monopoly rights on exported leaf tobacco. However it would be the sole manufacturer of Turkish cigarettes within the country.

Looking at the picture drawn above, one might wonder why the OPDA wanted to transfer its monopoly rights in spite of the growing potential of Turkish tobacco in the second half of the nineteenth century. According to the OPDA officials, there were basically four main reasons behind their decision to transfer the concession. First of all, to the OPDA, the banderole system was far from perfect, as there was considerable opportunity for fraud on the part of the officials in charge of weighing the tobacco, as well as the manufacturers. It was not unusual to sell tobacco of the first quality with a banderole of the third. The OPDA officials argued that the existing banderole system was hard to control, and in cases where fraud was detected, the factory owners bribed the OPDA inspectors with more than their yearly salary.[12] Hence, they pointed out the necessity of eliminating private cigarette factories in order to eliminate tax fraud. In this context, the OPDA officials were sympathetic to the new system proposed by the Régie officials. According to the proposal, all private factories would be abolished and the company would be the sole producer of Turkish cigarettes.

Secondly, tobacco revenues were threatened by smuggling activities and thus required strict control and surveillance. This generated a need for a specialized organization to fight smuggling. An OPDA report dating back to 1882–83 shows that from the beginning, the administration was concerned about the contraband activities in this sector and sought to remedy the problem. The same report argued that the Régie proposal, which aimed to transform the existing banderole system, included 'advantages of highest order'.[13] Thus, the OPDA was fully supportive of this proposal, while the consortium was seeking the government's approval.

Thirdly, the OPDA officials argued that the Régie system would enable them to establish more efficient control over the collection of the tobacco tithe revenues, which would remain under the control of the administration. The annual report of the OPDA in 1884 projected that LT 100,000 would be realized as tobacco tithe revenue, yielding a LT 32,000 increase over the previous year.[14]

Finally, by the terms of the concession, the OPDA was guaranteed a fixed annual payment of LT 750,000 – regardless of the Régie's revenues for any given year. OPDA officials welcomed this offer as 'a revenue equal if not superior to the net receipts of the best seasons'.[15] In addition to the LT 750,000 fixed annual payment, the administration would have a considerable share in the profits of the company. According to the terms specified in the concession, net profits of the company would be distributed as shown in Table 5.1.[16] As observed from the table, the government was given an increasing share of the profit. This was partly due to the company's and the OPDA's efforts to convince the government to accept the concession and partly to provide an incentive to the government for its cooperation in dealing with the smuggling activities.

The reasons laid out by the OPDA officials for the transfer of the concession discussed why the new administrative system proposed by the Régie was more beneficial. However, the OPDA did not specify why the administration itself did not initiate such a transition and keep the tobacco revenues under its control. The introduction of a provision to the decree (on the initiative of the BIO, which later owned 50 percent of the Régie, and other foreign representatives) regarding the farming out of the tobacco monopoly illustrates that the bondholders' representatives always considered this option. One possible argument is that the concession was made by the foreign bondholder groups to the BIO in return for giving up its administration of the six indirect revenues (ASIR) and agreeing to the terms of the debt settlement. It should be noted that as the largest creditor of the state, the BIO's approval was crucial for the debt settlement.[17]

The Régie Factory in Cıbali, Istanbul.. IU *Nadir Eserler Kütüphanesi*, 90553-001.

Table 5.1 Distribution of the net profits of the Régie Company

Net profit * (LT)	OPDA (%)	Ottoman Government (%)	Régie Company (%)
1-500,000	35	30	35
500,000-1,000,000	34	39	27
1,000,000-1,500,000	30	52	18
1,500,000-2,000,000	20	70	10
2,000,000	15	75	10

* Profit available for distribution after the payment of the LT 750,000 annual fee to the OPDA and the dividends.
Source: 'Régie Concession' in Doğruel and Doğruel, 2000.

Moreover, along with the BIO (a French-British partnership), Crédit Anstalt of Vienna and Berlin Bleichröder Bank were also represented in the Régie, with 30 percent and 20 percent shares respectively. This meant that four creditor countries, including all three of the major ones, were represented in the consortium. In addition, this transfer could be considered as a family affair since the bondholders of the Régie consortium were also the bondholders of the OPDA.

Finally, the Régie system proposed the abolition of private factories and the formation of an armed surveillance unit to fight smugglers. Both measures would surely cause serious public repercussions. Considering the magnitude of the OPDA's role in the Ottoman economy, it is possible that the OPDA officials did not want to be identified with the highly unpopular task of surveillance, which could lead to public hostility to the OPDA, and threaten the administration's activities in other sectors. Under the existing arrangements, the OPDA would receive a reasonable annual payment, without undertaking any risk. It would also have a share in the Régie's profits.

The terms of the concession granted the Régie Company monopoly rights for tobacco sales throughout the Empire wherever the banderole system was in use, with the exception of Eastern Rumelia.[18] However, the tobacco tithe (tax collected from the cultivators) still belonged to the OPDA until the liquidation of the debt. The company had no monopoly rights over tobacco exports. Nevertheless, to ensure accuracy in the registration, exported tobacco had to be sent abroad from the company's warehouses.

The Régie would also collect the duties from exports to Egypt, Samos, Tunisia, Montenegro, Serbia, Romania, Crete, Iran and Eastern Rumelia.[19] In addition, the company would collect the duties on tobacco imports, imposed in accordance with the trade agreements signed by the Ottoman government. Tax revenues from imported *tömbeki* would remain in the hands of the government.[20] According to the concession, the Régie was liable to buy all the tobacco produced in the domestic economy unless it was destined for export. Therefore, the monopoly aimed to restrict tobacco cultivation, which it was committed to buy, to places with the most suitable climate and soil for growing the crop. The concession required the abolition of tobacco production in several districts, mostly in İstanbul. Finally, the Régie would be the sole producer of tobacco in the Ottoman Empire and all other tobacco factories (workshops) would be abolished before the deadline announced by the company.

Organization of the Régie system

Despite the prominence of the Régie Company in the Ottoman economy for over three decades, it is difficult to find a detailed assessment of the Régie system; this is among the major shortcomings of the literature on the Ottoman economy. Previous studies of the company were based on fragmented pieces of information and data, discouraging further studies of the subject. This chapter aims to overcome this shortcoming by presenting a holistic picture of the Régie system and clarifying the functions of the company, the OPDA, the government and merchants in the tobacco economy, and the distribution of the tobacco revenues among these actors.

The establishment of the Régie system altered the pre-existing production, credit and distribution networks in the tobacco sector. Before the Régie, tobacco merchants and local landholding notables (*mültezim*), often working together, brought the product from the farm to the market. They also supplied credit to the producers in return for a certain portion of the harvest or for purchase below the market price.[21] After the concession, the company provided interest-free cultivator loans for up to 50 percent of the estimated value of the crop. These advances were no obstacle to the sale of the crop to a third party for export purposes, but had to be repaid by the producer before its export.[22] Hence, following the establishment of the Régie, all the previous credit arrangements collapsed. The former creditors, the *mültezims* and the tobacco merchants, were replaced by the tobacco monopoly itself.

In contrast to the previous banderole system, under the Régie cultivation, storage, distribution and the sale of tobacco was strictly controlled by the monopoly. Anyone intending to grow tobacco needed the Régie's permission. According to the initial agreement between the company and the government, all applicants would be granted the right to do so, with only one exception. Tobacco plantation was restricted to plots of at least one-half dönüm. By this restriction, the Régie aimed to discourage tobacco cultivation on tiny plots for personal use and sale to neighbors. According to Edgar Vincent, common representative of the British, Dutch and Belgian bondholders, this restriction was the keystone of the whole system.[23] After cultivation, the quantity and quality of the tobacco was registered both before and after the harvest. In addition, tobacco cultivation behind stone walls was strictly forbidden to facilitate the accuracy of the registration process and the monitoring of cultivation.

Following the harvest the crop was stored in the Régie warehouses. The owner of the crop was responsible for transportation expenses. However, the Régie was obligated to provide a warehouse in every village that produced 100,000 okka or more of tobacco; otherwise it had to provide a warehouse within ten hours distance. The Régie bore the cost of the first six months of storage and the grower paid for the rest of the storage period.

For the OPDA, one of the most favorable features of the concession was the warehouse procedure. Instead of collecting the tithes individually from cultivators in every village, under this system the tobacco tithe was collected from the central warehouses by a smaller number OPDA officials. In any case, the Régie had to establish warehouses to ensure the accuracy of the registration process and to prevent any leakage from the system. Hence, the OPDA did not have to bear the costs of providing the warehouses. In this regard, the Régie helped the OPDA and indirectly the government to collect the tobacco tithe properly and on a regular basis, minimizing collection expenses.

From the warehouses, the tobacco was either purchased by the Régie or sold to the tobacco merchants for export. As previously mentioned, having used the cultivator loan provided by the Régie, the tobacco producer was obliged to repay it before the crop was sold on to a third party. If the tobacco was to be exported to a country or a region excluded from the 1861 free trade agreement, the Régie would collect an export tax. If the tobacco was not sold to a merchant to be exported, it was bought by the company at a price established between the Régie and the growers with provisions for third party arbitration. The leaf tobacco purchased by the Régie was either exported by the Régie itself or sent to the factories owned by the monopoly.

Finally, the finished products were either exported or distributed to the tobacco shops licensed by the Régie and sold at the prices set by the company. At the end of the financial year, profits were distributed among the OPDA, the government, the Régie Company and its shareholders, as described in Table 5.1.

The Régie system radically altered the pre-existing networks in the tobacco sector. Besides the new restrictions and regulations regarding the cultivators, another crucial change in the production network was the elimination of the privately owned tobacco factories following the concession. In a year, the number of tobacco factories in the Empire dropped from between 300 and 450 to 12, all of which were operated by the company.[24] Hence, hundreds of businesses were closed or dislocated, and thousands of workers lost their jobs. There is no detailed information regarding the labor force employed in these factories. However, it is known that many Greek and Muslim factory owners moved their factories to Egypt, which later became one of the most prominent tobacco exporters.[25] As for the merchants, they lost the domestic market, but retained their position in regard to exports, since the Régie did not have monopoly rights over tobacco exports. However, the Régie formed an export company itself and became a major competitor. The company also wanted to extend its influence by entering the international markets from which it was excluded. To that end, it bought shares in the Tombac Company, a French-English monopoly on imported *tömbeki* from Iran, and also bought factories in Egypt for processing tobacco.

The Régie's employment policy

The armed surveillance units named *kolcus* were an essential part of the Régie's organizational schema. As mentioned in the previous chapter, the primary concern of the Régie was the tobacco smugglers. From the beginning, the Régie complained that despite the right to seizure, all penal powers and the right to taking legal action lay with the director of customs. For years, the OPDA and the Régie contested this decision, but the issue remained unresolved. However, besides legal conflicts between the company and the government there were more structural problems regarding tobacco contraband. Customs offices were only found along the coastline and not further inland, where most contraband trade was carried on. This generated a need for the creation of well organized surveillance forces to control the interior of the country.[26]

To combat smuggling the Régie formed the *kolcus*, who registered the crops before and after the harvest prior to escorting the crop to the warehouses. If the tobacco was to be exported, the *kolcus* would guard its transportation from warehouses to docks, where it would remain under their surveillance until shipped, consequently preventing tobacco from entering the domestic market. In fighting against smugglers these units were infamous for their brutality. They were held responsible for the death of more than 20,000 people.[27]

The Régie Company had a similar employment policy to the OPDA, which overwhelmingly employed Muslim Turks.[28] The company's personnel included a small number of European administrators placed at key positions, working through Ottoman intermediaries. According to company records 94 percent of the employees were Ottoman citizens in 1887 (78 percent of administrative personnel and all the surveillance forces). By 1899, the figure rose to 96 percent (85 percent of the administrative personnel and 99 percent of the surveillance personnel).[29] One obvious reason behind this employment policy was to dampen the prevailing anger over the company's pricing and surveillance policies.

The company's employment policy can be better understood by the following excerpt from an interview with Sir Edgar Vincent, General Director of the Ottoman Bank: 'The principle adopted is to leave the provincial executive entirely in the hands of natives, and to entrust only the duty of control and supervision to officials of foreign extraction … In a country like Turkey, there can be nothing more dangerous to the permanence of a system of collection than to levy heavy taxes by means of foreigners.'[30]

Figure 5.1 Organizational Schema of the Régie system

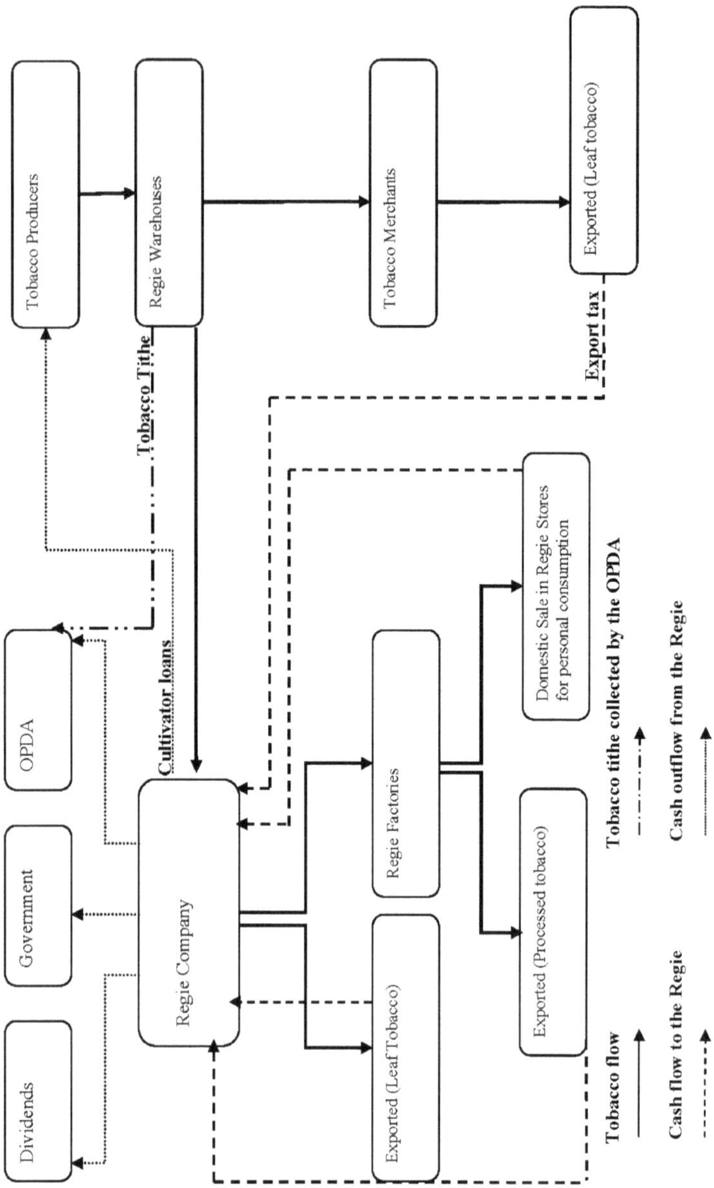

Manufacture of hand-rolled cigarettes in the the Régie Factory. IU *Nadir Eserler Kütüphanesi*, 90553-014.

Banderoling and price tagging of cigarettes. IU *Nadir Eserler Kütüphanesi*, 90553-0018.

Economic performance of the Régie Company

Figure 5.2 illustrates the trend in the annual net profits of the Régie, after the payment of the fixed annual loyalty to the OPDA. As the figure shows, the economic performance of the Régie Company, from its establishment in 1884 until the outbreak of the First World War in 1914, can be analyzed under four periods. First, the period of establishment and transition in 1884–87, during which the Régie failed to declare a net profit. Second, the period of takeoff in 1887–95, during which the company declared a net profit for the first time and started distributing dividends and profit shares. Third, the period of crisis in 1895–99, when the upward tendency in the company's economic performance was disrupted by political disorder particularly in the eastern *vilayets* of the Empire. In this period, the company's net profits plunged to their lowest level in ten years, and consequently the company was unable to distribute dividends. Finally, the period of recovery and growth in 1899–1914, during which the company's net profits reached unprecedented levels and the Ottoman tobacco monopoly turned into an attractive investment for foreign investors.

Figure 5.2 Net profits of the tobacco Régie: 1884–1912

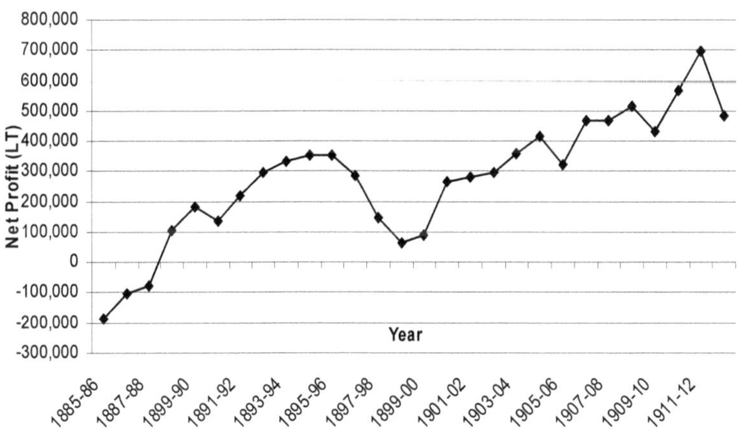

Source: Annual Reports of the Régie Company: 1884–1909.

Table 5.2 The Régie's balance in 1884-1912 (in LT)

Years	Sales revenue*	Others **	Total revenue	Expenses	Profit	Net profit ***
1884–85	978,789	245,116	1,223,905	725,758	498,147	-186,635
1885–86	1,415,493	232,907	1,648,400	1,000,626	647,774	-102,226
1886–87	1,410,408	181,709	1,592,117	917,803	674,314	-75,686
1887–88	1,579,700	196,677	1,776,377	921,013	855,364	105,364
1888–89	1,676,216	188,828	1,865,044	933,924	931,120	181,120
1899–90	1,651,412	195,308	1,846,720	959,723	886,997	136,997
1890–91	1,786,972	194,877	1,981,849	1,011,685	970,164	220,164
1891–92	1,966,433	184,894	2,151,327	1,103,135	1,048,192	298,192
1892–93	2,103,337	211,130	2,314,467	1,232,625	1,081,842	331,842
1893–94	2,208,214	227,502	2,435,716	1,334,017	1,101,699	351,699
1894–95	2,232,276	219,009	2,451,285	1,349,278	1,102,007	352,007
1895–96	2,171,416	211,793	2,383,209	1,345,010	1,038,199	288,199
1896–97	1,875,166	194,088	2,069,254	1,175,021	894,233	144,233
1897–98	1,652,176	226,518	1,878,694	1,064,719	813,975	63,975
1898–99	1,753,126	219,252	1,972,378	1,132,079	840,299	90,299
1899–00	1,948,212	240,125	2,188,337	1,172,398	1,015,939	265,939
1900–01	1,970,000	239,417	2,209,417	1,179,471	1,029,946	279,946
1901–02	2,003,605	240,252	2,243,857	1,194,566	1,049,291	299,291
1902–03	2,161,217	226,686	2,387,903	1,277,971	1,109,932	359,932
1903–04	2,271,242	244,138	2,515,380	1,347,096	1,168,283	418,283
1904–05	2,205,699	244,872	2,450,571	1,377,386	1,073,184	323,184
1905–06	2,350,149	259,149	2,609,298	1,393,836	1,215,461	465,461
1906–07	2,332,195	264,259	2,596,454	1,377,404	1,219,049	469,049
1907–08	2,390,066	270,829	2,660,895	1,396,864	1,264,030	514,030
1908–09	2,327,034	270,875	2,597,909	1,417,795	1,180,114	430,114
1909–10	2,410,132	376,920	2,787,052	1,469,204	1,317,848	567,848
1910–11	2,685,797	296,276	2,982,073	1,536,233	1,445,840	695,840
1911–12	2,517,940	286,477	2,804,417	1,570,152	1,234,265	484,265

Source: Annual Reports of the Régie Company: 1884-1909; McCarthy, 1982: 287.

* Until 1892-93, sales revenue includes the export figures, which comprise around 1 percent of the total sales. In July 1893 the Régie Export Company (REC) was established, thus after 1892-93 export figures are not shown in the annual reports of the company. The revenue obtained from the REC is included in the other revenues.

** Comprises import and export duties, revenue from retail sale permits, interest revenues and others, including the compensation paid by the OPDA for Egyptian Reftieh losses.

*** After the deduction of the LT 750,000 fixed loyalty paid to the OPDA. The fixed loyalty paid for the 11 months of operation in the first year was LT 684,782.

The period of establishment: 1884–87

Despite the vast expectations entertained by the foreign investors, the Régie's first year was a huge disappointment both for the company and the OPDA. As shown in Table 5.2, the company closed the first three fiscal years in the red. In their public statements, the company officials attributed the first year's LT 186,635 deficit to three causes.[31] Firstly, unforeseen expenses incurred while establishing the company. Secondly, Egypt's entering trade conventions with Greece subsequent to the formation of the Régie, whereby Turkish tobacco lost its former monopoly in the Egyptian market.

Finally, there were 'the inherent difficulties of supplanting an old system by new methods in a country whose population is of so conservative a turn of mind as that of Turkey'.[32] There is no doubt that the initial establishment costs were already accounted for by the foreign investors. The main sources of disappointment were the public reactions within the Empire to the establishment of the Régie system and the loss of monopoly in the Egyptian market. These two unanticipated developments remained the major obstacles to the success of the Régie Company throughout its operation. They also proved to be a persistent source of disagreement between the Régie, the government, and the OPDA.

Public reactions to the Régie

The immediate effect of the Régie on Ottoman tobacco production was a considerable fall in tobacco cultivation.[33] This was mostly due to the elimination of small producers as well as the high fees, low buying prices and excessive regulations applied on the remaining ones. Before the Régie, for the years 1881–82 and 1882–83, the total number of tobacco cultivators was reported as 246,961 and 226,700 respectively.[34] In the first year of the Régie, after the introduction of the restrictions on tobacco cultivation, the number of cultivators dropped instantly, down to 140,000 and then gradually down to 101,300 in 1887–88.[35]

On the other hand, as a natural outcome of monopolization, tobacco sale prices rose drastically, to the frustration of consumers. Figure 5.3. illustrates the trend in average tobacco purchase and sale prices under the tobacco monopoly. The Régie's already low purchase prices continued to fall in the first six years of the concession and remained below their initial level until

1893. In the same period, sale prices showed significant increases. After a brief period of recovery in 1893–96, purchase prices declined significantly and never reached their initial level until the 1910s. As observed from the figure, the large spread between sale and purchase prices of the company persisted and even widened throughout the practice of the monopoly.

Figure 5.3 Purchase and sale prices of the Régie in the domestic market: 1884–1912

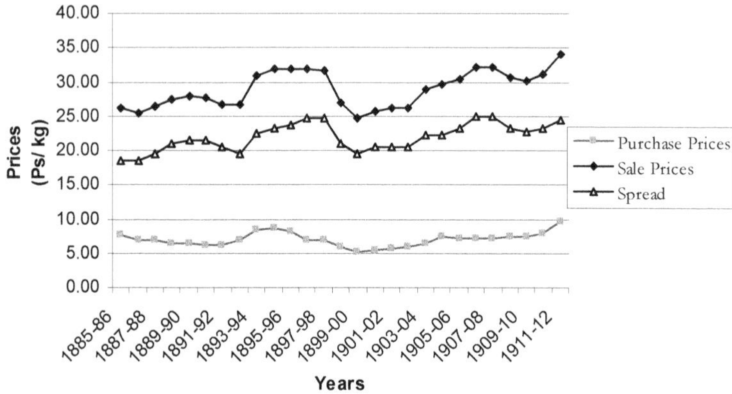

Source: Eldem, 1994: 79.

Under these circumstances, public frustrations with the company were expressed in three distinct forms. First, there were demonstrations and riots against the company. Second, lawsuits were filed against the monopoly. Finally, the large spread between low buying and high selling prices stimulated the expansion of the informal sector, and smuggling became rife.

Most of the demonstrations occurred in places where the economy was highly dependent on tobacco farming, such as Samsun, Trabzon, Giresun and Tokat. These demonstrations sometimes turned into attacks against Régie property and forces. Such was the case in Tokat, Zile and Harput.[36] In contrast to the anti-Régie movement in Iran, which had been successful in throwing out the monopoly, religious values played an insignificant role during the demonstrations within the Ottoman Empire.[37] Rather, it was economic demands that lay behind the opposition to the company.[38] In Giresun, a cleric named Hasan Hoca preached against tobacco consumption and the Régie, but people continued to smoke. Moreover, when theological students, *softas*, protested against the company, their major complaint was not that tobacco was harmful or sinful, but that it was sold for ten times the purchase price. In any case, the rioters were not all Muslim Turks. During the riots in Samsun, the majority of the activists were the Greek tobacco growers from the surrounding region.

The demands of the demonstrators can be better understood from court documents referring to numerous complaints regarding the Régie's practices. These documents focus on the following issues:[39]

1- Many cultivators filed complaints about the Régie's buying policy. They claimed that, in addition to the low level of the legally declared prices, the Régie was imposing methods to further depress them. Common malpractices included the arbitrary downgrading of the tobacco's quality during the registration process and under-weighing the crop at the point of its purchase.

2- Double standards during the registration of quality and amount before and after the harvest had other unfavorable consequences for the producers. In case of any difference between registrations, the producers were obliged to pay for the amount claimed to be missing.

3- High selling prices of tobacco formed another source of complaint, expressed vociferously during demonstrations.

4- It was also claimed that in some regions the Régie had been demanding 5 percent interest on loans to the cultivators, in clear violation of article 5 of the concession.

5- In some regions, the Régie did not provide the statutory storage depots. In such cases, the producers themselves often paid for transportation of the crop to the nearest warehouse.

6- The Régie was also accused of creating paperwork obstacles for registration to restrict the amount of tobacco it would have to buy. Apparently, the Régie aimed to replicate the legal framework practiced by other tobacco monopolies in Europe and North America. However, considering the low level of literacy in the Ottoman Empire, these requirements were, by and large, unrealistic. One common example was asking for a land title before issuing a license for tobacco cultivation.[40] With regard to land, private property had not been introduced until 1856, so a vast proportion of land remained untitled.

7- It was also common for the Régie to withhold licenses from growers who were suspected but not convicted of concealing tobacco. In such cases, the government insisted that the Régie had to provide substantiated evidence before denying a license.

Smuggling existed in the Ottoman tobacco sector well before the Régie. However, under the Régie system it expanded considerably and became more organized, as admitted in the company's first annual report.[41] The issue of contraband caused ongoing tensions between the government and the company throughout the concession. While the company accused the government of having an uncooperative attitude in fighting against the contraband, the government blamed the monopoly's restrictions and low prices for the increase in smuggling activities and eventual death of thousands in conflicts with the *kolcus*.[42]

It would actually be surprising if no contraband activity took place under the monopoly. However, considering its deadly consequences and the high proportion of the contraband tobacco compared with the legal domestic sale, one would expect smuggling to have been highly lucrative.[43] In 1890, official tobacco sales were six million kilograms while the contraband tobacco sale was estimated around 12 to 13 million kilograms. A French report in 1897 pointed out that the Régie was able to register around 70 percent to 80 percent of the tobacco produced in the major centers and only half of the amount produced in other regions.

The cultivators often sought to offset the losses incurred in transactions with the Régie, by cooperating with the contrabandists who worked with lower profit margins and offered 2–3 times the Régie price. For consumers, contraband tobacco was desirable because it was considerably cheaper. In the case of cigarettes, it was very difficult for the consumers to distinguish the contraband cigarettes, since the Régie trademarks on the cigarette paper were easily forged.

The Régie's immediate reaction to the boom in contraband activities was to increase the size of its surveillance force. As shown in Table 5.3, the number of *kolcus* increased steadily over time. From 3,617 in 1886, it reached 6,500 by 1895. However, despite growing investment in surveillance, the company failed to achieve significant increases in domestic sale figures. Since there was no reason for a significant decline in the total number of smokers during the period, it proves that contraband tobacco preserved its market share.

It has been noted that the Régie, expecting some increase in smuggling activities following the establishment of the monopoly, had given increasing shares from its profits to the government as an incentive for the government to cooperate in fighting the contraband activities. However, Sultan Abdülhamid, whose authority had already been damaged by the concession, did not want to be involved in the highly unpopular task of surveillance. As for the army, a significant number of the smugglers appeared to be drawn from its poorly and irregularly paid ranks.[44] Therefore, soldiers were also reluctant to fight against the smugglers. The same attitude towards the company can be observed in court records. Quataert points out that the courts seemed to be sympathetic to those accused of smuggling. In Samsun in 1893, more than 100 complaints against smugglers were dropped without examination.[45]

Table 5.3 Investment in prevention of tobacco smuggling: 1885–1909

Years	Tobacco seized (kg)	Surveillance expenses (LT)	Number of surveillance personnel
1885–86		126,582	
1886–87		118,762	
1887–88		115,389	3,617
1888–89		126,444	
1889–90		137,551	4,141
1890–91		143,823	4,622
1891–92		150,725	
1892–93		159,326	4,906
1893–94		163,336	
1894–95		143,483	
1895–96	191,725	161,883	5,950
1896–97	258,637	164,113	6,522
1897–98	314,141	188,470	6,701
1898–99	238,003	208,273	6,343
1899–00	196,786	204,671	6,533
1900–01	210,755	229,916	
1901–02	238,926	236,726	
1902–03	233,590	253,541	
1903–04	211,773	257,906	
1904–05	231,539	255,230	
1905–06	183,280	254,945	
1906–07	203,489	250,890	
1907–08	221,492	252,277	
1908–09	196,795	219,652	

Source: Annual Reports of the Régie: 1884–1909; Quataert, 1983: 22.[46]

Under these circumstances, the monopoly sought to counter contraband activities by offering incentives to targeted sections of the population. In

Bursa, unable to compete with the contraband prices, the company distributed high quality Yenice and Samsun tobacco seeds. The producers could either sell the crop to the Régie at a higher price or export their tobacco, thereby reducing their incentives to sell to smugglers. Again, in the early 1890s, the company aimed to gain the support of the local elite by handing over some of its commercial operations to contractors chosen from these notables.[47]

However, none of these attempts managed to reverse the general antipathy towards the Régie among the population. People often sided with the smugglers, who were praised as heroes.[48] This made it even harder for the company, particularly in terms of its legal stance against the accused smugglers before the courts. A good example was the case of search warrants. After many complaints concerning misbehavior by the *kolcus*, the government insisted that search warrants had to be issued before a property was searched; an extension of the investigation to neighboring households was permitted if there were reasonable grounds for suspicion.

Nevertheless, during searches *kolcus* had to be accompanied by the *muhtar* or the *imam* of the village and if no contraband was found the residents had the right to sue the company. In many cases, the Régie reported that both the *muhtar* and the *imam* had been hiding from the *kolcus*, to avoid involvement in the search process. This provided the smugglers with the extra time they needed to hide the contraband. For the company, it increased the prospect of being sued since the contraband was more likely to be moved somewhere else.[49]

After increasing complaints from the Régie, the state agreed to send the 'gendarmes' to accompany the *kolcus* in searches, the responsibility remaining with the Régie officials. However, the *kolcus* had evolved into an army in its own right and the monopoly had become a government within the government. In 1895, first the local administrations and finally the government decided to disarm the *kolcus*. In 1896, the Finance Ministry informed the Régie that the military would assume responsibility for suppressing contraband.

Despite the recurring demands of the Régie, the Ottoman government refrained from cooperating with the company to repress smuggling until after 1908. According to Quataert, the government was hostile to the company and essentially aimed to reduce the profitability of its monopoly.[50] After the change of government in 1908, the hostility between the government and the company was resolved. During the Young Turk Era, as Quataert notes, the government took an active stance against the smugglers. During this period the share of the salaries of the surveillance personnel in total salary expenses dropped to 55 percent as compared to over 60 percent in the preceding period. In addition, the surveillance expenditures as a proportion of the total expenditures dropped to 9.6 percent as compared to 12 percent in the earlier period.[51] Also, another major reason behind the decline in smuggling activities was the increase in export prices for tobacco, which will be discussed later in this chapter.

The loss of monopoly in the Egyptian market

Before the establishment of the Régie system, a major source of tobacco revenue was the export duties collected from tobacco exports to Egypt. In spite of the existence of a developing tobacco industry in the country, tobacco cultivation in Egypt was subject to harsh restrictions and high taxes. Furthermore high monetary penalties were imposed on illegally grown tobacco.[52] The only tobacco admitted into the country was Turkish tobacco, which was charged an export duty of Ps 10 per okka and an octroi duty of Ps 5 per okka on its arrival in Egypt.[53] Thus, Egypt's tobacco industry grew dependent on Turkish tobacco, making the potential for Turkish tobacco monopoly even more attractive.

However, a few months after the Régie Company commenced its monopoly, on 3 March 1884, a treaty of commerce was signed between Greece and British-controlled Egypt. The object of the treaty was 'to place the commercial relations of the two countries on a more satisfactory footing, more particularly with regard to tobacco, and to stimulate trade'.[54] High export duties on the Turkish tobacco that had a monopoly in the market had created an extensive smuggling trade into Egypt. The Egyptian government, unable to suppress the contraband, experienced a drastic fall in its receipts from tobacco imports. This was the main reason behind the Egyptian government's decision to open the market to Greek tobacco.[55]

Another crucial factor was the influence of the cigarette producers in Egypt. After the establishment of the Régie, all factory owners in the Ottoman Empire were forced to close their factories. After the signing of the Régie Concession in January 1883, many of these factory owners started moving their businesses to Egypt. Yet, the Régie's monopoly on tobacco exports to Egypt had a huge impact on their production costs. Hence, the factory owners pressured the Egyptian government to lower the barriers against tobacco imports from other countries. In this respect, the Greek-

Egyptian convention was closely linked with the establishment of the Régie system in the Ottoman Empire.

According to the Greek-Egyptian convention, no tax would be levied on tobacco upon its export from Greece and an import duty of Ps 5 per okka would be charged on its importation into Egypt. By the treaty, the Egyptian government aimed to increase its tobacco dues by legalizing tobacco imports from the second biggest exporter of the region and held the import duty at Ps 5 to minimize smuggling activities. The convention benefited the Egyptian government, leading to a sudden increase in tobacco revenues. The average monthly receipts from tobacco during April, May, June and July rose from LE 5,827 in 1883 to LE 12,981 in 1884, following the treaty. Table 5.4 illustrates the tobacco revenues of the Egyptian Customs House for the respective months in 1880–84.

Table 5.4 Tobacco revenues of the Egyptian Custom House (in LE)

Months	1880	1881	1882	1883	1884		
					Greek	Turkish	Total
April	4,563	9,324	9,956	7,200	4,277	14,188	18,466
May	4,227	7,134	5,896	6,314	7,613	4,741	12,354
June	3,006	6,776	2,373	7,245	6,989	4,917	11,907
July	3,950	5,987	752	2,552	4,708	4,489	9,197
Total	15,746	29,221	18,977	23,311	23,587	28,335	51,924
Monthly average	3,936	7,305	4,744	5,827	5,896	7,083	12,981

Source: CFB, 1884: 34.

The Greek-Egyptian convention brought a serious challenge to the monopoly of Turkish tobacco in Egyptian markets. Since there was a total of Ps 15 tax on Turkish tobacco, it was taxed three times as heavily as Greek tobacco. At first, the Régie hoped to maintain its position in the Egyptian market without serious losses, due to the superiority of Turkish tobacco over Greek tobacco.[56] The company was, however, unable to prevent contraband trade particularly in the Aegean region, which encouraged smugglers to move Turkish tobacco into Egypt from where it was exported to Egypt under the terms of the Greek-Egyptian Convention. Through this procedure, the exporters avoided the export taxes paid to the company and ultimately paid 5 percent on duties instead of 15 percent.

Due to these circumstances, in its first years of operation the Régie faced a sudden fall in the export duties collected from tobacco exports to Egypt.

After its first year of operation the company reported a loss of LT 91,262 – equal to nearly half of the total loss declared at the end of the first fiscal year – due to the loss of monopoly in the Egyptian market.[57] Following these losses, the Régie officials used all the means at their disposal to induce the OPDA and the Ottoman government to consent to a reduction in the fixed annual payment.[58] While the Régie demanded compensation for their losses from the OPDA (and indirectly from the government), the OPDA argued that the remedy lay in the hands of the Régie itself. According to Vincent Caillard, the president of the OPDA, who previously acted as the director of the Egyptian Custom House during the signing of the convention, the company could easily regain the monopoly of the trade by 'contenting itself with less profit per okka than the Ps 10, which form the export duty'.[59] Both arguments rested on valid grounds. After all, since both Greek and Turkish tobacco were subject to the same amount of import tax, the competitive advantage of the Greek tobacco came from the absence of an export tax. Considering the superiority of Turkish tobacco, the OPDA officials argued, the Régie could regain its monopoly in the Egyptian market by lowering the export tax. The Régie's counter-argument rested on the consortium having signed the concession contract with preconceived expectations, the Egyptian duty revenue being an important element. Eventually, the OPDA agreed to make certain advances to the Régie in order to alleviate its losses. From 1885–1888 the OPDA advanced a total of LT 210,562 to the Régie on the security of the future profits of the company.[60]

As can be observed from Table 5.5, the situation worsened in the second and third years of the concession. The annual revenue collected on tobacco exports to Egypt in 1886–87 fell to LT 32,000, which was about 20 percent of the annual revenue prior to 1884. Unable to reverse the continuing fall in the duty revenues, the Régie finally reached an agreement with the Egyptian government. According to the new agreement that became effective in February 1888, the Régie would no longer collect duty at Turkish ports on tobacco exports to Egypt. Concurrently, the Egyptian government would add a surcharge to import duty at the rate of Ps 4.5 per kilo to Turkish tobacco. The proceeds of the surcharge were split as follows: the Régie would receive the entire revenue derived from the first million kilos of tobacco and thereafter proceeds would be shared equally by the Régie and Egyptian government. By the agreement, the Egyptian government would also start to tax the tobacco production at LE 30 per *feddan* to deter the cultivation of inferior quality tobacco and increase tobacco imports from Turkey to at least 3,500 tons per year.[61]

Table 5.5 Tobacco export duties collected by the Régie Company: 1884–1909 (in LT)

Years	Duties from exports to Egypt	Other export duties*	Total export duties
1884–85	50,672	-	-
1885–86	35,380	815	42,145
1886–87	**32,000	-	45,521
1887–88	-	-	75,779
1888–89	-	-	58,232
1899–90	-	-	61,666
1890–91	-	-	51,612
1891–92	-	-	40,425
1892–93	-	-	47,365
1893–94	-	-	55,524
1894–95	-	-	66,391
1895–96	-	-	63,627
1896–97	68,225	8,356	76,581
1897–98	68,900	5,970	74,871
1898–99	65,962	10,499	76,461
1899–00	71,869	13,597	85,466
1900–01	72,534	7,519	80,053
1901–02	67,092	4,735	51,827
1902–03	65,995	1,446	67,441
1903–04	67,770	11218	78,988
1904–05	70,917	4849	75,766
1905–06	70,191	5415	75,606
1906–07	71,459	9396	80,855
1907–08	72,126	9506	81,632
1908–09	69,823	10,368	80,191

Source: Annual Reports of the Régie Company.[62]

*Comprises the export duties collected from Samos, Tunisia, Montenegro, Serbia, Romania, Eastern Rumelia, Crete and Iran under the terms of the concession.

**CFB, 1887: 168.

Later Régie reports patently show that that the tax of LE 30 per feddan imposed by the Egyptian government on tobacco-cultivated land did not bring the fall in tobacco cultivation anticipated by the Régie.[63] In 1887–97, Egyptian duty revenues were not shown separately in the Régie's annual reports. However, from the general trend of the total duty revenues it is understood that the situation was not reversed during the period.

In spite of the hopes entertained by the Régie officials, Egyptian duty revenues never reached the levels achieved before the establishment of the company. In 1888, the Régie, the OPDA, and the Ottoman government came to an agreement that the OPDA would make fixed annual payments to the Régie Company as compensation for the Egyptian Reftieh losses.[64]

Period of takeoff: 1887–95

The turning point for the Régie came in the fiscal year 1887–88 when a profit of LT 105,364 replaced the deficits that marked its previous history. As observed from Table 5.2, the increase in the net profits of the company in 1887–88 almost entirely comprised increases in domestic sales revenues. In the annual report of the CFB, this encouraging improvement was explained by the special powers granted to the Régie in dealing with smugglers.[65]

The following year the company declared a profit of LT 180,120, which enabled it to distribute shares from the profits to the OPDA and the Ottoman government, for the first time. The company's revenues continued to climb in the following years and by the end of 1894–95, the Régie's profits peaked at LT 352,003. This upward trend also boosted confidence in the company's stock on the European markets, resulting in the share price rising from Fr 100 to nearly four times that value during this period.[66]

Another factor that helped both the OPDA and the Régie in their fight against the smugglers in the Black Sea region was the sanitary cordon established in 1892 on the Black Sea, due to the prevalence of cholera in the Russian ports. The sanitary cordon was strictly controlled by cruisers that also made it very difficult for smugglers to operate by sea.[67]

In the fiscal year 1894, the Ottoman Empire faced an economic crisis caused by the fall in prices of agricultural produce and other raw materials in the world markets. Economic conditions were made worse by the spread of cholera over a considerable part of Anatolia and some parts of Rumelia. As a result, quarantine zones were established in many areas, which impaired transportation and communication within the Empire and 'caused trade and businesses of all kinds ... to be temporarily suspended'.[68]

Despite the general deterioration in the Ottoman economy in 1904–5, the Régie continued to prosper. This might seem contradictory at first glance. Two factors might have played crucial roles in this process. First of all, tobacco consumption has low income elasticity due to its addictive nature. Hence, it was probably one of the goods least affected by the economic crisis. Evidently, an increasing number of consumers could turn to cheaper contraband tobacco as a substitute. Nonetheless, the steady increase in the domestic sales figures of the company indicates that smuggling was seriously impaired by the firm government surveillance due to quarantines in a considerable part of the Empire.

The period of crisis: 1895–99

The Régie managed to escape the economic crisis until 1895–96 when the upward trend in the company's economic performance was disrupted by the escalating political disorder within the Empire. The Armenian revolt in Sasun, and its suppression by the Ottoman government in August 1884, inaugurated civil war conditions in the eastern *vilayets*. In the following years, the upheaval spread to the western regions. In 1895–97 more than 20 Armenian revolts took place, in different parts of the Empire.

The erosion of government authority during this period produced an upswing in tobacco smuggling.[69] During this period, the Régie filed several complaints of negligence against the government and urged the authorities to cooperate with the company in their effort to curb smuggling. However, the government, preoccupied with restoring order in the 'riot-torn' Empire, often ignored the company's demands.[70] Consequently the volume of tobacco sales, which had been climbing since 1885, dropped for three consecutive years until 1898, by 3 percent, 14 percent, and 12 percent respectively. A similar trend could be observed in the revenue from the retail sale permits, which declined 10 percent and plunged to their lowest level by 1897–98.[71] In the same year, the Régie announced only LT 63,975 of profit and failed to distribute shares to the OPDA and the government, for the first time in eight years.

Period of recovery and stable growth: 1899–1914

The Régie Company recovered from the crisis in the fiscal year 1899–1900, when its total sales revenue increased by 11 percent and it entered a path of stable growth. The most important dynamic behind the growth in this period was the increasing demand for Turkish tobacco in the world markets. The establishment of the American Tobacco Trust in 1901, which bought vast quantities of tobacco from the Ottoman market, also played a significant role in the expansion of the export market.[72] In 1902–3, after the trust began its purchases on the Ottoman market, the average export price rose rapidly, showing an 18 percent increase over the previous year. During the same year, average export price was around 50 percent more than the average purchase price offered by the Régie. In the following years, the Régie's purchase prices also showed significant increases but always remained around 13 percent to 35 percent below the average export prices until 1912.[73] Hence, the expanding export market provided an outlet for the cultivators where they could receive higher prices for their tobacco as compared to the prices set by the monopoly. The trend in the prices set by the Régie and the export prices can be followed from Table 5.6.

The burgeoning export market not only helped the cultivators, it benefited the Régie as well. The Régie's main focus had always been the domestic market where it had the monopoly. Export revenues had a negligible share in the company's total sales revenues. Before the transfer of its export operations to the Régie Export Company in 1893, export revenues made up only 1 percent of its total sales revenues.[74] The situation was not reversed until after the establishment of the company. Therefore, the Régie's main rivals were the contrabandists in the domestic market, not the exporters of unprocessed tobacco in world markets. As observed during the period of crisis, widespread consumption of contraband tobacco was the major limitation to the Régie's sale capacity. In this sense, rising export prices helped the company to advance its monopoly in the domestic market by diverting some tobacco that otherwise would have been sold in the domestic black market. Consequently, the increase in total export figures was accompanied by a rapid increase in the Régie's domestic sales figures as illustrated in Table 5.6.

Table 5.6 Tobacco economy under the Régie system: 1884–1914

Years	Production (tons)	Cult. land (*dönüm*)	No. of cult.	Exports (tons)	Exports (LT)	Régie Sales (tons)	Régie Sales (LT)	Exports/ D. sales	Purchase price (Ps/kg)	Sale price (Ps/kg)	Export price (Ps/kg)
1884–85	22,300	192,200	140,000								
1885–86	3,100	249,400	141,000	11,900	900,000	5,380	1,420,000	0.69	7.62	26.1	7.56
1886–87	17,200	250,500	138,600	11,500	900,000	5,540	1,410,000	0.67	6.84	25.32	7.83
1887–88	14,200	213,200	101,300	10,400	800,000	5,940	1,580,000	0.64	6.85	26.43	7.69
1888–89	19,100	249,000	111,000	8,100	600,000	6,060	1,680,000	0.57	6.52	27.46	7.41
1889–90	23,400	279,400	112,300	10,500	670,000	5,840	1,650,000	0.64	6.53	28.01	6.38
1890–91	20,300	299,300	109,000	13,400	830,000	6,400	1,790,000	0.68	6.17	27.6	6.19
1891–92	24,100	292,100	95,000	10,200	780,000	7,280	1,970,000	0.58	6.06	26.64	7.65
1892–93	25,400	324,200	106,000	13,800	950,000	7,820	2,100,000	0.64	7.03	26.63	6.88
1893–94	31,500	349,900	106,700	14,300	1,000,000	7,140	2,210,000	0.67	8.43	30.81	6.99
1894–95	23,100	346,400	109,200	13,600	960,000	7,020	2,230,000	0.66	8.53	31.81	7.06
1895–96	31,000	438,500	123,500	11,800	880,000	6,810	2,170,000	0.63	8.09	31.88	7.46
1896–97	29,400	407,000	123,100	14,800	1,100,000	5,910	1880,000	0.71	7.00	31.75	7.43
1897–98	28,400	373,600	122,100	15,900	1,210,000	5,250	1,650,000	0.75	6.80	31.5	7.61
1898–99	27,400	342,000	104,800	16,900	1,330,000	6,530	1,860,000	0.72	5.93	26.87	7.87
1899–00	26,400	326,000	102,400	19,400	1,490,000	7,870	1,950,000	0.71	5.22	24.75	7.68
1900–01	28,000	370,300	111,600	17,900	1,430,000	7,630	1,970,000	0.70	5.41	25.8	7.99
1901–02	31,800	386,200	112,800	19,100	1,420,000	7,650	2,000,000	0.71	5.78	26.18	7.43
1902–03	33,600	444,900	117,600	18,900	1,650,000	8,230	2,160,000	0.70	5.84	26.24	8.73
1903–04	48,900	632,900	171,200	20,700	1,720,000	7,880	2,270,000	0.72	6.52	28.81	8.31
1904–05	24,200	339,400	119,100	23,600	2,360,000	7,470	2,210,000	0.76	7.48	29.7	10.00
1905–06	34,100	463,400	132,000	16,600	1,490,000	7,790	2,350,000	0.68	7.07	30.33	8.98
1906–07	38,700	496,800	136,100	24,200	2,050,000	7,390	2,230,000	0.77	7.22	32.04	8.47
1907–08	41,800	525,200	140,400	23,900	2,130,000	7,520	2,390,000	0.76	7.12	32.04	8.91
1908–09	29,000	467,200	130,000	26,200	2,250,000	7,720	2330000	0.77	7.47	30.72	8.59
1909–10	34,700	520,200	157,300	31,700	2,850,000	8,260	2,410,000	0.79	7.38	30.16	8.99
1910–11	58,600	844,500	213,400	24,800	2,230,000	8,410	2,680,000	0.75	7.80	31.06	8.99
1911–12	63,400	814,100	243,600	38,500	3,100,000				9.60	34.07	8.05
1912–13	43,000	618,300	184,500							35.02	
1913–14	49,000	590,000	156,300	23,200	2,650,000	7,140	2,350,000	0.76	10.30	32.87	11.42

Sources: Annual Reports of the Règie: 1884–1909; Eldem, 1994: 79; McCarthy, 1982.

Presumably, another benefit of the expansion of the export market was the improvement in the quality of tobacco the Régie was compelled to buy. By the concession, the Régie had abolished tobacco cultivation in several places where the quality of tobacco was unsatisfactory. However, by itself this method fell short of completely eliminating the cultivation of low quality tobacco. To avoid having to buy low quality tobacco, the Régie occasionally distributed better quality seeds to the cultivators. In this sense, increasing export prices helped the monopoly by creating more incentives for cultivating better quality tobacco, which could be sold in world markets.

As a result of these favorable conditions, the Régie continued to prosper with the expansion of its export markets. In 1902–3, the shortage of crop probably even contributed to these developments and the monopoly announced a profit of LT 359,932, increasing its profits by 20 percent over the previous year. Thereafter, the company's profits never fell below LT 300,000 per annum and in 1908–9 surpassed the LT 500,000 limit set in the concession for the first time; allowing the company to deliver an increasing share of 39 percent to the government.

Tobacco revenues of the Ottoman government and OPDA under the Régie system

When the OPDA decided to farm out the tobacco monopoly, its officials persuaded the government and the bondholders by arguing that the Régie system could achieve significant increases in tobacco revenues, including the tobacco tithe, by means of the strict surveillance and control mechanisms under the proposed regime. Moreover, the monopoly of the company over the production of tobacco products would transfer the surplus previously obtained by private entrepreneurs to the monopoly. Both the government and the OPDA would receive shares from these profits. In addition, the OPDA would receive a LT 750,000 fixed annual payment, which was argued to equal the revenue of the best seasons. Thus, the OPDA officials argued that the concession would be advantageous for the bondholders. As far as the Ottoman government was concerned, it was not enthusiastic about the prospects of the Régie, which accounts for the lack of support given by the government to the fight against smugglers. As noted by Quataert, 'the state primarily viewed the corporation as an alien body draining away scarce Ottoman revenues and subjecting cultivators and consumers alike'.[75]

Table 5.7 Tobacco revenues of the OPDA and the government: 1882-1914

Years	Tobacco revenues of the OPDA		Government's share in Régie's profits (LT)
	Tobacco tithe (LT)	From the Régie (LT)	
1884–85	74,859	*724,297	0
1885–86	118,752	650,000	0
1886–87	-	688,582	0
1887–88	-	700,856	0
1888–89	-	712,000	10,215
1889–90	-	724,379	0
1890–91	-	700,000	19,143
1891–92	-	734,443	39,873
1892–93	-	771,744	48,397
1893–94	94,405	783,375	53,428
1894–95	103,115	796,134	53,173
1895–96	102,051	796,275	28,472
1896–97	90,960	768,680	783
1897–98	-	701,608	0
1898–99	91,240	700,000	0
1899–00	90,000	702,887	35,665
1900–01	113,003	720,607	35,087
1901–02	102,864	778,405	45,170
1902–03	165,666	760,957	62,453
1903–04	-	-	79,083
1904–05	153,624	833,510	51,979
1905–06	130,324	825,474	92,528
1906–07	183,026	829,879	93,551
1907–08	210,068	849,352	106,371
1908–09	221,273	819,243	82,454
1909–10	250,066	845,883	121,709
1910–11	343,017	890,900	158,186
1911–12	476,274	824,753	97,888
1912–13	348,122	813,980	-
1913–14	462,931	902,600	-

Source: Tobacco revenues of the OPDA are as reported in the Annual Report of the CFB. Tobacco revenues of the government are calculated from the Annual Reports of the Régie.[76]

* Comprises the Ps 3,951,446 collected by the OPDA between 13 March and 13 April, before the Régie commenced its operations, and the annual payment of 684,728 from the Régie for eleven months less one day of exercise in the first fiscal year (OPDA, 1884–85).

It is hard to argue that the Régie Company ever fulfilled the expectations of the OPDA officials, the bondholders or the government. Particularly before the period of growth after 1899, the company remained a major disappointment for foreign bondholders, as understood from the annual reports of the Council of Foreign Bondholders. A comparison between the tobacco revenues before and after the establishment of the Régie highlights the cause of this disappointment. Before the establishment of the OPDA, tobacco revenue was one of the six revenues handed over to the 'Administration of the Six Indirect Revenues' (ASIR) in 1879. Table 5.8 illustrates the tobacco revenues under the 'Administration of the Six Indirect Revenues,' in 1880–82, and during the first two years of the OPDA in 1882–84.

Table 5.8 Tobacco revenues before the establishment of the Régie system (in LT)

Years	Tobacco tithe	Revenue from the tobacco monopoly
1880–81		643,257
1881–82		728,403
1882–83	67,73	750,076
1883–84	77,08	689,477

Source: Annual Reports of the OPDA; Annual Reports of the CFB.

Though they would be helpful for comparison, reliable figures regarding the tobacco revenues of the Ottoman government are unavailable prior to 1880. Nevertheless, the historical accounts of the ASIR indicate that during its short period of operation the administration achieved significant increases in the collection of revenues as compared to the previous years. As observed from Table 5.8, in the second year of the ASIR revenues from the tobacco monopoly increased by more than 13 percent. The same trend continued throughout the first year of the OPDA, reaching its peak for the next ten years when the administration collected LT 750,076 from the tobacco monopoly.

However, this positive trend was interrupted in fiscal year 1883–84, when tobacco revenues of the OPDA fell by 8 percent, due to the disruption caused by the introduction of the Régie system. From the day when the establishment of the Régie system was declared by an Imperial decree, all transactions in tobacco fell off sharply, with both factories and tobacco sellers merely providing themselves with day to day stock, buying tobacco or banderoles in sufficient quantities to satisfy no more than their customers' immediate demands. As noted in the annual report of the OPDA, the fall in sales became more apparent as the date for the Régie to enter into force drew near.[77]

Trading patterns remained fairly static in the first year, at the end of which the Régie did not declare a profit and the OPDA received no more than its fixed annual payment. Thereafter, the situation deteriorated for the OPDA, which, following the loss of the Egyptian monopoly, was obliged to sacrifice part of its tobacco revenues in the form of advances or compensation to the Régie. Until 1892–93, the OPDA even failed to realize the LT 750,000 guaranteed by the initial agreement. After 1903–4, following the expansion of the export market, the revenue from the tobacco monopoly accruing to the OPDA improved significantly.

In spite of the Régie's better economic performance during the second part of the concession, the returns from the company remained far from satisfactory. In 1884–1914, the company remitted to the OPDA an average of LT 762,000 per annum. This amount was only LT 12,000 more than the amount collected by the OPDA in 1882–83 under the banderole system. Hence, the overall increase in the tobacco revenues after the establishment of the Régie was significantly below the increases achieved in the administration of other revenue sources during the same period.

As for the tobacco tithe revenues, a major change during the Régie era was the collection of the tithes from the warehouses. The OPDA officials believed that the company's involvement would result in accurate and regular collection of tithes, in the expectation that at least LT 100,000 would be generated, a 30 percent increase over the previous year.

In 1884–85, the Régie began its operations one month after the commencement of the fiscal year. The late inauguration of the company caused the already existing uncertainty to extend into the new fiscal year. As a result, tobacco operations were almost totally suspended during the first month. Therefore, during this year the tobacco tithe produced only about 75 percent of the LT 100,000 the OPDA had counted upon, falling below that of the previous year. The following years, however, saw the warehouse system yielding satisfactory results with a 58 percent increase in the tithe revenues reported in the company's second year. Until 1899–1900, the tobacco tithe produced around LT 95,000 on average. Following the expansion of the export market at the dawn of the new century, these revenues started to climb above the expected figures. In 1899–1900, they increased by 26 percent and in 1902–3 by 61 percent, over the previous year. This upward trend continued throughout the decade and by 1911–12 tithe revenues of the OPDA reached LT 476,274, showing a 518 percent increase over 1883–84, the last year before the inauguration of the Régie system.

As pointed out earlier, the Régie Company had given increasing shares of profit to the Ottoman government as an inducement to cooperate in the fight against smuggling. However, the share of profit accruing to the government was trivial. In 1887–88, the company was able to distribute a share of LT 10,215, for the first time since the commencement of the concession. Particularly until 1900s the Régie's contribution to the Ottoman treasury was negligible; LT 18,071 per annum, on average. From 1900–12 the company delivered around LT 85,538 per annum, far from satisfying the Young Turk Press which campaigned for the elimination of the Régie system.[78]

An assessment of the Régie system

Throughout its operation the Régie always remained a focus of public opposition, regarded as a symbol of Western imperialism and exploitation, mostly due to its controversial methods in dealing with the cultivators and its infamous surveillance unit, *kolcus*, which was held responsible for the death of thousands.

After the establishment of the Régie, a large number of Greek and Muslim tobacco producers emigrated to Egypt where there was no monopoly or any other kind of restriction on cigarette manufacture. Thus, Egyptian tobacco shops gradually expanded their business to include cigarette manufacturing. Initially most retailers started manufacturing 'made to order cigarettes'. These cigarettes were rolled on request for a fee. Therefore, it required a very low level of initial capital investment, bearing little risk. These 'made to order' cigarette shops owned by independent producers gradually evolved, first into small workshops employing a few workers producing ready-made cigarettes, and eventually into larger factories. Thus, many artisans turned into industrialists and the cigarette industry became one of the leading industries in Egypt, a prominent exporter of manufactured cigarettes.[79] On the other hand, in the Ottoman Empire, the same evolution process was disrupted by the establishment of the Régie, while the Ottoman immigrants who had fled from the monopoly formed the backbone of the Egyptian tobacco industry.

Another immediate effect of the Régie on the tobacco economy was a considerable fall in the number of tobacco cultivators. This was mostly due to the elimination of small plantations, as well as high fees, low purchase prices and excessive regulation of the remaining ones. While tobacco cultivators often complained about the low purchase prices of the monopoly and its pricing procedure, the high retail prices of tobacco frustrated the consumers. Smuggling flourished under these conditions and became a major obstacle to the success of the company.

While fighting the smugglers and illegal tobacco cultivation, the Régie occasionally complained that the state was favoring the interests of its subjects over those of the monopoly. In the annual reports of the OPDA and the Régie, particularly before 1908, the reluctance of the Sultan to cooperate with the monopoly was acknowledged as the major problem of the company. The Porte never fully supported the establishment of the Régie system. The Régie was rather imposed by the OPDA, which continued to support the company under all conditions, despite its disappointments and disagreements regarding the Egyptian Reftieh. In cases of non-compliance, the Ottoman government was repeatedly threatened with losing its access to the world capital markets.[80] Nevertheless, Sultan Abdülhamid, whose authority had already been challenged by the establishment of the OPDA, carefully distanced himself from the company and chose not to be involved in the highly unpopular task of surveillance.

A state, even an autocracy, has to protect the rights of its citizens to some extent for the autocrat to continue his rule. Therefore it has broader interests compared to those of any company whose only concern is to maximize its revenue. In this sense, there was a conflict of interest between the company and the government. Moreover, the tobacco revenues of the treasury – i.e. the government's share in the profits of the company – often remained negligible. As understood from Nuri Bey's report in 1890, the government believed that under state control its tobacco revenues would increase more than 50 percent.[81] Furthermore, the government held the company responsible for the boom in smuggling activities. Therefore, the government apparently did not feel much incentive to fully commit itself to a foreign monopoly that was fiercely opposed by the masses.

In some instances, 'non-compliance' on the part of the government had firm legal foundations. The government's attitude on disagreements between the Régie and the producers stemmed from the 1858 Ottoman land law stressing the priority of keeping the land under cultivation. Illegally planted grapevines or trees could not be destroyed if they reached maturity before discovery. Yet, the Régie insisted on burning the illegally cultivated tobacco.

In the 1900s, the expansion of the export market benefited the monopoly as well as the tobacco cultivators. Smuggling activities started to decline and the monopoly gradually increased its control over the domestic market. The decline in smuggling also relieved some of the tension between the government and the Régie, which significantly improved its financial position during this period.

In the last years of the concession, opposition to the company intensified. The Young Turk press was pressuring the government to abandon the monopoly in cigarette production in favor of a return to the banderole system, which they argued would relieve the burden on the impoverished cultivators and allow small entrepreneurs to establish their own factories. More importantly, it was argued that the elimination of the Régie would put an end to the extraction of the scarce resources of the country by a foreign company. However in 1912, under considerable economic strain on account of the Balkan war, the government received a loan from the Régie Company, and thus committed itself to extend the concession.

After the declaration of the Turkish Republic, the revenues and the properties of the company were transferred to the state. On 26 February 1925, the Turkish parliament passed a law abolishing the Régie Company and officially nationalized the tobacco monopoly. Hence, instead of switching to the banderole system, the new Turkish state chose to adapt the organizational framework practiced by the Régie. It should be noted that the young republic inherited most of the institutions created during the OPDA era. The largest state enterprise of the early Turkish Republic, TEKEL (the state monopoly on salt, tobacco and spirits), was established on these foundations.[82]

6

THE ROLE OF THE OPDA IN THE TRANSFORMATION OF THE OTTOMAN ECONOMY

Empirical studies in the world system theory argue that debt settlements served to restore the hegemony of the core over the periphery and to restructure the world economy in accordance with the growing needs of the core economies.[1] As these studies illustrate, the Ottoman default was far from being an isolated incident. In the mid-1870s and 1880s many debtor countries faced severe external debt service problems and eventually had to agree on new contracts for the settlement of their debts. The process always involved power asymmetries in favor of the creditors. In some cases the lenders were satisfied by certain institutional changes that secured the repayment of their loans and offered opportunities to further their economic or political gains. In other cases, the lenders went further and gained direct control over the fiscal revenues of debtor countries.[2]

This book has analyzed the aftermath of the debt settlement and the role of the resulting institutional structure in the peripheralization of the Ottoman Empire. The course of history transformed a series of profitable transactions for the core economies into an opportunity to establish a European financial administration in the Empire, through which they could safeguard their investments and extend their political control over the Ottoman Empire. As argued by Eldem, both the intensity and the nature of capital flows into the Empire changed radically in the OPDA era in a way that seemed to substantiate the Imperialism theories of the time:

> With the sharp turn of 1881, the nature of the financial relations between the West and the Ottoman Empire changed radically, both in intensity and in nature. A steady flow of Western capital started to penetrate the Ottoman market at an increasing rate, and most of all, in ways that entailed a greater control over some of the most crucial sectors of the economy. In short, from the 1890s on, Ottoman integration with Europe had started to take a substantially different course, much akin to imperialism.[3]

The characterization of the OPDA as an element of Western imperialism is not uncommon in the literature. However, these studies do not provide a fulfilling answer to the following questions: Why did the nature of capital flows into the Empire change after the OPDA? Why did foreign direct investment take place in this period, and not before? How did a government which had defaulted before, and hence already had a bad reputation as a borrower, regain access to foreign capital markets at considerably lower risk premiums? To be sure, a comprehensive answer to these questions would encompass the dynamics at the core of the world system. As argued by Lenin, foreign direct investment from core to the periphery was the distinguishing aspect of Western imperialism in the late nineteenth century.[4] However, besides the dynamics of the core economies, which have been overemphasized in the world system literature, one should also take into account the institutional changes in the periphery that facilitated this process. This would also enable us to understand why foreign capital flowed into certain peripheral economies and certain sectors, but not others. In this context, this book aimed to fill this gap by exploring the institutional background of the peripheralization process at the domestic level by focusing on the role of the OPDA.

From the early seventeenth century onward, the Ottoman Empire witnessed the weakening of the state institutions, a process that brought about a loss of control over both economic and political spheres. Until the second half of the sixteenth century, the traditional decentralized military structure based on the *timar* system functioned well and the Empire continued to expand. In this period, the financial position of the Ottoman state was considerably strengthened by the revenues obtained through rapid territorial expansion. However, in the late sixteenth century, developments in arms technology created the need for a modern central army. This not only brought the dissolution of the decentralized military structure, but also necessitated a cash flow collected at the center in order to finance the new army. For this purpose, the Ottoman government introduced a series of reforms, including the introduction of the *iltizam* system, which was based on tax-farm auctioning and subcontracting. As the financial problems of the state mounted, the government gradually increased the length of the tax-farming contracts and introduced new methods of tax collection.[5]

Nevertheless, none of these attempts to reform the tax collection system brought a long-term solution to the Ottoman budget deficits, which were often financed through debasements of the coinage. The capitulations contributed to the financial difficulties of the Porte by restricting its ability to pursue a protectionist development strategy and depriving the state of control over the customs duties, a considerable source of revenue for its European counterparts.[6] Moreover, the tax exemptions granted to foreign citizens and the protégés of the European powers, who dominated the most profitable economic activities in the period, imposed serious restrictions on the development of state revenues.

As the government could not overcome the increasing budget deficits through institutional reforms and frequent debasements, it turned to the Galata Bankers who provided the Ottoman government with short-term advances at often usurious rates. As the financial needs of the Empire grew, the Porte became more dependent on these bankers who borrowed from abroad and lent to the government, enjoying exceptionally high interests due to their unrivaled position in the domestic market and their connections within the government. From this perspective, the Porte's decision to turn to foreign capital markets for the issue of loans could also be seen as an attempt to break the monopoly of the domestic bankers and secure long-term loans at lower rates. Moreover, by the time a new loan was floated in the European markets, much of the money had in fact already been borrowed from the domestic market in the form of short-term advances, or would have to be borrowed in the near future in order to meet the payments on earlier loans. Hence, some foreign loans were simply a means for debt consolidation at more favorable terms.

Until 1854, the Ottoman government remained reluctant to seek foreign loans, mainly due to political concerns. The treasury crisis caused by the expenses of the Crimean War forced the Ottoman Empire to reconsider the borrowing opportunities in foreign markets. Under the official guarantee of its allies, Britain and France, the Ottoman state contracted its first loan in foreign markets – thus embarking on a path that would ultimately lead to its insolvency.

In order to float bonds in foreign markets, the debtor country must show some effective guarantees of its capacity for future repayment. In the Ottoman case, the Porte still had not established a budget system; the existing accounts of the treasury were unreliable and hardly monitorable. Under these circumstances, it was very difficult for the government to issue loans secured on the general revenues of the treasury and more revenues had to be pledged as collateral. For every attempt to raise a new loan, the Porte had to rely more on less attractive collaterals, which gradually brought an increase in the risk premiums charged on these loans. In the 1860s, the Porte initiated several institutional reforms in order to gain credibility in the European markets. These reforms included several measures aimed at improving the reliability and monitorability of the financial accounts. In some cases, the government went as far as delegating the collection of certain revenues of the central government to the BIO, or setting up a largely independent commission to control and approve the budgets. Nevertheless, European investors continued to question the sincerity of the government and risk premiums remained considerably higher on foreign loans during this period. The skepticism of the investors was often justified as the reforms were not fully carried through after securing the loans.

After 20 years of borrowing, the Ottoman government defaulted in 1875 and declared the Decree of *Muharrem* in 1881, which led to the establishment of the OPDA. By the terms of the decree, the Porte compromised its financial and political autonomy. Yet, the decree also helped to solve the Porte's short-term liquidity problems as the Ottoman government regained access to European financial markets at significantly lower risk premiums than ever before. Ottoman borrowing in the pre-OPDA period was marked by several reforms aimed at restoring eroding confidence in the Ottoman government. During the OPDA period, this trust problem was overcome by the constraints placed on the sovereignty of the government and the extension of OPDA control over the Ottoman economy. Hence, lending to the Ottoman government was no longer a matter of trust in the government itself. Rather, it was a matter of trust in an international commission established for the liquidation of the foreign debt. The extension of the OPDA's control of the Ottoman economy was surely a matter of concern for the government, but in need of short-term liquidity it often resorted to foreign loans, despite the fact that each loan agreement brought more constraints on the economic sovereignty of the Porte.

The establishment of the OPDA encouraged not only foreign lending but also foreign direct investment in the Empire. A considerable amount of the FDI in this period went to railway schemes that not only facilitated domestic economic activities but also encouraged the penetration of Western goods into the interior of the country. Hence, the construction of the railways was one of the major dynamics behind the peripheralization of the Ottoman economy in this period. The OPDA played a crucial role in the railway investments. European capitalists who sought profits amidst the disorder that prevailed in the country often asked for the protection or the cooperation of the OPDA. The involvement of the administration in the railway projects secured their investments to a large degree, minimized their risks and enabled them to enjoy handsome profits. As Blaisdell notes:

> The opening-up of the Ottoman Empire to Europe and the world was accompanied by the realization of profits whose production was assured by the interposition of the Public Debt Council.[7]

Under the terms of the decree, the revenues from the salt and tobacco monopolies, the stamps and spirits tax, the fish tax, and the silk tithe in certain districts as well as the Bulgaria tribute, the revenue from Eastern Rumelia and the surplus of the Cyprus revenue were irrevocably ceded to the OPDA, until liquidation of the debt. The administrative system introduced by the OPDA, in many respects, formed a great contrast to the financial administration of the Ottoman government. The OPDA introduced new technologies to the relevant sectors under its responsibility, improved the regulations and made the necessary legislative changes concerning the development of its revenues. Improvements in the revenues under its control and the introduction of new institutions in the relevant sectors also created positive externalities for other sectors of the economy. It is also important to note that in salt, silk and spirits revenues, the OPDA achieved significant increases by creating export markets for these articles. This was one reason for the growth in exports from the Empire in this period. Finally, the international treaties imposed on the Porte by the European powers also restricted the administration's ability to improve its revenues. In several cases, for example the stamp law, wine duties and patent law, the OPDA officials complained of unfair conditions imposed by these treaties and asked for revisions. In some cases they managed to convince the European powers to make minor modifications.

The most important revenue of the OPDA, the tobacco monopoly, was farmed out to the Régie Company, which turned out to be not only the largest foreign investment in the country, but also the largest corporation. The establishment of the Régie system altered the pre-existing production, credit and distribution networks in the tobacco sector. One immediate effect of the Régie on the tobacco economy was a considerable drop in the number of tobacco cultivators. This was mostly due to the elimination of small producers, as well as the high license fees, low purchase prices, and excessive regulations applied on the remaining growers. Smuggling flourished under these conditions and became a major obstacle to the success of the company.

After the establishment of the Régie, a large number of Greek and Muslim tobacco producers emigrated to Egypt, where no restrictions existed on cigarette manufacture. These immigrants initially established small workshops employing a few workers rolling cigarettes. Their small workshops gradually evolved into larger factories selling ready-made cigarettes. During this process, many artisans turned into industrialists and the cigarette industry became one of the leading industries in Egypt, a prominent exporter of manufactured cigarettes. By contrast, in the Ottoman Empire, the same evolution process was disrupted by the establishment of the Régie, while Ottoman immigrants who fled from the monopoly formed the backbone of the Egyptian tobacco industry.

Throughout its existence, the Régie was a focus of public opposition. It was regarded as a symbol of Western imperialism and exploitation, mostly due to its controversial methods in dealing with the cultivators and its infamous surveillance unit, *kolcus*, held responsible for the deaths of thousands. After the establishment of the republic, one of the priorities of the economic agenda, as discussed at the economic congress, was the abolition of the monopoly system. In this context, the new Turkish parliament passed a law abolishing the foreign monopoly, and officially nationalized the tobacco monopoly. However, instead of switching to the banderole system, the new Turkish state chose to adapt the organizational framework practiced by the Régie. Significantly, the new republic inherited most of the institutions created during the OPDA era. TEKEL (the state monopoly on salt, tobacco and spirits), the largest state enterprise of the Turkish Republic, was established on these foundations.

The OPDA's role in risk reduction

The theoretical contribution of this book to the existing literature on the OPDA is twofold. First, it introduces a game theoretical framework to analyze the institutional background of Ottoman borrowing. This model explains how foreign investors made their risk assignments; how the risk premiums on individual loan issues were determined in the international markets. The model is then used to highlight the sources of decline in risk premiums on loans issued in the OPDA era. The model illustrates that the constraints placed on the sovereignty of the Porte by the Decree of *Muharrem* enabled the government to borrow from international markets at lower risk premiums.

There were basically two main factors that affected the risk assignments of the creditors. The first was the perceived higher probability of debt service in the OPDA era. The reliability and monitorability of the financial accounts of the OPDA reduced the uncertainty about the repayment of debt and brought about a considerable fall in the risk premiums. The second factor was the increase in expected net returns in case of insolvency. The key function of the OPDA was the maintenance of coordination among the Ottoman bondholders. The coalitional stability of the creditors formed an important enforcement mechanism by creating a wider international consensus on the legitimacy of the OPDA. Hence, as the perceived probability of government intervention in case of default increased, expected returns from lending to the Ottoman government rose considerably. This lowered the risk premium charged on loans issued by the Ottomans.

The dual role of the OPDA

The second theoretical contribution of this book to the literature on the OPDA is that it provides a novel interpretation of the administration's function in the peripheralization of the Empire by emphasizing its 'dual role' in the process. In contrast to the previous accounts, portraying the OPDA merely as an aggressive outpost of Western imperialism or an agent of European powers pursuing hegemony in an Empire on the brink of collapse, this book also points out the role of the OPDA in the modernization of the Turkish state.

The OPDA played a crucial role in the transfer of economic surplus from the Empire to the core economies. It certainly secured and furthered the interests of the countries directly or indirectly represented in the administration. The main purpose of the OPDA was the collection of taxes to pay the shares of the foreign bondholders. More efficient tax collection meant a bigger tax burden on the impoverished agricultural population and a greater capital outflow from the economy. Significantly, most members of the OPDA also held additional posts in other foreign corporations operating in the Ottoman Empire. In case of a disagreement between the Ottoman government and these corporations, the administration usually sided with the interests of the latter. Perhaps most important of all, by limiting the state's control over the appropriation and utilization of the economic surplus, the establishment of the OPDA terminated the sporadic efforts of the palace to recreate Ottoman centralism. In these respects, the role of the OPDA lends support to the 'colonization through lending' arguments.

Yet, this book also demonstrates another aspect of the OPDA that has been previously overlooked in most historical accounts. With the Decree of *Muharrem*, the OPDA received the right to administer, collect, and hold in deposit the revenues resulting from the development of the sources of income ceded to the bondholders. In this framework, the OPDA initiated several measures including administrative reforms and technology transfers that not only facilitated growth in the sectors under its responsibility, but also generated positive externalities for other sectors. The administrative reforms initiated by the OPDA also set examples for the Ottoman state. Double-entry bookkeeping, first introduced by the Ottoman Bank and then by the OPDA to state accounting, was later adopted by the Ottoman state as the standard accounting principle. The institutional reforms initiated by the administration contributed to the development and modernization of state entrepreneurship in the Empire. The backbone of the early republican economy owes much to these reforms.

While analyzing the role of the OPDA in the penetration of Western capitalism into the Empire, this book also challenges several arguments previously developed by nationalist historical accounts of the administration. In this literature, the OPDA is often portrayed simply as an official agent of foreign powers or Western capitalism. This approach perceives Western capitalism as a monolithic entity and overlooks the fact that different capitalist groups, even with the same country of origin, might have conflicting interests on a variety of issues. OPDA members were directly appointed by the bondholder organizations of the respective countries. Hence, they were responsible above all to the bondholders.

These representatives were undoubtedly under the influence of their governments, and sometimes even handpicked by them. But on many occasions they also opposed the general policies of their governments to protect the interests of their bondholders, which were closely tied to the performance of the Ottoman economy. For instance, while foreign merchants and governments pressed for lower tariffs on European goods and the extension of the tax privileges granted to foreign subjects, the OPDA asked for trade protection and the abolishment of tax privileges for foreigners. In some cases, the impositions of the foreign powers posed serious restrictions on the development of the OPDA's revenues.

Another argument observed in the nationalist critiques of the period is that foreigners forced loans on the government at usurious rates. This book has shown that the high rates on foreign loans stemmed mostly from a lack of trust in the Ottoman finances and the attempts at reform. After the OPDA, the risk premiums on foreign loans declined drastically due to the strong enforcement mechanisms for sovereign compliance. Moreover, unable to command confidence in the financial markets by its own means, the government aimed to benefit from the credibility of the OPDA. Therefore, when necessary, the government voluntarily transferred more revenue sources to the control of the OPDA in order to raise new loans at more favorable terms. Hence, in a similar way to that described in North and Weingast's seminal paper on the economic consequences of the Glorious Revolution, the constraints on the sovereign enabled the Ottoman government to regain access to foreign capital markets with lower risk premiums.[8] One notable difference between these cases was that in Britain the constraints were imposed by the internal dynamics of the country while in the Ottoman case they were imposed from outside nearly 200 years later. In the 'age of high imperialism', this delay made the Ottoman Empire even more vulnerable to political and economic exploitation by the European powers. The reason why the internal dynamics of the Ottoman Empire could not develop a similar set of institutions as in Britain is beyond the scope of this book. However, it is surely crucial in understanding the Ottoman Empire's later subordination to the European powers.

Absence of reforms in the Ottoman Empire

One crucial point that requires further attention is the striking disparity between the performances of the government and the OPDA (or the Régie) in the administration of the revenues. Why could the Ottoman state not initiate, on its own, the administrative reforms, technology transfers and organizational renovations that helped the OPDA to drastically raise the revenues previously controlled by the government? In the case of the administration's success in wiping out the contraband, the answer is relatively simple. The OPDA did not function as a governmental organization, but rather as a private company controlled by foreign creditors, who did not have responsibilities towards the local population. For instance, the government might have overlooked the sale of contraband salt in poor districts or contraband activities of unpaid army personnel in the tobacco sector to avoid social disturbances. For the government, all these activities were part of a larger equation. Using force to fight smuggling could lead to unfavorable political consequences. The OPDA, on the other hand, simply worked as a private company pursuing the maximization of its own profits. It was much less interested in the political consequences. Hence, at least in the case of contraband, the main reason for the disparity between the economic performances of the OPDA and the government was not the inability of the latter to use similar methods. Faced with a tradeoff between economic and political objectives, the government chose to tolerate some level of contraband despite its economic costs.

In other cases, however, the drastic increases achieved by the OPDA revealed the inefficiency and the backwardness of the management of the Ottoman finances as compared to its Western counterparts. The underdevelopment of the state enterprises or the state finances was closely related to the underdevelopment of private enterprise and the organization of economic life in general. In the West, many developments in business organization and administration, such as the introduction of double-entry bookkeeping, first occurred in the private sector and were later adopted by the public sector. However, in the Ottoman Empire, the development of the private sector was much slower.

Kuran's work on the economic consequences of the Islamic inheritance system offers a compelling explanation for the underdevelopment of the Ottoman enterprises as compared to their Western counterparts.[9] According to Kuran, the egalitarian Islamic inheritance system limited the size and duration of partnerships, while primogeniture, a widely used inheritance practice in Europe, facilitated enterprise preservation and growth. Islamic law, requiring the division of estates among numerous heirs upon the death of a partner, inadvertently raised the costs of liquidating a partnership prematurely. Accordingly, Middle Eastern merchants minimized the risk of premature liquidation by limiting the size and duration of their partnerships. In Europe, on the other hand, large partnerships evolved into modern joint-stock companies, enjoyed economies of scale, developed new methods and invested in new technologies in order to improve their productivity and efficiency.

The late adoption of double-entry bookkeeping by the Ottoman state was also closely related to the underdevelopment of private enterprises. In Europe, the history of double-entry bookkeeping dated back to the thirteenth century. It grew rapidly, particularly among large firms, and gradually replaced single-entry bookkeeping due to several features that facilitated the monitoring of financial flows, enabled the detection of fraud as well as the sources of loss or profit, and increased the reliability of financial statements.[10] This accounting principle not only facilitated the endurance of large partnerships and the working of the credit markets by bringing credibility to the financial statements issued by the firms or debtors, but also improved the efficiency of companies.

As pointed out by Kuran, the development of double-entry bookkeeping in Europe as a standard accounting principle was a response to the developing needs of large partnerships. In the Ottoman Empire, on the other hand, due to the Islamic inheritance system, commercial enterprises generally remained small and short-lived. Members of small partnerships did not feel the need to develop the type of sophisticated or standardized accounting techniques that become necessary to facilitate communication and coordination among large numbers of bondholders. Hence, the absence of double-entry bookkeeping in the Middle East until the late nineteenth century can be explained by the atomistic nature of the private sector.[11]

Unlike the European experience, in the Ottoman Empire double-entry bookkeeping developed first in the state sector.[12] After the establishment of the OPDA, the state had two separate budgets, one covering the revenues of the Ministry of Finance and the other concerning the revenues controlled by the OPDA. While the OPDA used double-entry bookkeeping in its financial records, the state continued to use single-entry bookkeeping. From Güvemli's accounts, we understand that the Ottoman authorities had observed the precision and accuracy of double-entry bookkeeping used by the BIO in the 1860s, and considered the adoption of this principle in 1880.[13] However, due to a lack of trained personnel, this modern accounting principle could not be adopted by the Ministry of Finance until as late as the 1910s. Although it goes unmentioned in the literature, there is no doubt that the OPDA, by introducing this modern accounting principle to state finances, played a crucial role in the adoption of double-entry bookkeeping by the Ministry of Finance.

Foreign archives and the OPDA as sources of historical information

Finally, this book also contributes to the existing literature on the OPDA through extensive research on the primary sources that were partly used by early foreign writers such as Blaisdell, Du Velay and Roumani, but largely ignored by Turkish studies of the period. A valuable source for an analysis of the administration is the Annual Reports of the OPDA. These reports contain detailed information about the organization of the OPDA, its conflicts with both the Ottoman government and foreign embassies, the development of the revenues ceded to the administration, and the payments made to the bondholders. Each source of revenue is analyzed under separate sections, with special focus on the changing circumstances that affected the development of these revenues. These archives also provide fairly consistent and accurate data regarding the sectors controlled by the administration, which is absent from previous Ottoman accounts of these sectors.

The second major archival source used in this work is that of the Council of Foreign Bondholders (CFB), formed in 1868 to protect the interests of British holders of foreign bonds. While similar bondholders' associations were established in other countries at various times in history, the CFB was the longest-lived, best known, and most important of these institutions, mostly due to London's pre-eminence as the main financial center during the period of interest here. The Annual Reports of the Council of Foreign Bondholders include the council's annual assessments regarding financial, political and economic developments in the Ottoman Empire as well as other debtor countries that issued bonds in London. Another important source of information found in the Council's archives is the newspaper cutting files of the CFB. In the early 1870s, the Council's officers began systematically to collect and retain printed material, primarily newspaper cuttings, to supply basic information to the Council's negotiators and provide background material for country reports. The cuttings are in English taken mainly from British daily newspapers, the weeklies and the financial press. These archives enable us to identify the obstacles faced by foreign investors in the Ottoman Empire and understand their reactions to the economic reforms and other changing economic or political circumstances in the country. More importantly, these archives, particularly the letters written by foreign investors in the country, provide the reader with comparisons between Western and Ottoman economic life from the foreigners' perspective.

Another archival source used in this work is the Annual Reports of the Régie Company. Printed in French, these reports contain detailed information about the development of the revenues and the expenditures of the company. They also yield insights into the sources of these changes and the obstacles encountered by the tobacco monopoly. Despite the Régie's significant place in the Ottoman economy during the last four decades of the Empire, the literature offers no thorough study of the company. By introducing original data gathered from these archives, this book aims to encourage further studies of the company, which was the largest, yet also the most controversial, enterprise of the late Ottoman Empire.

Further research

This book will hopefully spark a renewed interest in the OPDA and encourage further studies of the administration. One major difficulty during this research was the lack of reliable data regarding the administration of indirect revenues before the establishment of the ASIR. This made it impossible to measure the real magnitude of the improvements achieved by the OPDA in different sectors. In order to extend our knowledge beyond the archives of the OPDA, further studies of the administration should focus on local sources in regions where the OPDA policies became influential.

Recently, both scholarly and popular discourses in Turkey have witnessed a growing emphasis on the similarities between the OPDA and the IMF and their role in the transformation of Turkish economy, following two external debt crises a century apart. However, a satisfactory comparative analysis of the Turkish experience with these two organizations is still lacking. While there is a striking resemblance between the role of the OPDA (and similar creditor organizations established in other debtor countries in 1880s) and the IMF (such as the introduction of strong enforcement mechanisms for sovereign compliance with debt contracts and transparency in state finances), there are also essential differences between these organizations. The former had vested interests in the country and in some cases even defended protectionist government policies when they coincided with its interests. The latter, however, has a global agenda that includes maintaining global financial stability, as well as facilitating international trade. A comparative study of these organizations would also help us identify the structural changes in the core-periphery relationship within the last century.

Finally, the newspaper cutting files of the CFB contain foreign investors' accounts of their individual experiences in the Empire. Despite the prevalence of strong orientalist prejudices, these accounts also include valuable observations about the dysfunctional organization of the Ottoman bureaucracy, the backwardness of the Ottoman financial institutions, and comparisons with European institutions. While the Ottoman accounts of the period take many institutions as given, such as the existing accounting or budgetary principles of the state (mostly due to the lack of knowledge of modern methods), the accounts of the foreign observers draw attention to the distinguishing features of the Ottoman finances. In this context, studies that aim to transcend the traditional 'military crisis' explanations and scrutinize the institutional roots of the crisis in Ottoman finance would surely benefit from these archives.

NOTES

1. Introduction

[1] Viner, 1924; Iversen, 1936.
[2] Avramovic, 1964; Chenery and Strout, 1966; Bardhan, 1967; Agarwala and Singh, 1958; Meier, 1970; Sachs, 1984.
[3] Hobson, 1902; Hilferding, 1910; Luxemburg, 1913; Lenin, 1916; Bukharin, 1917.
[4] Amin, 1976; Arrighi, 1994; Frank, 1998; Wallerstein, 1974.
[5] Up to this stage, the statement may mean that the economy in the core is 'self sufficient', causing a one-dimensional understanding of the core-periphery relationship. Aware of such risk and the determining role of external trade in terms of capitalist accumulation, Amin adds, 'auto-centric accumulation does not mean autarchy' (Amin, 1976: 191). But again the rules of the game are determined by the core. External trade is dependent upon capital accumulation in the core, yet, at the same time, constitutes a means of achieving this. In short, auto-centric economies impose an unequal international specialization on the periphery that serves their own interests.
[6] İslamoğlu and Keyder, 1987: 60.
[7] Eichengreen, 1989; Eichengreen and Portes, 1989; Fishlow, 1985; Stallings, 1987; Suter, 1992.
[8] Suter, 1992. For a detailed account of business cycles and their international policy implications, also see Bergesen and Schoenberg, 1980; Modelski, 1977, 1987; Wallerstein, 1974, 1999.
[9] Suter, 1989 and 1992; Suter and Stamm, 1992.
[10] The Westphalian model refers to the modern state system introduced by the Peace of Westphalia in 1648, which ended the Thirty Years' War in Europe and led

to the birth of several small sovereign states out of the Holy Roman Empire. The treaty brought an end to the idea of the Holy Roman Empire having secular dominion over the entire Christian world. More importantly, it introduced the notion of an international system based on fully sovereign states which recognize no superior authority, and have the right to freely choose and develop their own political, social, economic, and cultural systems (Griffiths and O'Callaghan, 2000: 296–299).

[11] Krasner, 1999: 131.

[12] Krasner, 1999: 132.

[13] North, 1990: 134.

[14] The bargaining position of the Ottoman Empire was considerably better than that of many other debtor countries. In the nineteenth century the Empire was one of the key players in the European military balance. This allowed the Turkish ruling class to maintain domestic sovereignty to a certain extent. Therefore the bureaucratic apparatus of the Empire never totally collapsed.

[15] 'Young Turks' was the name given to Turkish constitutionalist groups mainly formed by army officers, military students and intellectuals. After the establishment of the Committee of Union and Progress (CUP) in 1906, Young Turks became members of this party. In 1908, Young Turks rebelled against the rule of Sultan Abdulhamid II and forced the Sultan to summon a parliament.

[16] Parvus Efendi's real name was Alexander Helpland. He was a Russian socialist who was exiled to Siberia by the tsarist regime due to his role in the 1905 revolution. Parvus later fled to the Ottoman Empire. Between 1910 and 1914, he wrote articles in the nationalist *Türk Yurdu* journal published by the Young Turks. For a collection of Parvus Efendi's articles, see Parvus Efendi, 1977.

[17] Blaisdell, 1929; Du Velay, 1978 [1903]; Morawitz, 1978 [1902]; Novichev, 1979 [1937]; Roumani, 1927.

[18] Gürsoy, 1984; Kazgan, 1985; Keskinkılıç, 1997; Kömürcan, 1948; Önsoy, 1999; Yeniay, 1964; Yılmaz, 1996.

[19] For widely influential critiques of the OPDA as an agent of Western imperialism, see Avcıoğlu, 1973; Berkes, 1975.

[20] Güvemli, 2000: 53–55, 221–22; Karaarslan, 2004.

[21] Sunar, 1987: 78–84.

[22] Sunar, 1987: 78.

[23] Decdeli, Kasaba and Wallerstein, 1987: 89.

[24] İnalcık, 1964.

[25] Avcıoğlu, 1973: 125.

[26] While foreign merchants and governments pressed for lower tariffs on European goods and the extension of the tax privileges granted to foreign subjects, the OPDA asked for trade protection and the abolition of tax privileges for foreigners. These impositions posed serious restrictions on the development of the OPDA's revenues.

[27] Mutluçağ, 1967.

[28] North and Weingast, 1989. One notable difference was that in Britain these constraints were imposed by the internal dynamics of the country while in the Ottoman case they were imposed from outside nearly 200 years later, which made the country, in the 'age of high imperialism', even more vulnerable to political and economic exploitation by the European powers. The reason why the internal dynamics of the Ottoman Empire could not develop a similar set of institutions as in Britain is beyond the scope of this work. However, it is surely crucial in understanding the Empire's future subordination to the European powers.

[29] Wallerstein, Decdeli and Kasaba point out that determining the dating of the transformation of the Ottoman Empire into a peripheral structure is controversial and difficult. For contradictory claims about the periodization, see Decdeli, Kasaba and Wallerstein, 1987: 95–97. On one extreme, Pamuk argues that until the nineteenth century the Ottoman Empire could be defined as a self contained unit of reproduction, largely isolated from the dynamics of the world economy (Pamuk, 1994: 151).

[30] Yücekök, 1968.

2. Ottoman borrowing in the pre-OPDA period: The path to the Decree of *Muharrem*

[1] In order to understand the extent of the Sultan's control over this administrative structure, we should note that the administrative position *sipahi* was not hereditary, and the Sultan could remove the *sipahi* at any time (Karpat, 1973).

[2] Coşgel and Miceli, 2005.

[3] Until the mid-nineteenth century, before they were replaced by modern joint-stock banks, banking operations in Europe were mainly carried on by banking houses owned by private individuals, families or small partnerships. In Britain, it was prohibited for the private banks to have more than six partners (a requirement for the formation of a joint-stock company), as part of the privileges granted to the Bank of England. Moreover, as opposed to the limited shareholder liability in modern joint-stock banks, private bankers had unlimited liability, which posed a serious restriction on the expansion of their banking operations and made them

extremely vulnerable to economic crises. During this period, it was widely believed that limited liability would lead to excessive risk taking and moral hazard on the part of both managers and owners. This was the underlying logic of the Bubble Act in Britain, which banned the formation of new limited liability companies in 1720. The restriction on the formation of joint-stock banks in Britain lasted until 1825, when the Banking Co-Partnership Regulation Act (1825) was enacted after the spiraling bank failures. This act permitted banks to form freely as joint-stock companies and enjoy all the privileges usually associated with incorporation, except limitation of liability. Generalized limited liability was first introduced in Sweden in 1844, and then in England in 1856, with the Joint Stock Company Act. However, limited liabilities for banks and insurance companies were introduced later on (in 1856 and 1862 respectively) (Acheson and Turner, 2006; Chang, 2002: 86–87; Hildreth, 2001 [1837]: 22–23).

4 Kuran points out the risk-return tradeoff faced by the Ottoman state in the conversion of short-term tax farms into longer-term or even life-term tax farms. The longer the tax farm period, the greater the bids of potential tax farmers, hence the greater the returns from the auctions. On the other hand, as the period lengthened, the probability of the tax farmer gaining political autonomy grew accordingly. As a result, tax farmers increased their political power, claiming the right to bequeath farms to their descendants. This threatened the central authority of the government. In 1812, the government started to take over the management of tax farms in order to restore the central authority (Kuran, 2005b).

5 Genç, 1987. Pamuk notes that in the long term the *malikane* system fell short of fulfilling expectations and was gradually phased out in the 1840s. One obvious reason was the state's inability to regain control of the revenue sources after the death of the individuals who purchased them (Pamuk, 2002). We should also note that none of these changes in the tax collection system altered the legal basis of land ownership. Until the nineteenth century, state ownership continued to be the key institution of the Ottoman order.

6 Shaw, 1975: 422.

7 Shaw, 1975: 422. Coşgel and Miceli bring a transaction cost explanation to the practice of tax farming. The authors argue that if the central government collected taxes through hired agents, they would have lacked the knowledge of local production technologies and units of measurement to accurately calculate the variable tax bases, both in terms of quality and quantity. Moreover, they did not have the incentives to measure the tax bases accurately since their income was independent of the tax revenue. Tax farmers, on the other hand, had the knowledge, ability and high incentives for accurate measurement of the variable tax revenue

(Coşgel and Miceli, 2005). The failure of *muhassıls* in the *Tanzimat* period supports this argument. We should also point out that the authors analyze the problem from the perspective of the recipient and disregard its consequences for the taxpayer. The tax farming system also created an incentive for over-taxation, causing disturbances among the peasants (Shaw, 1975: 424–426). However, as the term of the tax farm contracts were extended, it naturally provided the tax farmer with the incentive to set the taxes at an optimal level that would allow the expansion of the economic activities in the province, and maximize his tax revenues in the long run.

[8] Shaw, 1975: 429.

[9] The history of capitulations dates back to the ninth century, when the caliph Harun-al-Rashid granted guarantees and commercial facilities to the Franks. After the break-up of the Frankish empire, similar concessions were made to some of the Italian city states that flourished on its ruins. The Byzantine emperors followed this example, and Genoa, Pisa and Venice all obtained capitulations. The Ottoman Empire continued the existing system as various non-Muslim peoples were allowed their semi-autonomy in matters affecting their personal status, and the Genoese of Galata were confirmed in their privileges. However, the first capitulation granted to a foreign state was that of 1535, granted to the French (*Encyclopedia Britannica*, 1911, Vol. 5: 284).

For competing explanations on the logic of capitulations, see Kuran, 2005a. According to Kuran, the early capitulations were essentially aimed at reducing tariff discrimination against foreign subjects and allowing them to settle internal disputes through their own legal systems. The first provision enhanced economic efficiency by stimulating competition. The second, on the other hand, allowed foreigners to settle disputes through arbitration, without the involvement of the local judicial system. Since arbitration requires the consent of all parties involved in the dispute, at initiation, each party must expect to do at least as well as in a formal court, hence it is efficient. Therefore, the ruler, by granting legal autonomy to foreign subjects, allowed for internal dispute resolution mechanisms to be brought in, which lowered the transaction costs and ultimately benefited the ruler by facilitating external trade and raising customs revenues (Kuran, 2005a: 5–6).

[10] Kuran argues that the capitulations benefited the Ottoman rulers by allowing Western merchants to operate under their own legal systems, which served to minimize transaction costs and facilitated the external trade of the Empire. During the period, Westerners were developing institutions aimed at 'enhancing contract credibility, reducing arbitrary taxation, and aligning individual effort with individual

rewards'. Kuran also points out that the capitulations enabled the transplant of various institutional innovations to the Middle East (Kuran, 2005a).

[11] Adam Block, 'The Commercial Independence of Turkey', *Times*, 14 December 1908. CFB, Reel 207, Vol. 32.

[12] Morawitz, 1904: 204–206.

[13] In most European powers customs duties on imports varied between 15 and 25 percent, whereas the Ottomans were not allowed to exceed 8 percent (Morawitz, 1904: 201). In the 1820s, average tariff rates on manufactured products were around 50 percent in Britain (Chang, 2002: 17).

Similar unequal treaties were imposed in almost all peripheral economies. For a detailed account of the unequal treaties imposed on the peripheral economies and the protectionist policies adopted by the core economies in their early development stages, see Chang, 2002.

[14] Shaw, 1975: 444.

[15] *Ibid.* The early capitulations were voluntary grants of the Sultan rather than impositions by the foreign powers. The existence of the protective measures on exports rather than imports suggests that the greatest concern of the palace during the period was the scarcity of essential goods, particularly in urban areas, which could lead to public unrest. Imports, on the other hand, were encouraged as they added to the number of available goods in the urban markets (Pamuk, 2002). This is also consistent with the provisionalism principle, which Genç argues to be one of the key principles of the traditional Ottoman state (Genç, 2000: 68–86). In this context, Ottoman provisionalism stood in great contrast to European mercantilism based on lowering export duties and increasing import duties. From the works of Naima, an early eighteenth century historian who defended mercantilist ideas, we understand that the Ottomans were not completely unaware of mercantilism. An important reason why mercantilism had little impact on Ottoman economic policy was the limited influence of the merchants and the domestic producers on the state as compared to Europe (Naima, 1968).

Later on, in the nineteenth century, witnessing the steady decline of the local production under the fierce rivalry of their Western counterparts and the growing budget deficits of the state, more Ottoman intellectuals became acquainted with the idea of trade protectionism. Particularly after the second half of the nineteenth century the Ottoman state constantly appealed to the European powers for modification of the treaties. For a detailed account of the evolution of trade protectionism in Ottoman economic thought, see Sayar, 1986.

[16] Bailey notes that it was not a coincidence that the period of rapid development in Britain between 1825 and 1850 was also the period in which British interest in the

Ottoman market was the greatest. Particularly during the second quarter of the nineteenth century, Britain's exports to other European states remained fairly limited due to the protective trade barriers. Under these circumstances, Turkey served as an important outlet for the British manufactured goods. Over the ten years following the 1838 trade agreement British exports to the Ottoman Empire grew by more than 260 percent and reached £7,619,106 in 1848, which made up more than 5 percent of total British exports. According to the same figures, Ottoman exports to Britain grew by 35 percent between 1837 and 1845 (Bailey, 1940: 457–461).

17 For strategic considerations behind the 1838 Trade Agreement, see Yücekök, 1968: 399–401. For details of the agreement, also see Issawi, 1966: 38–39.

18 In his reports, the Austrian consul described the 1838 treaty as 'more hostile' to Ottoman industry than the previous capitulations due to the privileging of foreign merchandise over the indigenous industry (Issawi, 1966: 41).

19 CFB, 1909–10: 32.

20 For the obstacles posed by the capitulations to the Ottoman attempts at industrialization, see the following accounts of the textile factories in the Empire: Issawi, 1966: 46–59; Pamuk, 1994: 146–150.

21 Adam Block, 'The Commercial Independence of Turkey', *Times*, 14 December 1908. CFB, Reel 207, Vol. 32.

22 These protégés, who could enjoy the tax privileges granted to foreign subjects, controlled a vast proportion of commercial activities, as well as those in the modern economic sectors such as banking and insurance. 'In 1882, "foreign subjects" accounted for 112,000 of the 237,000 residents of Galata, İstanbul's leading commercial district; most were natives' (Kuran, 2004: 501–502). For a detailed explanation of the incentives for seeking foreign protection, see Kuran, 2004.

23 Morawitz, 1904: 205.

24 For details on debasements and their political impacts, see Pamuk, 2004.

25 Clay, 2000: 20–21.

26 Toprak, 1995: 4.

27 Clay, 2000: 19.

28 Both Clay and Suvla note that substantial profits were made by the bankers through the encashment of *eshams* and *sergis* (Clay, 2000: 20; Suvla: 1966: 96). However, they do not provide specific information regarding the size of these profits. It is hard to estimate the exact magnitude of the profits, due to the fact that the encashment process often involved 'commissions' paid to bureaucrats that were never documented.

[29] Suvla notes that when the state was in financial crisis, the brokers lent money to the treasury at very high rates of interest and commission, and at the end of the term of loan, they collected their money by bribing the authorities (Suvla, 1966: 96).
[30] *Times*, 16 December 1880. CFB, Reel 200, Vol. XVII.
[31] *Times*, 10 December 1879. CFB, Reel 200, Vol. XV.
[32] Baltazzi, Tubini, Camondo and Zarifi were some of the bankers who had established branches in European financial centers (Clay, 2000: 19). For detailed information on Zarifi, see Hulkiender, 2003.
[33] Suvla, 1966; Blaisdell, 1929.
[34] The government paid an indemnity of Fr 2.2 million for the cancellation of the contract (Suvla, 1966).
[35] After the default, some newspapers held the government morally responsible against the bondholders of the 1854 loan who 'put their trust in their government'. For details, see Blaisdell, 1929: 48–49.
[36] See, Önsoy, 1999; Suvla, 1966; Yeniay, 1964.
[37] Clay, 2000: 9.
[38] Blaisdell, 1929: 28.
[39] Suvla, 1966: 99.
[40] Clay, 2000: 12.
[41] *The Navy*, 26 September 1874. CFB, Reel 193, Vol. III.
[42] Adam Smith describes the practice of hypothecated loans in the following manner: 'Nations, like private men, have generally begun to borrow upon what may be called personal credit, without assigning or mortgaging any particular fund for the payment of the debt; and when this resource has failed them, they have gone on to borrow upon assignments or mortgages of particular funds' (Smith, 1998 [1776]: 460).

The practice of pledging revenue for the security of the government debt was used at least as early as 1187, when a Venetian loan was secured on the revenues derived from salt and seignorage. Other early uses of pledging revenues include a loan to Florence in 1307 for the war of Arezzo, and in 1515 in France for a loan issued by Francis I, the first French king to raise loans by hypothecating revenues. The practice of pledging revenues was not uncommon in Britain either. Before the Revolution of 1689, the kings often secured funds by pledging jewels and mortgaging revenues. After the revolution the importance of this device gradually declined due to the improving credit of the constitutional government (Coleman, 1936).

[43] Shortly after the loan contract, Jules Mirès was arrested by French authorities for embezzlement and rumors of bribery in high circles. Subsequently, the vice

governor of the Bank of France, Baron Doyen, was dispatched to İstanbul to cancel the contract and settle the accounts with Porte while the drafts already accepted by Mirès were paid by the Bank of France (Raccagni, 1980: 346–347).

[44] Many historians regard 1860–61 as the first budget of the Empire in the modern sense, because it was prepared in advance of the fiscal year (Shaw, 1975 and 1978; Giray, 2001: 133).

[45] Clay, 2000: 62. Fuat Paşa resigned from his post in 1863 and thus failed to realize many of his reforms. For a more detailed account of the reforms initiated by Fuat Paşa, see Clay, 2000: 60–73.

[46] Shaw, 1975 and 1978.

[47] For the Turkish translation of the report, see 'Osmanlı Maliyesi Hakkında İngiliz Raporları: 1861–92'. Hobart and Foster also noted the reluctance of Turkish officials to share any information with the representatives of a foreign country.

[48] Vincent Caillard, 'The Truth About Turkish Finances'. *Fortnightly Review*, September 1885. CFB Reel 202, Vol. 23.

[49] *Ibid.* In reality the system described by Caillard was very similar to central planning as understood today. In Caillard's language the term 'decentralization' had a negative connotation, emphasizing the information asymmetry between the central and local authorities and the unreliable information flow from *vilayets* to the capital, which naturally led to a seriously flawed budget system.

[50] According to Du Velay, similar payment orders were issued in France when the treasury had difficulty in fulfilling its financial obligations to contractors. However, in the Ottoman Empire, due to the uncertainty about the payment date, contractors often charged very high interest on these drafts. For details of the *havale* system, see Du Velay, 1978: 470–472. Blaisdell does not give a detailed account of the *havale* system. However, he implies that the bureaucrats received commissions in return for larger discounts on these payment orders made to contractors. Also, since the payment orders made by the ministries required the approval of the ministry of finance, he argues that the system involved 'favoritism' among the ministries as well (Blaisdell, 1929: 14–15).

[51] Feis, 1974: 313.

[52] Blaisdell, 1929: 15, notes that 'the extravagant tastes of Medjid (Sultan Abdülmecit) and Aziz (Sultan Abdülaziz) during the middle of the nineteenth century had necessitated a series of incumbents ingenious enough to meet royal demands'.

[53] See Kazgan, 1985.

[54] 'The New Turkish Budget', *Economist*, 25 April 1874. CFB, Reel 193, Vol. III.

[55] For a detailed account of the previous attempts see Clay, 2000: 14–60.

[56] In theory multiple currencies can exist. However, the existence of a continuously depreciating currency would lead individuals to spend in terms of this currency and save in terms of the other. Consequently, the 'bad money' would drive the 'good money' out of circulation. Another reason for the bank's insistence on the complete withdrawal of *kaimes* could be the bank's lack of confidence in the government. As noted by Clay, 'Had the withdrawal been anything less than complete, then given the Ottoman political system, a new set of ministers would probably sooner or later have increased the volume in circulation again' (Clay, 2000: 62).

[57] Pamuk, 2004: 25.

[58] Clay, 2000: 73.

[59] Clay, 2000: 74.

[60] Clay, 2000: 73–78.

[61] Feis, 1974: 322.

[62] For the Turkish transliterations of the original texts of the loan contracts underwritten by the BIO, see Ölçer, 1989.

[63] Eldem, 2005: 438. The 1862 loan was considered successful due to the fact that the effective interest rate charged on this loan was 0.8 percent lower than the previous loan contract in 1860, which was hypothecated on almost the same revenues.

[64] See Figure 3.6 for the spread between the yield of British consols and Ottoman bonds.

[65] *The Navy*, 26 September 1874. CFB, Reel 193, Vol. III.

[66] Blaisdell, 1929: 77.

[67] *Times*, 26 September 1874. CFB, Reel 193, Vol. III.

[68] *The Navy*, 26 September 1874. CFB, Reel 193, Vol. III.

[69] Clay, 2000: 234.

[70] 'Turkish Finance: Report of the Financial Commission', *Financier*, 11 May 1874. CFB, Reel 193, Vol. III.

[71] The functions bestowed on the bank were extremely far reaching. As argued by T.C. Bruce, the chairman of the BIO's London committee, 'the proposed arrangement was without parallel in the history of independent companies or financial institutions in the world' (Clay, 2000: 239). Despite the fact that that these arrangements were never fully practiced, this example itself suffices to illustrate the extent of financial difficulties experienced by the Porte. In order to borrow from abroad, the Porte was left with no other option but to propose an arrangement that was not witnessed even in colonial regimes.

[72] *Navy*, 26 September 1874. CFB, Reel 193, Vol. III; Yerasimos, 1976: 819–821; Blaisdell, 1929: 68–69.
[73] *Times*, 26 September 1874. CFB, Reel 193, Vol. III.
[74] In 1874, the BIO was also heavily criticized in the European press for not preventing future borrowings of the Ottoman government but instead helping it and thus risking the assets of the European bondholders. However, this policy was completely in accord with the bank's short-term interests since the bank received a sizeable commission from each loan issue contracted by the bank (Blaisdell, 1929: 69).
[75] 'The New Turkish Budget', *Economist*, 25 April 1874. CFB, Reel 193, Vol. III. For similar views on the reliability of the budget, see 'The Latest Turkish Reform Programme', *Stock Exchange Review*, April 1874. CFB, Reel 193, Vol. III.
[76] *Times*, 26 September 1874. CFB, Reel 193, Vol. III. Double-entry bookkeeping is an accounting technique that records each transaction as both a credit and a debit. Credit entries represent the sources of financing, and the debit entries represent the uses of that financing. Since each credit has one or more corresponding debits and vice versa, the system of double-entry bookkeeping always leads to a set of balanced ledger credit and debit accounts. The history of double-entry bookkeeping dates back to thirteenth century. As noted by historians, it was first practiced in Genoa for precision purposes. It grew rapidly, particularly among large firms, and gradually replaced single-entry bookkeeping. For the creditors it made it easier to monitor the movements in the debtor's accounts and increased the reliability of the financial statements made by the debtor.

As pointed out by Kuran, the development of double-entry bookkeeping in Europe as a standard accounting principle was in response to the developing needs of the large partnerships. In the Ottoman Empire, on the other hand, due to the Islamic inheritance system, commercial enterprises generally remained small and short-lived. Members of small partnerships did not feel the need to develop sophisticated or standardized accounting techniques required to facilitate communication and coordination among large numbers of bondholders. Hence, the absence of double-entry bookkeeping in the Middle East until the late nineteenth century can be explained by the absence of large partnerships (Kuran, 2005b).

According to Kuran, it was the egalitarian Islamic inheritance system that limited the size and duration of partnerships, while primogeniture, a widely used inheritance practice in Europe, facilitated the preservation and growth of enterprises. Islamic law, requiring the division of estates among numerous heirs upon the death of a partner, inadvertently raised the costs of liquidating a partnership prematurely.

Accordingly, Middle Eastern merchants minimized the risk of premature liquidation by limiting the size and duration of their partnerships. For details on how the Islamic inheritance system hindered the development of large partnerships, also see Kuran, 2004.

In the Ottoman Empire, the development of double-entry bookkeeping was in the state sector (Güvemli, 2000). After the establishment of the OPDA, the state had two separate budgets: one concerning the revenues of the Ministry of Finance and the other concerning revenues controlled by the OPDA. While the OPDA used double-entry bookkeeping in its financial records, the state continued to use single-entry bookkeeping. From Güvemli's accounts, we understand that the Ottoman authorities had observed the precision and accuracy of double-entry bookkeeping used by the BIO in 1860s, and considered the adoption of this principle in 1880 (Güvemli, 2000: 222). However, due to a lack of trained personnel this modern accounting principle could not be adopted by the Ministry of Finance until as late as the 1910s. Although it often goes unmentioned in the literature, there is no doubt that the OPDA, by introducing this modern accounting principle to the state finances, played a crucial role in its adoption by the Ministry of Finance.

77 *Times*, 26 September 1874. CFB, Reel 193, Vol. III. For details of the convention, see 'The Convention Between the Turkish Government and the Imperial Ottoman Bank', *Financier*, 31 March 1875, CFB, Reel 193, Vol. IV.

78 Clay, 2000: 591.

79 Blaisdell, 1929: 76.

80 Clay, 2000: 280.

81 Clay: 2000: 297.

82 Blaisdell, 1929: 80–81.

83 For the default to occur state expenditures should grow faster than the revenues. In the Ottoman case, with the exception of the 1870 loan that was allocated to the construction of the Rumeli Railway, none of the loans were apportioned to infrastructural investments that could facilitate economic growth and lead to an increase in state revenues. As illustrated in Table 1.1., other loans contracted in the pre-OPDA era were allocated to the following areas: military expenditure, luxury expenditures by the Sultan, debt repayments and the recurring budget deficits. For a critique of the Ottoman policy of foreign borrowing for consumption purposes, see Kazgan, 1982.

84 Apparently this view found supporters in the capital. After Nedim Paşa was taken off the power the Mithat Paşa government established a commission to investigate the charges on the ex- Grand Vezir. Yeniay, 1964.

85 *Times* 13 July 1877. CFB, Reel 193, Vol. II.

[86] 'Advantages of the 1854 bondholders: Meeting of the Bondholders', *Standard*, 10 April 1877. CFB, Reel 196, Vol. IX.
[87] Letter to the editor, *Daily Telegraph*, 29 March 1877 : CFB ; Reel 193, VI:9
[88] Letter to the editor, *Daily Telegraph*, 30 March 1877: Newspaper Cutting files CFB; Reel 193, Vol. I.
[89] *Times*, 7 July 1877. Newspaper Cutting files CFB, Reel 193, Vol. II. For details of the Egyptian tribute loans. See the 'Egyptian Tribute: A Short History of the Tribute Loans' issued by the Office of Egyptian Tribute Bondholder's League. Newspaper Cutting files CFB, Reel 193,Vol. II.
[90] The Turkish Debt: Meeting of the 1854 Bondholders, *Bullionist*, 14 April 1877. CFB, Reel 193, Vol. II.
[91] Memo from Mr Palmer to the Earl of Derby, November, 1875. F.O. 434/035:75.
[92] Letter to the Editor, *Times*, 2 April 1877. CFB, Reel 193,Vol. I.
[93] *Hornet*, 19 July 1877. CFB, Reel 193, Vol. II.
[94] The guaranteed loan of 1855 was partly secured on the tribute and partly on other revenues. For the full service of the loans the government would have to pay this amount from other sources to the holders of the 1854 loan (Clay, 2000: 370).
[95] Clay, 2000: 370.
[96] Declaration of the Loan by the London Agency of the Imperial Ottoman Bank, 8 December 1877. CFB, Reel 197, Vol. XI.
[97] *Truth*, 31 May, 1877. CFB, Reel 197, Vol. XI. For the reactions to the issue of the 1877 loan also see *Times* 13 July 1877. CFB, Reel 193, Vol. II.
[98] 'A New Turkish Loan', *Bullionist,* 19 May 1877. CFB, Reel 197, Vol. XI.
[99] 'Letter to the Editor', *Daily Telegraph*, 4 April 1877. CFB, Reel 193, Vol. II.
[100] While most people were reluctant to accept *kaime*s that were rapidly depreciating, the civil servants and the military personnel who received their wages in *kaimes* had no alternative. In the case of contractors working for the state, their mistrust of *kaimes* certainly led them to charge significantly higher prices when paid in these banknotes.
[101] For details see Clay, 2000: 350–351.
[102] Pamuk, 2004: 23.
[103] Pamuk, 2004: 25.
[104] Clay, 2000: 367.
[105] For details on how the Islamic inheritance system hindered the development of large partnerships, see Kuran, 2004.
[106] Clay, 2000: 367.
[107] Suvla, 1966: 102.

[108] Amount outstanding during the signing of the convention. Including LT 120,000 advance made as a prerequisite of the convention. See the table in Clay, 2000: 460–461.

[109] See 'The History of the Turkish External Debt' in the Annual Reports of the CFB.

[110] 'The Ottoman Loan of 1862', *Bullionist*, 6 December 1879. CFB, Reel 200, Vol. XV.

[111] According to the calculations of Guedella, the chairman of the English Committee of the General Debt, foreign bondholders would receive only 0.5 percent on the nominal value of their loans which would be divided (Clay, 2000: 462).

[112] Clay, 2000: 470.

[113] Clay, 2000: 473.

[114] Clay, 2000: 479.

[115] *Financier*, 15 October 1875.

[116] *Daily Telegraph*, 16 May 1876. CFB, Reel 196, Vol. IX.

[117] Clay, 2004: 483.

[118] Mauro and Yafeh, 2003: 17

[119] Wynne, 1951: 49.

[120] While issuing a bond hypothecated on a certain source of revenue, the government issued a financial statement of the revenues obtained from this collateral in the past years and estimations for the future. In order to convince the investors for a second mortgage, these revenues were often overstated. Nevertheless, these successive pledges were often met with suspicion in the financial markets and led to high risk premiums.

[121] See Pamuk, 1994.

[122] 1872 Treasury Bonds, which were also issued without security, are not included because of the provision that they were to be converted into 5 percent General Debt specially created for this purpose. For details, see Clay, 2000: 469.

[123] Clay, 2000: 200.

[124] 'Last Words and Warnings to the Various Classes of Bondholders', by H. Guedella, Chairman of the English Committee of the General Debt of Turkey, CFB. May 1881, Reel 200, Vol. 17.

[125] *Ibid.*

[126] *Ibid.*

[127] Total estimated revenue of the Ottoman treasury in 1874–75 was Ps 2,480,742,000. However, this hardly serves as a precise measure to understand the magnitude of the debt. As mentioned before, treasury revenues in this period were

often overstated and actual collections were not reported at the end of the fiscal year. The 1874–75 budget figures, despite the establishment of a private commission in charge of controlling the accuracy of the budget, seems to be overstated since it estimates an approximate 20 percent increase in revenues as compared to the estimations for 1872–73. From the figures reported by Shaw, it can be observed that until 1903–4, the actual revenues of the treasury did not exceed Ps 1,900,000,000 (Shaw, 1975: 451). Hence, the actual ratio of the annual revenues of the treasury to the total foreign debt should be considerably less than 9 percent.

128 'Mr. Bourke's Report', *Statist*, 14 January 1881. CFB, Reel 201, Vol. 20.

129 During the negotiations, the government proposed that a reduction be made on the basis of the amount received by the government for each loan, excluding the commissions paid to underwriters. The representatives of bondholders, on the other hand, insisted that the outstanding totals be reduced according to the issue prices figured in the prospectuses of each loan. For details, see the 'History of Turkish Debt' in the Annual Reports of the CFB: 1902–3, 1903–4. A detailed account of the negotiations can also be found in Clay, 2002 and Blaisdell, 1929.

130 According to the report of the British representative, the Porte also demanded that the war indemnity and the floating debt be included in the negotiations. However, the creditors were determined to make no further compromise and these issues were left out. 'Mr. Bourke's Report', *Statist*, 14 January 1881. CFB, Reel 201, Vol. 20. Also see 'Turkey and Her Creditors', *Economist*, 11 January 1881. CFB, Reel 201, Vol. 20.

131 It was unlikely that the conceded revenues would yield any surplus over the maximum charges defined in the decree. This provision was included as a 'sop to the government's pride' (Blaisdell, 1929: 93). In 1903, with the consent of the OPDA, a supplementary decree was issued introducing new provisions under which the government might profit (Annual Report of the CFB, 1903–4).

132 Eldem, 2005: 443.

133 Blaisdell, 1929: 97.

134 Blaisdell, 1929: 99.

135 Clay, 2000: 508.

136 As discussed earlier in this chapter, during the *Tanzimat* period the government attempted to establish a centralized tax system. However, the salaried agents of the central government who were sent out to the countryside faced many difficulties due to their lack of local knowledge and connections. Consequently, the new system failed to fulfill expectations, forcing the government to revert to the tax farming system.

[137] Clay, 2000: 479.
[138] On the British side of the consortium Layard and Glyn Co. was the largest shareholder. The French side comprised several banks and bankers headed by the Credit Mobilier. For details on the members of the consortium and the general committee of the bank, see Autheman, 2002.
[139] Clay, 2000: 472.
[140] Clay, 2000: 482.
[141] For critiques of Bourke's mission and the Decree of *Muharrem* see City Notes *Pall Mall Gazette*, 25 September 1881. CFB, Reel 201, Vol. 20; Joseph Nelson's letter to the Bondholders, 13 December 1881. CFB, Reel 201. Vol. 20; 'Turkey and Her Creditors', *Economist*, 11 January 1882. CFB, Reel 201, Vol. 20; 'Mr. Bourke's Report', *Statist*, 14 January 1882. CFB, Reel 201, Vol. 20; 'Mr. Bourke's Story', *Money*, 17 January 1882. CFB, Reel 201, Vol. 20.

3. Coordination, commitment and enforcement: Making sense of the OPDA

[1] Tomz, 1998
[2] Cole, Dow and English, 1995; Cole and Kehoe, 1994; Dixit and Londreagan, 2000; Eaton and Gersovitz, 1981; Grossmand and Huyck, 1988; Atkeson, 1991; Tomz, 1998, 1999, 2000; Schultz and Weingast, 1998.
[3] Tomz, 1998.
[4] North and Weingast, 1989.
[5] At the heart of Bulow and Rogoff's model is the observation that the capital market can provide a richer set of opportunities than just lending contracts. Hence, the defaulting country cannot be cut off from international capital markets entirely. Although it may no longer be able to borrow for domestic investment, it can still buy consumption-insurance contracts under which a country makes a payment upfront in return for a state contingent, non-negative future payment. The authors then prove that there are states of nature in which the sovereign will be better off by defaulting and using the amount due as debt service to make an upfront payment to another financial intermediary in exchange for a stream of contingent payments in the future (an insurance contract). This leads the authors to the conclusion that a pure reputational debt contract cannot be sustained in equilibrium (Bulow and Rogoff, 1989).
[6] Cole and Kehoe, 1995.
[7] Aggarwal, 1996.
[8] Hirschleifer, 1983.
[9] Eaton and Fernandez, 1995.
[10] Bulow and Rogoff , 1989a, 1989b.

[11] Rose, 2002.

[12] The reason behind the contradictory findings is that while Rose measures the effects of trade sanctions by using the bilateral trade variable, Martinez and Sandleris use total trade variable for the same purpose. If the total trade volume of the defaulter remains the same, then a fall in bilateral trade between the creditor and the debtor would not mean much as an indicator of effectiveness of the punishment mechanisms (Martinez and Sandleris, 2004). This empirical fact also highlights the importance of coordination between governments in punishing the debtors. If coordination cannot be maintained among the defaulting country's trade partners, then the creditor might even end up punishing itself without inflicting any costs on the debtor, depending on the nature of bilateral trade between the countries.

[13] Authors define supersanctions as instances where external military pressure or political pressure was imposed on defaulting nations (Mitchener and Weidenmier, 2004).

[14] Borchard, 1951; Suter and Stamm, 1992; Suter, 1992.

[15] Lindert and Morton, 1989; Lipson, 1989; Mauro and Yafeh, 2003; Tomz, 1998.

[16] Kaletsky, 1985.

[17] The reason for the discrepancies among these findings was that most economic models in sovereign debt literature restricted their analysis to economic parameters while ignoring the political ones. This ahistorical approach could partly work in analyzing the default incidents in the latter half of the twentieth century, when the use of military power to enforce compliance with debt contracts was almost unthinkable. However, as emphasized by Mitchener and Weidenmier (2004), until the end of the First World War, use of military power functioned as a major enforcement mechanism.

[18] Frieden, 1994.

[19] Tomz, 1998.

[20] Eaton and Fernandez, 1995.

[21] *Ibid.*

[22] Goodhart, 1972.

[23] Clemens and Williamson, 2004.

[24] *Ibid.*

[25] Eichengreen and Bordo, 2001.

[26] *Ibid.*

[27] The situation was no different in the Ottoman case. As noted by historians, state revenues were often exaggerated in the general budget for the issue of new bonds.

Kazgan, 1985 offers an example from the 1875 budget which shows a tremendous increase in state revenues.

28 Blaisdell, 1929: 44–45.

29 A similar cost-benefit analysis was made by the British government, which occupied Egypt after the default, but nevertheless refused to intervene on behalf of the Ottoman bondholders. This double standard was explained by the Foreign Secretary, Lord Salisbury, who argued that the intervention in the former case was not made merely to protect the bondholders, but also because it coincided with the 'high political interests' of the Empire. For details, see 'Lord Salisbury on Interference for Foreign Bondholders', *Statist*, 15 January 1880. CFB, Reel 200, Vol. XV.

30 Mauro and Yafeh, 2003.

31 In the annual report of the CFB its chief objects were defined as 'the vindication and protection of the rights and interests of the holders of foreign bonds, and the maintenance of the public credit of foreign governments by the propagation of sound doctrines with respect to the punctual fulfillment of their financial engagements, especially towards foreign creditors' (CFB Annual Report, 1874: 8). The CFB's revenues came from two sources. Firstly, the annual fees paid by the permanent members and the annual subscribers. Secondly, the commissions paid by debtor governments after debt settlement agreements (CFB Annual Report, 1874: 8–10).

32 For this purpose, a reading room was prepared for members, providing financial periodicals, newspapers and journals from all countries that had contracted loans in England. Moreover, it organized periodic lectures and discussions, inviting experts on issues of interest to the bondholders. The council also appointed agents to various countries in whose financial position the bondholders were interested. The periodic reports of these agents were available to all the members. All information at the disposal of the CFB was reported back to the members, who could apply to the council verbally or in writing to ask for material on any issue relating to foreign bonds (CFB Annual Report, 1874: 8–10).

33 Mauro and Yafeh, 2003: 13.

34 Wright, 2000.

35 The council stopped stock exchanges listing new Mexican issues in 1874 and new Turkish issues in 1877 until arrears were cleared. For a more detailed account of these instances see Mauro and Yafeh, 2003.

36 Suvla, 1966; Blaisdell, 1929.

37 Blaisdell, 1929: 105.

38 Feis, 1974: 337.

39 Blaisdell, 1929: 105.
40 'The Latest Turkish Reform Programme', *Stock Exchange Review*, April 1874. CFB, Reel 193, Vol. III.
41 'Turkey and Her Creditors', *Economist*, 11 January 1882. CFB, Reel 201, Vol. 20.
42 'Perhaps no impression is more widespread or more deeply seated than that Turkey is at her last gasp for money; that of all the maladies with which she is generally supposed to be afflicted, that of financial depletion is the most hopeless. The uncertainty of the elements ordinarily obtainable for arriving at any idea of the financial state of the country, and the veil of secrecy intentionally thrown by the government over its financial position render it an easy task to pessimists to maintain their depressing thesis, for contradiction is difficult. .... Thus the worst suppositions are those which find the greatest favor, and the less encouraging an estimate may be, the more truth it is supposed to contain' (Vincent Caillard, 'The Truth About Turkish Finances', *Fortnightly Review*, September 1885. CFB, Reel 202, Vol. 23).
43 The OPDA used double-entry bookkeeping, which records each transaction as both a credit and a debit. Credit entries represent the sources of financing, and the debit entries represent the uses of that financing. This system enabled both the administration and the creditors to track the specific sources of increase or decrease in revenues. The Ottoman state, on the other hand, still used single-entry bookkeeping, in which each transaction was entered as either debit or credit and was followed under the same column. This system made it difficult for the state, as well as the creditors, even when the financial records were available, to assess the sources of gain or loss in specific revenues. From the official documents of the Ministry of Finance we understand that the ministry decided to adopt this principle in 1880s in order to gain a 'real grasp of revenues and expenditures' (Güvemli, 2000: 222). However, the lack of trained personnel delayed this transition in state accounting until the 1910s (Karaarslan, 2004).
44 Some revenue sources were easier to publicize than others. For instance, in case of the Egyptian tribute a fixed sum was paid annually by the Egyptian Khedive to the central treasury. However, the collection of tithes was decentralized and details of these revenues were not easily obtainable.
45 *The Times*, 26 July 1865.
46 'Turkey and Her Creditors', *Economist*, 11 January 1882. CFB, Reel 201, Vol. 20; Mr. Bourke's Report, *Statist*, 14 January 1882. CFB, Reel 201, Vol. 20.
47 Edgar Vincent's Report to English, Dutch and Belgian Bondholders, 1882: 21.
48 'Turkey and Her Creditors', *Economist*, 11 January 1882. CFB, Reel 200, Vol. 17.

49 *Bullionist*, 16 May, 1874. CFB, Reel 193, Vol. III.
50 Blaisdell, 1929: 3.
51 Blaisdell, 1929: 152.
52 North and Weingast, 1989.
53 The term the 'age of high imperialism' was used by Scott B. Cook to denote the period between 1880 and 1914 (Cook, 1996).
54 For instance, if a bond with £100 face value bearing 4 percent nominal interest is issued at £80, this means that the effective interest on this particular bond is 5 percent.
55 UK consols were the pre-eminent debt issues of the eighteenth and nineteenth centuries. Hence, in the literature British consols are widely accepted as the indicator of the interest rate on the risk-free investment and as the base for risk premium (Mitchener, 2005).
56 CFB, 1908–1909: 32.
57 *Ibid.* The reliability of the budget stemmed mostly from the fact that it was drawn up under the guidance of a French expert suggested by the French government. As illustrated in Table 3.1, the subsequent LT 7,000,000 loan was issued in France. It should be noted that the 1909–1910 budget was the first budget published in the CFB annual reports. From 1909 onwards, Ottoman budgets continued to appear in these reports.
58 Yeniay, 1964; Suvla, 1966.
59 CFB, 1895–1896: 328–329.
60 Blaisdell, 1929: 152.
61 Suvla, 1966: 102.
62 For a detailed portrayal of the lavish expenditures of the Ottoman central bureaucracy in the pre-OPDA period, see Kazgan, 1982.
63 Issawi, 1980: 204.
64 Issawi, 1980: 200.
65 Blaisdell, 1929: 152.
66 *Times*, 16 December 1880. CFB, Reel 200, Vol. XVII.
67 Blaisdell, 1929: 125.
68 *Stock Exchange Review*, April 1874. CFB, Reel 193, Vol. III. For a Western perspective on the working of Turkish bureaucracy also see 'Business prospects in Turkey', *Financial News*, 4 March 1910. CFB, Reel 207, Vol. 32.
69 Morawitz, 1902: 288.
70 Blaisdell, 1929: 125.
71 Pamuk, 1994: 197–200.

[72] For the data on capital outflow arising from foreign loans, see Pamuk, 1994: 66. The role of the OPDA in the realization of surplus generated in the core economies and the transfer of resources from periphery to the core serves as one of the key case studies forming the basis of Rosa Luxemburg's theory of imperialism (Luxemburg, 1951). For similar argument also see Blaisdell, 1929; Feis, 1974; Issawi, 1980; Novichev, 1979; Owen, 1993; Parvus, 1977; Suter, 1992.
[73] Toprak, 1995: 115.
[74] Pamuk, 1994: 76.
[75] From the military perspective, the effect of the railway investments was twofold. On one hand, it would make it easier for the government to mobilize the army from one front to the other. This would enable the Porte to respond quickly to local revolts and strengthen the central authority even in remote regions. However, it would also make the Empire more vulnerable to foreign occupation by the European powers. This fact was also one of the strategic considerations behind foreign interest in the Ottoman railways. Nevertheless, the Porte's persistence in railway construction shows that the government believed the benefits of these projects far outweighed the potential costs.
[76] Özyüksel, 2000. For a monograph on the Anatolian Baghdad Railway, also see Özyüksel, 1988.
[77] Feis, 1973: 317.
[78] Blaisdell, 1929: 129.
[79] Owen, 1993: 196–197.
[80] To give just one example out of many, in 1903 the French government had delayed the progress of an Ottoman debt conversion scheme until the Turkish authorities had met the claims of a French railway company, agreed to leave the control of the docks of Istanbul in French hands and given orders for the supply of their military equipments to French factories (Owen, 1993: 198).
[81] Blaisdell, 1929: 215–224 enumerates these connections in detail. Also see Feis, 1978: 338.
[82] Blaisdell, 1929: 7.
[83] Pamuk, 1994: 81; Quataert, 1977: 159.
[84] Eldem, 1994: 93

4. Organizational structure of the OPDA and the administration of the indirect revenues

[1] Based on the budget figures reported by Shaw, 1975: 451.

[2] In 1910–11, the revenues apportioned to the service of public debt made up more than 32 percent of total state revenues. For details see CFB, 1911: 379–380.

[3] Blaisdell, 1929.

[4] Blaisdell: 1929: 6–7.

[5] Annual Report of the OPDA, 1883: 8–9.

[6] Edgar Vincent, 1882, Turkish Debt: Report to English, Dutch and Belgian Bondholders. CFB, Reel 201, Vol. 21.

[7] *Ibid.*

[8] Data regarding the gross receipts of the OPDA were obtained from Annual Reports of the OPDA and the CFB.

[9] By 1906–7 the increase in total gross receipts of the OPDA was only 66 percent, significantly below the 90 percent growth in the indirect contributions (CFB, 1906–1907: 409).

[10] These permanent assignments were the Eastern Rumelian Tribute, the bills on customs of Cyprus and *tömbeki* revenues.

[11] This revision in the commercial treaties brought an additional LT 918,438 in 1908–9, the first year it was practiced for the whole 12 months. This amount made up around 25 percent of the OPDA's gross receipts for the same year (CFB, 1908–1909: 357).

[12] For an example of the complaints of the OPDA officials about these treaties see Adam Block's article, 'The Commercial Independence of Turkey', *Times*, 14 December 1908.

[13] Morawitz, 1978: 222.

[14] For instance, the circumference of the salt lake in Koçhisar was approximately 120 miles. The situation was similar in Aleppo and İzmir where the salt works consisted of several small salt lakes spread over a sea coast about 45 miles in length and separated from one another by marshes (OPDA, 1884: 11–12).

[15] For instance the sale price of salt in Basra was ten times the price in Aleppo, where some of the salt works were located (Du Velay, 1978: 310–311).

[16] Blaisdell, 1929: 109.

[17] CFB, 1906–1907: 396.

[18] Morawitz, 1978: 222.

[19] OPDA, 1886: 34.

[20] OPDA, 1885: 32; CFB, 1892–1893: 10.

[21] OPDA, 1883: 10.

[22] CFB, 1892–1893: 10.

[23] Blaisdell, 1929: 111.

[24] CFB, 1910–1911: 363; Du Velay, 1978: 312.

[25] CFB, 1907–08: 401.

[26] OPDA, 1884: 10–11.

[27] CFB, 1906–07: 396. A contract was signed with the Comptoir Nationale D'Escompte for the export of salt to India; CFB: 1892–1893: 10.

[28] *Economist*, 12 November 1892.

[29] Blaisdell, 1929: 110. According to the statistics for the year 1910–11, around 95 percent of the exports went to India. The rest was exported to Serbia, Montenegro, Bulgaria and Romania (Mc Carthy, 1982: 237). In 1908–9 export revenues made up around 10 percent of the OPDA's salt revenues. To give an idea of the magnitude of these revenues, the monthly salary of a ministry official was around LT 14 for the same year. Computations are based on the personal files of 366 officials of the Ottoman foreign ministry (Findley, 1986: 84).

[30] Blaisdell, 1929: 110.

[31] CFB, 1914–1915: 328.

[32] Issawi, 1980: 253–254.

[33] Issawi, 1880: 254.

[34] Some silkraisers and merchants in Bursa had traveled to France to observe the Pasteur technique in its birthplace and implement it back home. Quataert notes that 'even with direct access to the source of the innovation and in the presence of a permanent French colony at Bursa, the technology transfer was unsuccessful' (Quataert, 1992: 50). The individual experiences of the Bursa merchants suggest that the prevention of the disease required a more institutionalized effort such as the one during the OPDA era.

[35] Quataert, 1992: 51.

[36] OPDA, 1884: 14.

[37] The OPDA administered the silk tithe revenues of the districts contiguous with İstanbul: Bursa, Samsun and Edirne.

[38] OPDA, 1884: 14.

[39] Blaisdell, 1929: 111.

[40] 'Silk Culture in Turkey: The Benefits of M. Pasteur's Discovery', *Daily Times*, 5 December 1893.

[41] The silkworms fed on mulberry leaves. CFB, 1907–1908.

[42] Blaisdell, 1929: 111.

[43] Quataert, 1992: 52.
[44] Quataert, 1992: 52–53.
[45] Du Velay, 1978: 325.
[46] Quataert, 1992: 53.
[47] The territorial losses included Salonica, one of the silk centers of the Empire, where the OPDA made considerable investments in order to stimulate silk production.
[48] Blaisdell, 1929: 111.
[49] The OPDA was assigned the administration of the silk tithe in certain provinces such as Bursa, Samsun, İstanbul, Edirne, İzmit (OPDA, 1882: 5–6). Beirut was another important silk-producing center but it was outside the responsibility of the OPDA, so the OPDA regulations were not enforced on the silk producers there.
[50] Only right before the First World War, when the profit margins of the industry were severely squeezed, did it become possible to break the monopoly of the imported eggs with a significant number of locally produced ones. These eggs, though cheap, were not subject to the same quality control system as the one implemented by the Pasteur Institute in Anatolia (Owen, 1993: 252).
[51] Shaw, 1975: 434–435.
[52] In some cases the penalty was applied as 3 percent of the original value of the document (Shaw, 1975: 436).
[53] In terms of the stamp law, unstamped contracts were unenforceable if a conflict arose between the parties (Shaw, 1975: 435).
[54] Blaisdell, 1929: 112. The reports of the OPDA do not give further information on why written contracts were used mostly among minorities and almost only in urban areas. A plausible explanation can be developed based on Kuran's argument that the Islamic inheritance system limited the size and durability of Islamic partnerships (Kuran, 2004). Simple forms of businesses did not require written contracts that would raise the transaction costs, and relied on verbal contracts traditionally ended with a handshake. The enforcement of these contracts often worked through reputational mechanisms, particularly in rural areas, where the reputational costs of defection would be much higher due to the smaller size of the business community. Also, widespread illiteracy among the Muslim population was surely another cause of the disproportionate reliance of Muslims on verbal contracts.
[55] 'In 1882, "foreign subjects" accounted for 112,000 of the 237,000 residents of Galata, İstanbul's leading commercial district; most were natives' (Kuran, 2004: 501–502). For a detailed explanation of the incentives for seeking foreign protection, see Kuran, 2004.

[56] Adam Block, 'The Commercial Independence of Turkey', *Times* 14 December 1908.
[57] OPDA, 1883: 11.
[58] OPDA, 1884: 12.
[59] Vincent, 1882: 15; OPDA, 1885: 32; OPDA, 1886: 36–37.
[60] CFB, 1905–1906: 38–39.
[61] Avcıoğlu, 1973: 125.
[62] CFB, 1900–1901: 403.
[63] *Ibid.*
[64] CFB, 1901–2: 399; CFB, 1902–3: 385.
[65] OPDA, 1885: 33.
[66] Önsoy, 1999: 198.
[67] CFB, 1907–08: 408.
[68] CFB, 1910–1911: 363.
[69] Shaw, 1975: 441–442.
[70] During the eighteenth century various *örfi* levies were imposed on grapes as they were shipped. A new prohibitions tax was also imposed on spirits sold in the market. The revenues were primarily farmed out to non-Muslim money lenders (Shaw, 1975: 442).
[71] Shaw, 1975: 443.
[72] Önsoy, 1999: 188–189.
[73] Blaisdell, 1929: 112; Önsoy, 1999: 189–190.
[74] In 1892, the *Economist* noted that the increase in the French tariff on wines had caused serious disturbances among the vine growers (*Economist*, 12 November 1892).
[75] CFB, 1906–07: 397; CFB, 1909–1910: 32.
[76] CFB, 1907: 408.
[77] According to the new law, the first 20 percent of the beer sold each month would be exempted from tax, while the rest of the sales would be subjected to the 15 percent sales tax applied to all other alcoholic beverages (Shaw, 1975: 443).
[78] CFB, 1910–1911: 363.
[79] Coverage of the OPDA's taxation rights in the fishing industry were extended in 1888, following the foreign loan contracted by Deutsche Bank, including other lakes, rivers and seas in the Empire. However, this arrangement excluded the fishery revenues collected by the *Hazine-i Hassa* (treasury of the Sultan) (Önsoy, 1999: 189).
[80] Blaisdell, 1929: 113.
[81] CFB, 1906–1907: 397.

[82] Önsoy, 1999: 199–200.
[83] CFB, 1909–1910: 32.
[84] CFB, 1910–1911: 363.

5. The tobacco sector and the Régie Company

[1] From Katip Çelebi in Issawi, 1980: 249.
[2] Doğruel and Doğruel, 2000: 26. Historical accounts do not specify the reasons behind the legalization of tobacco. One possible reason is that the rapid growth in tobacco consumption, due to its addictive nature, must have made the enforcement of harsh penalties even more difficult, forcing the state to back down. Also, as the size of the tobacco sector continued to grow, it should have led to the emergence of a lobby that had vested interests in the legalization of tobacco, such as tobacco producers, the *mültezims* who collected taxes in tobacco-producing regions, and tobacco sellers. Even though there is no specific information regarding the role of this lobby in the legalization of tobacco consumption, it might have played a role in the process. Finally, if cultivators chose to cultivate tobacco despite heavy restrictions on its consumption, this was due to the fact that it was more profitable than other alternative crops. In this context, legalization of tobacco consumption would lead to an increase in the auction prices of the tax farms in the tobacco-producing regions and ultimately benefit the government in economic terms.
[3] Schechter, 2003: 60; Doğruel and Doğruel, 2000: 25.
[4] http://www.tobacco.org/resources/history/Tobacco_History.html
[5] Schechter, 2003: 60; Cox, 2000: 22.
[6] The *Los Angeles Times* said that a significant proportion of Americans were 'passive supporters of the Crescent' who were opposed to the disintegration of the Turkish Empire, not because they love the Christians less, just that they love the cigarettes more (*Los Angeles Times*, 17 October 1912).
[7] Edgar Vincent's Report to English, Dutch and Belgian Bondholders in 1882, CFB, Reel 201, Vol. 21.
[8] Article 9 of the Decree of *Muharrem*.
[9] Starting capital of the company was LT 4,400,000 of which the Ottoman Bank owned 50 percent while the Crédit Anstalt and Bleichröder bank groups owned 30 percent and 20 percent respectively.
[10] From the table in Yerasimos, 1977: 960.
[11] Quataert, 1983: 14.
[12] Vincent, 1882: 13–14.
[13] Blaisdell, 1929: 114.

[14] OPDA, 1884: 8–9.
[15] OPDA, 1883.
[16] Based on Article 7 of the Régie Concession. For a transliterated version of the concession see Doğruel and Doğruel 2000: 331–337.
[17] For details of the BIO's interest in the Régie Concession, see Clay, 2000.
[18] Eastern Rumelia was not included in the monopoly due to the terms of the Treaty of Berlin in 1878. The company collected duties from tobacco exports to Eastern Rumelia.
[19] The amount of taxes on exports to other countries was negligible due to the 1861 trade agreement.
[20] Régie Concession in Doğruel and Doğruel, 2000: 331–337.
[21] Quataert, 1983: 15–16.
[22] Article 15 of the Régie Concession.
[23] 'If the company, assisted by the government, cannot enforce it, the Régie is sure to fail as every peasant will grow a few okes (okkas) of tobacco for his own consumption' (Vincent, 1882: 12).
[24] Thobie (1977) and Quataert (1983: 17) reports the number of private factories shut down during this period as 300. According to Novichev (1979: 89) this number was around 450.
[25] Novichev, 1979: 89, Owen, 1993: 152.
[26] Annual Report of the Council of Foreign Bondholders, 1884.
[27] Mutluçağ, 1967. According to another source, from 1884–1908 the death toll was between 50 and 60 thousand (Zeki, 1928: 17, in Doğruel and Doğruel, 2000: 83).
[28] As of 1881 out of 5,704 officers employed at the OPDA only 88 were of foreign nationality. The vast majority of the Ottomans employed in the administration were Muslims (Vincent, 1882: 8).
[29] Quataert, 1983: 160.
[30] Vincent, 1882: 8–9.
[31] OPDA, 1884–1885: 11
[32] *Ibid.*
[33] Issawi, 1966: 60–61.
[34] *Statist*, 5 May, 1883. CFB, Vol. 22.
[35] After this year, the number of cultivators fluctuated below 140,000, with the exception of 1903–4, until after 1909–10 (Eldem, 1994: 70). For details see Table 4.7.
[36] For a more complete account of the demonstrations and riots against the Régie, see Quataert, 1983.

[37] Quataert (1983) and Keskinkılıç (2000) report a failed attempt to link the anti-Régie movement in the Ottoman Empire to that of Iran, which was suppressed by the government before it gained any public support.
[38] Quataert, 1983: 19–20.
[39] Quataert , 1983; Doğruel and Doğruel, 2000.
[40] Doğruel and Doğruel, 2000: 93.
[41] Quataert, 1983: 19.
[42] Quataert, 1983: 34.
[43] Quataert, 1983: 21
[44] Quataert (1983) and Doğruel and Doğruel (2000) report several incidents pointing to the involvement of army members in contraband activities.
[45] Quataert, 1983: 31. Since Quataert does not report the total number of complaints filed by the Régie, it is difficult to grasp the real magnitude of the court's disregard toward the Régie's complaints.
[46] Surveillance expenses were reported as LT 154,057 for the year 1895 in the annual report published in 1896 but corrected as LT 161,883 in the annual report in 1896. Surveillance expenses were reported as LT 150,725 for the year 1891 in the annual report published in 1892 but corrected as LT 150,723 in the annual report in 1893.
[47] Quataert, 1983: 25.
[48] Çakırcalı Mehmet Efe (1872–1911) was a regional heroic figure who was involved in smuggling activities until his death during a shootout (Paksoy, 2003). Several songs in Turkish folklore praise the fight of these smugglers against the *kolcus.*
[49] Quataert, 1983: 27; Doğruel and Doğruel, 2000: 96. After several complaints from the Régie, the government decided that surveillance forces could be accompanied by the village elders if neither the imam nor the *muhtar* was around. But then both would be fined if they could not report a valid reason for their absence.
[50] Quataert, 1983: 25.
[51] Quataert, 1983: 162.
[52] There were basically two reasons for the Egyptian government's harsh restrictions on domestic tobacco cultivation. First of all the the Egyptians found it rather costly and more difficult to tax the cultivators as compared to imposing duties on imports. Secondly, tobacco importers formed a powerful financial elite that had been pressuring the government to create further restrictions on domestic cultivation. To this end, they petitioned the government arguing that low taxes on tobacco cultivation would cause a decline in state revenues (Schecter, 2003: 54–56).
[53] CFB, 1884: 31–32.
[54] CFB, 1884: 31.

[55] Lowering the Egyptian duties on Turkish tobacco would not have much impact on the existing circumstances, under which smuggling had flourished. The Egyptian duties on Turkish tobacco were already set as low as 5 percent. The real cause of the problem was the 10 percent duty imposed by the Régie. The company did not agree to lower the export duty due to its monopoly in the market. As discussed later, the loss of monopoly in Egyptian market was also the main cause of the company's demand for compensation from the OPDA.
[56] CFB, 1884: 6.
[57] The average of the Egyptian duty revenues for the previous three years was LT 154,838. For the eleven months of operation during the first year of the concession, this corresponds to an estimated revenue of LT 141,934. However, actual revenue obtained during these eleven months was only LT 50,672. The Régie reported the LT 91,262 difference between the estimated and actual revenues as the loss suffered due to the loss of Egyptian monopoly (Annual Report of the Régie, 1885: 7–8; OPDA, 1884–1885: 11). We should also note that, in the first annual report of the Régie Company, the duty revenue from Egypt and the loss caused by the Greek-Egyptian convention were declared as LT 49,388 and LT 88,949. respectively. The disparity between the figures above and the ones mentioned in the first report was due to the difference in the conversion rates employed in the first and later reports of the Régie. In the first annual report, the conversion rate was LT 1= Ps 102.6, while in later reports the same figures were converted to LT based on the LT 1= Ps 100 conversion rate. To maintain consistency throughout this text, all figures are converted to LT by using the LT 1= Ps 100 conversion rate.
[58] CFB, 1884: 6–7.
[59] OPDA, 1884–1885: 11. For a detailed account of Vincent's career in Egypt and in the Ottoman Empire, see Auchterlonie, 2000. The article examines the concept of 'gentlemanly capitalism' as embodied in the career of Sir Edgar Vincent, who, despite his noble background, chose to spend 20 years of his life in the middle east as a financier and imperial administrator promoting 'the civilizing mission of Britain' in the region.
[60] Total amount of advances breaks down as follows, LT 100,000 in 1885–1886, LT 61,418 in 1886–1887, and LT 49,144 in 1887–1888 (Annual Reports of the Régie 1886, 1887, and 1888). We should also note that in the annual reports of the Régie, these advances were treated as ordinary revenues. Hence for the respective years the company's revenues were overstated.
[61] CFB, 1887: 168.

62 After 1896–97, export duty revenues stated in the Annual Reports of the Régie include the LT 50,000 annual compensation paid by the OPDA. To reach the actual duty revenues, this amount is deducted from the figures stated in the original reports.

63 CFB, 1887: 160.

64 LT 38,000 in 1888–89, LT 44,000 in 1889–90 and LT 50,000 later on. Annual Reports of the Régie.

65 CFB, 1887: 167.

66 'The Turkish Tobacco Régie', *Financial Times*, 16 August 1892; 'Turkey and the Régie', *Financial News*, 23 September 1897.

67 In 1892, the salt revenue of the OPDA from the sales in the Black Sea region increased by 50 percent as a consequence of the decline in smuggling activities in the region (CFB, 1892: 10).

68 CFB, 1894: 17.

69 CFB, 1895: 325.

70 Quataert, 1983: 30–35.

71 Annual Reports of the Régie, 1898–99.

72 Quataert, 1983: 36.

73 The spread between the average export prices and the Régie's average purchase prices could partly be explained by the fact that under the terms of the tobacco concession the company was compelled to buy all the tobacco produced in the Empire, which also meant buying low quality tobacco in some cases. Consequently purchase of low quality tobacco would pull down the average purchase prices. However, the tremendous increase in the annual exported tobacco figures suggest that the cultivators found it more profitable to sell their tobacco to exporters.

74 Annual Reports of the Régie.

75 Quataert, 1983: 37.

76 The OPDA's revenue from the tobacco monopoly comprises an LT 750,000 annual payment of the Régie, 25 percent of the 5 percent founders' share in the profits of the previous year, repayment of advances in respective years, one-third of the remaining profits of the previous year until 1895–96 and a share in dividends. Later on, the OPDA received 35 percent of the profits of the previous year while the government's share was dropped to 30 percent. Beginning from 1904–5 figures reported in CFB reports are based on the current year's profits. From 1901–10, the OPDA's share in the Egyptian duties collected by the company was added to this amount. Finally, net receipts were obtained after the advances (from 1885–88), and the compensation paid by the OPDA (from 1888–1914) were subtracted from the total amount. Also note that the distribution of the founders' share, the repayment

of the advances and the distribution of the profits were made, in the mentioned order, after the deduction of 8 percent interest on capital, equal to LT140,800 for each year (Annual Reports of the Council of Foreign Bondholders).

In the 1894–95 annual CFB report, OPDA's revenue from the tobacco monopoly was reported as LT 791,941 and was corrected as LT 796,250 in the later report. Discrepancies between the figures under this heading in the 1895–96 report and those given in the 1894–95 report were due to the final accounts not having been closed when the 1894–95 report was published. In the interests of accuracy, the figures in the 1895–96 report have been taken into account.

77 OPDA, 1884: 188.

78 See Parvus Efendi, 1977 [1910].

79 Owen, 1993: 152

80 In 1897, reporting the lack of government cooperation in fighting against the tobacco smugglers, *Financial News* noted, 'As the Sultan contemplates to borrow abroad, it should not be difficult to induce him to correct his ways' ('Turkey and the Régie,' *Financial News*, 23 September 1897.

81 For details of the report, see Quataert, 1983: 26.

82 During the 1930s, TEKEL's revenues made up around 15 percent of total state revenues. By 1944, its share peaked at 20 percent (Doğruel and Doğruel, 2000: 183).

6. The role of the OPDA in the transformation of the Ottoman Economy

1 Suter, 1989 and 1992; Suter and Stamm, 1992.

2 Some defaults led to foreign occupation of the debtor countries such as Tunisia in 1881, Egypt in 1882 and Morocco in 1912 (Issawi, 1966: 94).

3 Eldem, 2005: 13.

4 Lenin, 1965 [1916].

5 Kuran points out the risk-return tradeoff faced by the Ottoman state in the conversion of short-term tax farms into longer-term or even life-term tax farms. The longer the tax farm period, the greater the bids of potential tax farmers, hence the greater the returns from the auctions. On the other hand, as the period lengthened, the probability of the tax farmer gaining political autonomy grew accordingly. As a result, tax farmers increased their political power and began claiming the right to bequeath farms to their descendants. This threatened the central authority of the government. In 1812, the government started to take over the management of tax farms in order to restore the central authority (Kuran, 2005b).

[6] In most European powers customs duties on imports varied between 15 and 25 percent, whereas the Ottomans were not allowed to exceed 8 percent (Morawitz, 1904: 201). In the 1820s, average tariff rates on manufactured products were around 50 percent in Britain (Chang, 2002: 17).

[7] Blaisdell, 1929: 153.

[8] North and Weingast, 1989.

[9] Kuran, 2004.

[10] One important feature of double-entry bookkeeping was the 'error catching' and antifraud feature. For instance, if a company inflated the cash on its books, due to the matching principle of double-entry bookkeeping, another account such as 'accounts receivable' needed to be adjusted. Since more than one account was affected by a false entry there was a greater chance of detecting fraud as compared to single-entry bookkeeping. Secondly, the dual nature of accounts enabled the auditor to understand the relationship between accounts and identify the sources of changes in revenues or expenses. For instance, an increase in cash could not be recorded without first identifying a credit account; hence it required the specification of the sources of cash flow.

[11] Kuran, 2005b.

[12] Güvemli, 2000.

[13] Güvemli, 2000: 222.

BIBLIOGRAPHY

Açba, S. 1989. *Osmanlı Devleti'nin Dış Borçlanması (1854–1914)*. Afyon: Anadolu Üniversitesi İ.İ.B.F.

Acheson, G.G. and J.D. Turner 2006. 'The Impact of Limited Liability on Ownership and Control: Irish Banking, 1877–1914.' *Economic History Review* 59(2): 265–433.

Agarwala, A.N. and S.P. Singh (eds) 1958. *The Economics of Underdevelopment*. New York: Oxford University Press.

Aggarwal, V.K. 1996. *Debt Games: Strategic Interaction in International Debt Rescheduling*. Cambridge: Cambridge University Press.

Akpınar, M. 2002. 'Reji Uygulamalarına Bir Tepki: Tütün Kaçakçılığı.' *Türkler* 14: 305–312.

Alavi, H. 1972. 'The State in Post-Colonial Societies: Pakistan and Bangladesh.' *New Left Review* 74: 59–81.

Amin, S. 1976. *Unequal Development*. New York: Monthly Review Press.

Arrighi, G. 1994. *The Long Twentieth Century*. London: Verso.

Atkeson, A. 1991. 'International Lending with Moral Hazard and Risk of Repudiation.' *Econometrica* 59: 1069–1089.

Avcıoğlu, D. 1973. *Türkiye'nin Düzeni*. İstanbul: Cem Yayınevi.

Avramovic. D. 1964. *Economic Growth and External Debt*. Baltimore: Johns Hopkins.

Auchterlonie, P. 2000. 'A Turk of the West: Sir Edgar Vincent's Career in Egypt and the Ottoman Empire.' *British Journal of Middle Eastern Studies* 27(1): 49–67.

Bailey, F.E. 1940. 'The Economics of British Foreign Policy, 1825–50.' *The Journal of Modern History* 12: 449–484.

Bardhan, P.K. 1967. 'Optimal Foreign Borrowing,' in *Essays on the Theory of Optimal Growth*, edited by K. Shell, 117–128. Cambridge, MA: MIT.

Bergesen A. and R. Schoenberg. 1980. 'Long Waves of Colonial Expansion and Contraction, 1415–1969,' in *Studies of the Modern World System, edited by* A. Bergesen, 231–277. New York: Academic.

Berkes, N. 1975. *Türk Düşününde Batı Sorunu*. Ankara: Bilgi Yayınevi.

Blaisdell, D. 1929. *European Financial Control in the Ottoman Empire: A Study of the Establishment, Activities, and Significance of the Administration of the Ottoman Public Debt*. New York: Columbia University Press.

Bukharin, N. 1987 [1917]. *Imperialism and World Economy*. London: Merlin Press.

Bulow, J. and K. Rogoff. 1989. 'Sovereign Debt: Is to Forgive to Forget?' *American Economic Review* 79: 43–50.

Caillard, V. 1885. 'The Truth About Turkish Finances.' *Fortnightly Review* September.

Cameron, R.A. 1993. *Concise Economic History of the World: From Paleolithic Times to the Present*. Second Edition. Oxford: Oxford University Press.

Cezar, Y. 1986. *Osmanlı Maliyesinde Bunalım ve Değişim Dönemi*. İstanbul: Alan Yayıncılık.

Chang, Ha-Joon. 2002. *Kicking Away the Ladder: Development Strategies in Historical Perspective*. London: Anthem Press.

Chase-Dunn, C. 1989. *Global Formation: Structures of the World Economy*. Cambridge and Oxford: Basil Blackwell.

Chase-Dunn, C. and P. Grimes 1995. 'World-System Analysis.' *Annual Review of Sociology* 21: 387–417.

Chenery, H.B. and A.B. Strout 1966. 'Foreign Assistance and Economic Development.' *American Economic Review* 56: 679–733.

Chew, S.C. and R.A Denmark 1996. 'On Development and Underdevelopment,' in *The Underdevelopment of Development: Essays In Honor of Andre Gunder Frank*, edited by S.C. Chew and R.A. Denmark, 1–16. California: Sage Publications.

Clay, C. 2000. *Gold for the Sultan*. London: I.B.Tauris.

Clemens, M. and J. Williamson 2004. 'Wealth Bias in the First Global Capital Market Boom 1870–1913.' *Economic Journal* 114 (April 2004): 311–44.

Cole, H. and P.J. Kehoe 1994. 'Reputation Spillover Across Relationships with Enduring and Transient Benefits: Reviving Reputation

Models of Debt.' Federal Reserve Bank of Minneapolis Research Department Staff Report 137/JV.

Cole, H., Dow, J. and W.B. English 1995. 'Default, Settlement, and Signalling: Lending Resumption in a Reputational Model of Sovereign Debt.' *International Economic Review* 36: 365–385.

Coleman, R.W. 1936. 'Pledged Revenue as Security for Government Bonds.' *The American Economic Review* 26(4): 667–682.

Cook, S. 1996. *Colonial Encounters in the Age of High Imperialism.* NY: Talman Company.

Coşgel, M. and T.J. Miceli 2005. 'Risk, Transaction Costs, and Tax Assignment: Government Finance in the Ottoman Empire.' *Journal of Economic History* 65(3): 806-821.

Council of Foreign Bondholders. Annual Reports of the Council of Foreign Bondholders, 1873-1914.

Council of Foreign Bondholders. Newspaper Cutting Files of the Council of Foreign Bondholders, 1870-1914.

Cox, H. 2000. *The Global Cigarette: Origins and Evolution of British American Tobacco 1880-1945.* Oxford: Oxford University Press.

Çizakça, M. 1987. 'Price History and the Bursa Silk Industry: A Study in Ottoman Industrial Decline,' in *The Ottoman Empire and the World Economy,* edited by H.İ. İnan, 1550–1650. Cambridge: Cambridge University Press.

Decdeli, H., I. Wallerstein and R. Kasaba 1987. 'The Incorporation of the Ottoman Empire into the World Economy,' in *The Ottoman Empire and the World Economy*, edited by H.İ. İnan, 88–102. Cambridge: Cambridge University Press.

Dixit, A and J. Londregan 2000. 'Political Power and the Credibility of Government Debt.' *Journal of Economic Theory* 94: 80–105.

Doğruel, F. and S. Doğruel 2000. *Osmanlı'dan Günümüze Tekel.* İstanbul: Tarih Vakfı Yayınları.

Du Velay, A. 1978 [1903]. *Türkiye Maliye Tarihi.* Translated by Maliye Tetkik Kurulu. Ankara: Maliye Bakanlığı Yayınları.

Eaton J. and R. Fernandez 1995. 'Sovereign Debt.' NBER Working Paper No. 5131.

Eichengreen, B. 1989 'Resolving Debt Crisis: An Historical Perspective,' in *The Latin American Debt Crisis,* edited by S. Edwards and F.Larrain. Oxford: Blackwell.

Eichengreen, B. and Bordo, M. 2001. 'Crises Now and Then: What Lessons from the Last Era of Financial Globalization.' NBER Working Paper No: 8716.

Eichengreen, B. and R. Portes 1989. 'After the Deluge: Default, Negotiation, and Readjustment during the Interwar Years,' in *International Debt Crisis in Historical Perspective,* edited by B. Eichengreen and P.H. Lindert, 12–47. Cambridge, MA: MIT Press.

Eldem, E. 1999. *Osmanlı Bankası Tarihi.* Translated by Ayşe Berktay. İstanbul: Osmanlı Bankası ve Tarih Vakfı Ortak Yayını.

—2005. 'Ottoman Financial Integration with Europe: Foreign Loans, the Ottoman Bank and the Ottoman Public Debt.' *European Review* 13(3): 431–445.

Eldem,V. 1994. *Osmanlı İmparatorluğu'nun İktisadi Şartları Hakkında Bir Tetkik.* Ankara: Türk Tarih Kurumu Basımevi.

Feis, H. 1974. *Europe the World's Banker, 1870–1914: An Account of European Foreign Investment and the Connection of World Finance With Diplomacy Before the War.* Clifton: Augustus M. Kelley Publishers.

Findley, C.V. 1986. 'Economic Bases of Revolution and Repression in the Late Ottoman Empire.' *Comparative Studies in Society and History* 28(1): 81–106.

Fishlow, A. 1985. 'Lessons From the Past: Capital Markets During the Nineteenth Century and the Interwar Period.' *International Organization* 39(3): 383–439.

Fişek, K. 1968. 'Osmanlı Dış Borçları Üzerine Düşünceler.' *Ankara Üniversitesi Siyasal Bilgiler Fakültesi Dergisi* 22(3).

Frank, A.G. 1998. *ReOrient: Global Economy in the Asian Age.* Berkeley: University of California Press.

Freiden, J. 1994. 'International Investment and Colonial Control: A New Interpretation.' *International Organization* 48: 559–593.

Genç, M. 1987. 'A Study of the Feasibility of Using Eighteenth Century Ottoman Financial Records as an Indicator of Economic Activity,' in *The Ottoman Empire and the World Economy,* edited by H.İ. İnan, 345–373. Cambridge: Cambridge University Press.

—2000. *Osmanlı İmparatorluğunda Devlet ve Ekonomi.* İstanbul: Ötüken Yayınları.

Giray, F. 2001. *Maliye Tarihi.* Bursa: Ezgi Kitabevi.

Goodhart, C. 1972. *The Business of Banking, 1891–1914.* London: Weidenfeld and Nicolson.

Griffiths, M. and T. O'Callaghan. *International Relations: The Key Concepts.* London: Routledge, 2002.

Grossman, H and J.V. Huyck 1988. 'Sovereign Debt as a Contingent Claim: Excusable Default, Repudiation, and Reputation.' *American Economic Review* 78: 1088–97.

Gürsoy, B. 1984. 'Düyun-u Umumiye İdaresi Üzerine Bir Değerlendirme.' *İstanbul Üniversitesi İktisat Fakültesi Mecmuası* 40(1–4).

Güvemli, O. 2000. *Türk Muhasebe Tarihi.* Vol.3. İstanbul: YMM Odası Yayınları.

Hildreth, R. 2001 [1837]. *The History of Banks.* Kitchener: Batoche Books Limited.

Hilferding, R. 1981 [1910]. *Finance Capital: A Study of the Latest Phase of Capitalist Development.* London, Boston : Routledge & Kegan Paul.

Hirshleifer, J. 1983. 'From Weakest Link to Best Shot: The Voluntary Provision of Public Goods.' *Public Choice* 41: 371–386.

Hobson, J.A. 1938 [1902]. *Imperialism: A Study.* London: G. Allen & Unwin Ltd.

Hulkiender, H. 2003. *Bir Galata Bankeri'nin Portresi: 1806–1884.* İstanbul: Osmanlı Bankası Arşiv Araştırma Merkezi.

Issawi, C. 1966. *The Economic History of the Middle East, 1800–1914.* Chicago: The University of Chicago Press.

—1980. *The Economic History of Turkey, 1800–1914.* Chicago: The University of Chicago Press.

Iversen, C. 1936. *Aspects of the Theory of the International Capital Movements.* Copenhagen: Levin & Munksgrad.

İnalcık, H. 1964. 'The Nature of Traditional Society,' in *Political Modernization in Japan and Turkey,* edited by R. Ward and D. Rustow. Princeton, NJ: Princeton University Press.

—1970. 'The Ottoman Economic Mind and Aspects of the Ottoman Economy,' in *Studies in the Economic History of the Middle East,* edited by M. Cook. London: Oxford University Press.

İnalcık, H. and D. Quataert 1994. *An Economic and Social History of the Ottoman Empire, 1300–1914.* Cambridge: Cambridge University Press.

İnan, H.İ. (ed.) 1987. *The Ottoman Empire and the World Economy.* Cambridge: Cambridge University Press.

İnan, H.İ. and Ç. Keyder 1987. 'Agenda for Ottoman History,' in *The Ottoman Empire and the World Economy*, edited by H.İ. İnan, 42–62. Cambridge: Cambridge University Press.

Jones, E.L. 1987. *The European Miracle, Environments, Economies and Geopolitics in the History of Europe and Asia.* Second Edition. Cambridge: Cambridge University Press.

Kahler, M. 1986. *Politics of International Debt.* Ithaca: Cornell University Press.

Kararaslan, E. 2004. 'Ülkemizde Devlet Muhasebesinin Serüveni.' *Sayıştay Dergisi* 54: 37–76.

Karamursal, Z. 1989. *Osmanlı Mali Tarihi Hakkında Tetkikler.* Second Edition. Ankara: Türk Tarih Kurumu.

Karpat, K.H. 1973. 'Structural Change, Historical Stages of Modernization, and the Role of Social Groups in Turkish Politics,' in *Social Change and Politics in Turkey*, edited by K. Karpat, 11–92. Leiden: E.J. Brill.

Kasaba, R. 1987. 'Incorporation of the Ottoman Empire, 1750–1820.' *Review (Journal of the Fernand Braudel Center)* 10(5/6): 805–847.

—1988. *The Ottoman Empire and the World Economy: The Nineteenth Century.* Albany: State University of New York.

Kazgan, H. 1982. 'Osmanlı Modeli Tüketim İçin Borçlanma.' *İstanbul Üniversitesi İktisat Fakültesi Mecmuası* 35(1–4).

—1985. 'Düyun-u Umumiye,' in *Tanzimattan Cumhuriyete Türkiye Ansiklopedisi*, 691–716. İstanbul: İletişim Yayınları.

—1991.*Galata Bankerleri.* İstanbul: TEB Yayıncılık.

Keskinkılıç, E. 1997. *Osmanlı Düyun-u Umumiye İdaresi'nin Kuruluşu, Gelişimi, Çalişmasi Safhalari ve Osmanlı Ekonomisine Etkileri.* Unpublished Dissertation, Ankara.

Keskinkılıç, E. 2000. 'Reji İdaresi ve Kuruluşu.' *Akademik Arastırmalar Dergisi Osmanlı Özel Sayısı* 4–5: 657–676.

Keyder, Ç. 1980. 'Ottoman Economy and Finances 1881–1918,' in *Social and Economic History of Turkey 1071–1920,* edited by O. Okyar and H. İnalcık, 323–328. Ankara: Meteksan.

Keyder, Ç. 1981. *The Definition of a Peripheral Economy: Turkey 1923–1929.* Cambridge: Cambridge University Press.

Keyder, Ç. 1987. *State and Class in Turkey: A Study of Capitalist Development.* London: Verso.

Keyder, Ç. 1988. 'Bureaucracy and Bourgeoisie: Reform and Revolution in the Age of Imperialism.' *Review (Journal of the Fernand Braudel Center)* 11(2): 151–165.

Kıray, E. 1999. *Osmanlı'da Ekonomik Yapı ve Dış Borçlar.* Second Edition. İstanbul: İletişim Yayıncılık.

Kömürcan, K. 1948. *Türkiye İmparatorluk Devri Borçlar Tarihçesi: Düyun-u Umumiye Tarihçesi.* İstanbul: İstanbul Yüksek Ekonomi ve Ticaret Okulu Yayınları.

Koraltürk, M. 1995. 'Osmanlı Dış Borçları ve 1875 Moratoryumu (6 Ekim 1875).' *Tarih ve Toplum Dergisi* 24(142): 50–55.

Krasner, S. 1999. *Sovereignty: Organized Hypocrisy.* Princeton, NJ: Princeton University Press.

Kuran, T. 2003. 'The Islamic Commercial Crisis: Institutional Roots of Economic Underdevelopment in the Middle East.' *Journal of Economic History*, 63 (June 2003): 414–46.

Kuran, T. 2004. 'The Economic Ascent of the Middle East's Religious Minorities: The Role of Islamic Legal Pluralism.' *Journal of Legal Studies*, 33 (June 2004): 475–515.

Kuran, T. 2005a. 'The Logic of the Ottoman Capitulations.' Chapter 10 of *Islam and Economic Underdevelopment* (unpublished book manuscript).

Kuran, T. 2005b. 'The Absence of Corporation in Islamic Law: Origins and Persistence.' *American Journal of Comparative Law* 53 (July 2005): 785–834.

Kuran, T. 2005c. 'The Logic of Financial Westernization in the Middle East.' *Journal of Economic Behavior and Organization* 56 (April 2005): 593–615.

Kurdakul, N. 1985. 'Osmanlı İstikrazları ve Abdulhamid'e İki Uyarı Mektubu.' *Tarih ve Toplum Dergisi* 4(22): 55–56.

Kurmuş, O. 1987. 'The Cotton Famine and its Effects on the Ottoman Empire,' in *The Ottoman Empire and the World Economy*, edited by H.İ. İnan, 160–169. Cambridge: Cambridge University Press.

Landes, D. 1998. *The Wealth of Poverty of Nations: Why Some Are So Rich and Some So Poor?* New York: W.W. Norton and Co.

Lenin, V.I. 1965 [1916]. *Imperialism, the Highest Stage of Capitalism.* Peking: Foreign Languages Press.

Luxemburg, R. 1968 [1913]. *The Accumulation of Capital.* New York: Monthly Review Press.

Martinez, J.V. and G. Sandleris 2004. 'Is it Punishment? Sovereign Defaults and the Decline in Trade'. Unpublished paper.

Mauro, P. and Y. Yafeh 2003. 'The Corporation of Foreign Bondholders'. IMF Working Papers No. 03/107.

McCarthy, J. 1982. *The Arab World, Turkey, and the Balkans (1878–1914): A Handbook of Historical Statistics.* Boston: G.K. Hall.

Meier, G.M. 1970. *Leading Issues in Economic Development: Studies in International Poverty*. New York: Oxford University Press.

Mensh , G. 1978. *Stalemate in Technology*. Cambridge, MA: Ballinger.

Mitchener, K.J. and M. Weidenmier. 2004. 'How are Sovereign Debtors Punished? Evidence from the Gold Standard Era.' Unpublished paper.

Modelski, G. 1977. 'The Long Cycle of Global Politics and the Nation State.' *Comparative Studies in Society and History* 20: 214–235.

Modelski, G. 1987. *Long Cycles in World Politics*. Basingstoke: Macmillan.

Morawitz, C. 1978 [1902]. *Osmanlı Maliyesi*. Ankara: Maliye Tetkik Kurulu Yayınları.

Morawitz, C. 1902. 'Public Debt of Turkey.' *The North American Review* 175: 275–288.

Morawitz, C. 1904. 'Obstacles to Reform in Turkey.' *The North American Review* 179: 194–206.

Mutluçağ, H. 1967. 'Düyun-u Umumiye ve Reji Soygunu.' *Belgelerle Türk Tarihi Dergisi* 1: 33–39.

Naima. 1968. *Tarih-i Naima*. Zuhuri Danışman, ed. İstanbul: Danışman Yayınevi.

North, D. 1990. *Institutions, Institutional Change and Economic Performance*. Cambridge: Cambridge University Press.

North, D. and B. Weingast 1989. 'Constitutions and Commitment: The Evolution of Institutions Governing Public Choice in Seventeenth-Century England.' *Journal of Economic History* 49: 803–832.

Novichev, A.D. 1979 [1937]. *Osmanlı İmparatorluğu'nun Yarı Sömürgeleşmesi*. Ankara: Onur Yayınları.

Ottoman Public Debt Administration. Annual Reports of the Ottoman Public Debt Administration, 1882–1914.

Owen, R. 1993. *The Middle East in the World Economy, 1800–1914*. London: I.B.Tauris.

Ölçer, C. 1989. *Osmanlı Bankası Aracılığıyla Yapılan Borç Anlaşmaları: Metinler*. İstanbul: Yenilik Basımevi.

Önsoy, R. 1999. *Mali Tutsaklığa Giden Yol: Osmanlı Borçları (1854–1914)*. Ankara: Turhan Kitabevi.

Özyüksel, M. 1988. *Anadolu Bağdat Demiryolları*. İstanbul: Arba Yayınları.

Özyüksel, M. 2000. *Hicaz Demiryolu*. İstanbul: Tarih Vakfı Yurt Yayınları.

Paksoy, H.B. 2003. 'Views of the "Outlaw Concept" in Comparative Perspective: The American West and the Zeybeks in the Turk

Lands.' Paper presented at the West Texas Historical Association Annual Meeting.

Pamuk, Ş. 1987. 'Commodity Production for the World Markets and Relations of Production in Ottoman Agriculture, 1840–1913,' in *The Ottoman Empire and the World Economy*, edited by H.İ. İnan, 88–100. Cambridge: Cambridge University Press.

Pamuk, Ş. 1988. 'The Ottoman Empire in Comparative Perspective.' *Review (Journal of the Fernand Braudel Center)* 11(2): 127–149.

Pamuk, Ş. 1994. *Osmanlı Ekonomisinde Bağımlılık ve Büyüme*. Second Edition. İstanbul: Türkiye Toplumsal Tarih Vakfı.

Pamuk, Ş. 2002. 'The Evolution of Fiscal Institutions in the Ottoman Empire, 1500–1914.' Paper presented at the session on 'The Formation and Efficiency of Fiscal States in Europe and Asia, 1500–1914' of the Thirteenth Economic History Congress, Buenos Aires.

Parvus Efendi (Alexander Israel Helphand). 1977 [1910]. *Türkiye'nin Mali Tutsaklığı*. İstanbul: May Yayınları.

Pfister, U. and C. Suter 1989. 'Global Debt Cycles and the Role of Political Regimes,' in *Markets, Politics and Change in Global Economy*, edited by W.P. Avery and D. Rapkin, vol. 4, 17–55. Boulder: Lynne Rienner.

Quataert, D. 1977. 'Limited Revolution: The Impact of the Anatolian Railway on Turkish Transportation and the Provisioning of Istanbul, 1890–1908.' *Business History Review* 51: 38–55.

Quataert, D. 1983. *Social Disintegration and Popular Resistance in the Ottoman Empire, 1881–1908: Reactions to European Economic Penetration*. New York: New York University Press.

—1987. 'The Silk Industry of Bursa, 1880–1914,' in *The Ottoman Empire and the World Economy*, edited by H.İ. İnan, 284–289. Cambridge: Cambridge University Press.

—1992. *Manufacturing and Technology Transfer in the Ottoman Empire, 1800–1914*. İstanbul, Strasbourg: Isis Press.

Raccagni, M. 1980. 'The French Economic Interests in the Ottoman Empire.' *International Journal of Middle East Studies* 11(3): 339–376.

Régie Company. Annual Reports of the Régie Company, 1884–1910.

Rose, A.K. 'One Reason Why Countries Repay Their Debts: Renegotiation and International Trade'. NBER Working Paper No.8853.

Roumani, A. 1927. *Essai Historique et Technique sur la Dette Publique Ottomane*. Paris: M. Giard.

Sachs, J. 1984. *Theoretical Issues in International Borrowing.* Princeton University Department of Economics Princeton Studies in International Finance No.54.

Sayar, A.G. 1996. *Osmanlı İktisat Düşüncesinin Çağdaşlaşması.* İstanbul: Ötüken.

Sayar, N.S. 1977. *Türkiye İmparatorluk Dönemi Olayları.* İstanbul: İTİA Vakfi Yayınları.

Schultz, K. and B. Weingast 1998. 'Limited Governments, Powerful States,' in *Strategic Politicians, Institutions and Foreign Policy*, edited by R. M. Siverson. Ann Arbor: University of Michigan Press.

Shaw, S.J. 1975. 'The Nineteenth Century Ottoman Tax Reforms and Revenue System.' *International Journal of Middle East Studies* 6: 421–459.

—1978. 'Ottoman Expenditures and Budgets in the Late Nineteenth and Early Twentieth Centuries.' *International Journal of Middle East Studies* 9: 373–378.

Shechter, R. 2003. 'Selling Luxury: The Rise of the Egyptian Cigarette and the Transformation of the Egyptian Tobacco Market, 1850–1914.' *International Journal of Middle East Studies* 35(1): 51–75.

Similianskaya, I.M. 1966. 'From Subsistence to Market Economy, 1850s' in *The Middle East in the World Economy, 1800–1914,* edited by R. Owen. London: I.B. Tauris.

Smith, A. 1998 [1776]. *An Inquiry into the Nature and Causes of the Wealth of Nations.* Oxford: Oxford University Press.

Stallings, B. 1987. *Banker to the Third World: U.S. Portfolio Investment in Latin America, 1900–1986.* Berkeley: University of California Press.

Sunar, İ. 1987. 'State and Economy in the Ottoman Empire,' in *The Ottoman Empire and the World Economy,* edited by H.İ. İnan, 63–87. Cambridge: Cambridge University Press.

Suter, C. and H. Stamm 1992. 'Coping with Global Debt Crises Debt Settlements, 1820 to 1986.' *Comparative Studies in Society and History* 34(4): 645–678.

Suter, C. 1989. 'Long Waves in the International Financial System: Debt Default Cycles of Foreign Borrowers.' *Review (Journal of the Fernand Braudel Center)* 12:1–49.

—1992. *Debt Cycles in the World Economy: Foreign Loans Financial Crises, and Debt Settlements, 1820–1990.* Chicago: Westview Press.

Suvla, R.S. 1966. 'Debts During the Tanzimat Period,' in *The Middle East in the World Economy, 1800–1914*, edited by C. Issawi, 95–106. Chicago and London: University of Chicago Press.

Thobie, J. 1985. 'Osmanlı Devletinde Yabancı Sermaye,' in *Tanzimat'tan Cumhuriyet'e Türkiye Ansiklopedisi*, translated by Merih İpek, Vol. 3, 724–739. İstanbul: İletişim Yayınları.

Tomz, M. 1998. 'Do Creditors Ignore History? Reputation in International Markets.' Paper presented at the Annual Meeting of Latin American Studies Association.

—2001. 'How do Reputations Form? New and Seasoned Borrowers in International Capital Markets.' Paper presented at the Annual Meeting of the American Political Science Association, San Francisco, September 2001.

Toprak, Z. 1995. *Milli İktisat Milli Burjuvazi*. İstanbul:Tarih Vakfı Yurt Yayınları.

—1995. 'From Imperial Debt to Global Offerings.' İstanbul: Mepa.

Ülgener, S.F. 1951. *İktisadi İnhitat Tarihimizin Ahlak ve Zihniyet Meseleleri*. İstanbul: İstanbul İktisat Fakultesi.

Varcan, N. (ed.) 2000. *Osmanlı Maliyesi Hakkında İngiliz Raporları: 1861–1892*. Ankara: Maliye Bakanlığı.

Viner, J. 1924. *Canada's Balance of International Indebtedness, 1900–1913*. Cambridge, MA: Harvard University Press

Wallerstein, I. 1974. *The Modern World-System Volume 1*. New York: Academic.

—1999. *The End of the World as We Know It*. Minneapolis: University of Minnesota Press.

Wynne, W. 1951. *State Insolvency and Foreign Bondholders: Volume No. 2, Selected Case Histories of Governmental Foreign Defaults and Debt Readjustments*. New Haven, CT: Yale University Press.

Yeniay, İ.H. 1964. *Yeni Osmanlı Borçları Tarihi*. İ.Ü. İktisat Fakültesi Maliye Enstitüsü Yayınları No. 15. İstanbul: Ekin Basımevi.

Yerasimos, S. 1976. *Azgelişmişlik Sürecinde Türkiye*. İstanbul: Gözlem Yayınları.

Yılmaz, F. 1996. *Devlet Borçlanması ve Osmanlı'dan Cumhuriyete Dış Borçlar*. İstanbul: Birleşik Yayıncılık.

Yücekök, A. 1968. 'Emperyalizm Yörüngesinde Osmanlı İmparatorluğu: 1838 Ticaret Sözleşmeleri.' *A.Ü. Siyasal Bilgiler Fakültesi Dergisi* 23(1).

INDEX

Page numbers in bold type indicate figures or tables

www.ingramcontent.com/pod-product-compliance
Ingram Content Group UK Ltd.
Pitfield, Milton Keynes, MK11 3LW, UK
UKHW020206290926
15470UKWH00001B/30

9 781848 852983